Also by David Owen

Sheetrock & Shellac

A THINKING PERSON'S GUIDE TO
THE ART AND SCIENCE OF
HOME IMPROVEMENT

DAVID OWEN

SIMON & SCHUSTER
NEW YORK   LONDON   TORONTO   SYDNEY

SIMON & SCHUSTER
Rockefeller Center
1230 Avenue of the Americas
New York, NY 10020

For information about special discounts for bulk purchases,
please contact Simon & Schuster Special Sales at
1-800-456-6798 or business@simonandschuster.com

Designed by C. Linda Dingler

Manufactured in the United States of America

10 9 8 7 6 5 4 3 2 1

Library of Congress Cataloging-in-Publication Data
Owen, David, date.
Sheetrock & shellac : a thinking person's guide to the
art and science of home improvement / David Owen.
p.   cm.
Includes bibliographical references.
1. Dwellings—Remodeling—Amateurs' manuals.
I. Title: Sheetrock and shellac. II. Title.
TH4816.O945   2006
643'.7—DC22   2006042330
ISBN-13: 978-0-7432-5119-8
ISBN-10: 0-7432-5119-9

CONTENTS

Sheetrock & Shellac

1

ROOMS AND DREAMS

THE BEST-SELLING POET in America in the nineteen-thirties was also a newspaper columnist, a small-time actor, and a successful designer of Hawaii-themed dinnerware. His name was Don Blanding. He wore an oversized fedora and had a Clark Gable mustache, and he described himself as an "artist by nature, actor by instinct, poet by accident, vagabond by choice." He was born in Kingfisher, Oklahoma Territory, in 1894. In 1912, he saved the life of a six-year-old neighbor, Billie Cassin, who grew up to be the actress Joan Crawford. In 1915, he briefly shared an apartment in Chicago with the novelist and playwright Sherwood Anderson. For a few years in the nineteen-forties, he was married to the crayon heiress Dorothy Binney. He was famous for having no fixed address, but he kept turning up in certain favorite warm-weather locales, mainly in Florida, Hawaii, and California. He died in 1957, at the age of sixty-two. In 1986, the musician Jimmy Buffett borrowed the title of one of his poetry collections, *Floridays,* for a song (which he dedicated partly to Blanding) and an album.

I first heard about Blanding from a friend, who had bought one of his books at a flea market and thought that I would get a kick out of it. The book is called *Vagabond's House.* It was first published in 1928, was reprinted more than fifty times during the next couple of decades, and is still in print today, though only barely. I bought my own copy from a used-book dealer; the flyleaf is inscribed "Aloha Don Blanding." The book is—well, the book is virtually unreadable. And the illustrations, which are also by Blanding, are on the creepy side, full of statuesque naked ladies and dated-looking silhouettes. But the title poem is kind of captivating:

When I have a house . . . as I sometime may . . .
I'll suit my fancy in every way.
I'll fill it with things that have caught my eye
In drifting from Iceland to Molokai.
It won't be correct or to period style
But . . . oh, I've thought for a long, long while
Of all the corners and all the nooks,
Of all the bookshelves and all the books,
The great big table, the deep soft chairs
And the Chinese rug at the foot of the stairs,
(it's an old, old rug from far Chow Wan
that a Chinese princess once walked on).

My house will stand on the side of a hill
By a slow broad river, deep and still,
With a tall lone pine on guard nearby
Where the birds can sing and the storm winds cry.
A flagstone walk with lazy curves
Will lead to the door where a Pan's head serves
As a knocker there like a vibrant drum
To let me know that a friend has come,
And the door will squeak as I swing it wide
To welcome you to the cheer inside.

And there are a couple hundred more lines, all written in the same merrily sprung anapestic blandometer. I've never drifted from Iceland to Molokai, and I don't own a Chinese rug or a Pan's head door knocker (although I now sporadically search for both on eBay), and some of Blanding's decorating touches are mildly disturbing—"An impressionistic smear called 'Sin,' / a nude on a striped zebra skin," "a nook / For a savage idol that I took / from a ruined temple in Peru, / A demon-chaser named Mang-Chu"—but the impulse that drove his fantasy must be close to universal. The theme of Blanding's poem is the same happy daydreaming that leads to the construction of tree houses, backyard forts, ice-fishing shacks, cottages at the beach, and three-bedroom raised ranches in suburban New Jersey. The Vagabond's reverie is a reverie of shelter.

Don Blanding is unrelated to Jim Blandings, the fictional protagonist of Eric Hodgins's 1946 novel, *Mr. Blandings Builds His Dream House* (which was made into a movie, starring Cary Grant and Myrna Loy, in 1948, and was remade, as *The Money Pit*, in 1986), but Blanding and Blandings share a belief in salvation by home improvement—and so do I. Anyone who has spent a happy hour wandering the aisles of the Home Depot, or has looked covetously at a neighbor's brand-new pressure-treated garbage-can enclosure, or has used two hooks to hang a picture on a freshly painted living-room wall and then stepped back to admire the completed project from various distances and angles, understands how a drifter like Blanding could take comfort in the idea of a fixed anchorage, and why a sensible urbanite like Blandings might yearn to upend his life by buying a decrepit country place on the verge of collapsing into its cellar. All shelters, even real ones, have fanciful dimensions as well as structural ones. All houses are also houses of the mind.

There's a second poem about the Vagabond's House in *Vagabond's House,* just seventeen pages after the first one. It begins:

> *I wrote of a house of dreams one day,*
> *My "Vagabond's House." I told of the way*
> *That the rugs were laid across the floor,*
> *I told of the walls and the paneled door, . . .*
> *The jars of spices along a shelf,*
> *I told of the things I chose myself*
> *To grace my house . . . those priceless things*
> *That an hour of idle dreaming brings.*
>
> *So vividly real it sometimes seemed*
> *That I quite forgot that I only dreamed;*
> *. . . So I wrote as though the house were real.*

The book went forth and made appeal
To some far person in some far land.
I know, for a letter came to hand. . . .
"Dear Friend," it said. "I don't know you,
But I am a dreamer and a vagabond, too,
And the house you built of fragile stuff
Is the same as mine. If we dream enough,
If we strive and work, I truly feel
That we can make our houses real.
And if mine comes true and I build some day
A house of wood and stone or clay
In a summer land by a drowsy sea
I hope you will come and visit me
For the door will open to rooms beyond
For poet and artist and vagabond.

Forced rhymes aside, I feel the same way (except for the last bit, about dropping by for visits). Home improvement is a powerful creative act, maybe the most ambitious creative act that all but the true artists among us will ever undertake. Remodeling a room, building an addition, planting a garden, even installing a bathroom sink are all forms of three-dimensional self-expression. Over time, houses evolve into structural extensions of the people who live inside them: our shelters become projections of our selves. I still have an almost physical memory of the houses of all my best friends when I was growing up. Each of those houses was a unique micro-environment, with its own topography, smell, ambience, quality of light, and temperature of parental authority, and each had features that came to seem indivisible from the personalities of its inhabitants. My memories of my grandmothers, who died more than fifteen years ago, are partly memories of their houses, which I visited often when I was little and which seemed to me, and still seem to me, as much a part of them as their potent perfume and their soft, fascinating skin. My memories of my own childhood are scenes in which the scenery is often a room. A nautilus is a living creature, not a shell, but when we think of the creature what we picture is the shell.

MY DIRECT ADULT relationship with home improvement began a week after I got married, in 1978, when I was twenty-three and my wife, whose name is Ann Hodgman, was not quite twenty-two. We had just graduated from college. On the Saturday of Labor Day weekend, we loaded our belongings into a small Ryder truck in Rochester, New York, said good-bye to Ann's parents and their dog, and drove to New York City, where we had rented the unfurnished one-bedroom apartment in which we would begin our married lives. I took the wrong expressway exit in Manhattan, and we nervously drove, for what seemed like several hours, down an avenue that neither of us had seen before. At some point earlier in the day, a short circuit had developed in the truck's steering column, and periodically it caused the horn to blare unexpectedly, sometimes for many seconds. The only way to stop the horn, I had discovered, was to pound the center of the steering wheel with my fist. At the corner of 120th Street, while we were waiting at a traffic light, the horn suddenly started, and when the people in the crosswalk looked up to see what the problem was they saw me, in the cab of our Ryder truck, face red with aggravation, pounding the center of the steering wheel with my fist.

Somehow, we got where we were going. Two friends from college helped us move in. The move didn't take very long. The friends went home. The sun went down. The power in our apartment hadn't been turned on yet, and we learned from the building's superintendent that no one from Con Ed would be able to turn it on until Tuesday, after the holiday, three days from now. The phone didn't work, either. We couldn't afford to go out. There was hardly anywhere to sit, because we didn't own a couch yet. Our apartment that night seemed as big and blank and dark as the formless future. The empty rooms were no longer quite empty, since we had heaped our boxes on the floors, but the apartment was not in any sense inhabited.

We lived in that apartment for seven years, and, little by little, we turned it into our home, initially just by filling it with possessions: our shell grew around us, chamber by chamber. We bought a couch, then some bookcases, then some other things, then a cheap metal table to hold the sole piece of office equipment that we owned in those days: a used IBM Selectric typewriter, which I had bought in college. Ann's parents gave us some old curtains. We hung pictures on the walls. After a few months, I could no longer quite recall what the apartment had looked like when it was truly empty—could no longer re-experience the sense of portentous excitement and anxiety I had felt when the rental agent first unlocked the door and walked Ann and me through the starkly unlived-in rooms. Week by week, my brain overwrote the old memory files. The shiny expanse of parquet flooring receded beneath rugs and furniture and laundry, and the blank walls pulled away. Gradually, the rooms acquired an identity that, in the minds of our friends and neighbors, and even in our own minds, was no longer easily separable from us. Our apartment became our living shell, our first joint act of home improvement.

Eventually, that shell became so crowded with stuff that Ann and I sometimes had to walk sideways and step over stacks of magazines to change channels on our TV. A friend remarked that our place was decorated more like a yacht than like a house because our chairs and tables appeared to have been stowed rather than arranged. Our living room was like the trailer of some circus performers I met once, who had crammed so many boxes and old clothes and papers under their couch that the couch seemed less like a piece of furniture than like the topmost item in a pile. Ann and I didn't actually own that many things, but space was scarce and the things we did own filled virtually all of it.

In 1984, a few months before our first child was born, we decided to have the apartment painted—to impress the baby, I guess. The superintendent told me to move all our furniture at least three feet from any paintable surface, and this forced me, among other things, to remove all the books from each bookcase and stack them on the couch, then move the now empty bookcase three feet toward the center of the room, then put all the books back on the shelves so that I could load the couch with the books from another bookcase, etc.—a tedious process that had to be repeated in reverse when the painter had finished (about fifteen minutes after he arrived, with a single huge bucket of extremely white paint). Disassembling the rooms in this way was jarring, like rearranging the features of a familiar face. Very briefly, the upended apartment became a window through which it was possible to glimpse our younger selves, during the long-ago week when our still-sealed moving boxes had been piled on the floor. Then the painter left, and I put everything back, and the present re-swallowed the past.

The one major physical renovation project that we undertook during those seven years was also baby-related. Our apartment contained about seven hundred and fifty square feet of living space. It had a decent-size bedroom, a small bathroom, a tiny kitchen, and a living room that had a box-like dining alcove at one end—the kind of place that New York City real estate agents sometimes describe as having four rooms, but that in most other parts of the country would not be credited with more than two and a half. The dining alcove was so compact that when we had guests for dinner we sometimes had to take apart my home office—which occupied one dark corner—and move the living-room couch a foot closer to the TV. Yet the cramped alcove seemed to be the only conceivable parking space for a baby. Several months before our daughter was born, we moved the dining table behind the living-room couch, moved my office next to it, and turned the alcove into an official room, by walling it off. We also carpeted the new room's floor, and discovered that wall-to-wall carpeting can make a small space appear larger—a useful trick of the eye.

The partition with which we created our new room was actually a wall unit—a floor-to-ceiling bank of bookcases, with a real hung door in the middle. It was built to fit by a company for which I'd seen an advertisement in the *Village Voice,* and it was installed by a trio of surly workers. It consisted of four thirty-inch-wide floor-to-ceiling sections, one of which contained the door. These sections were bolted to each other, and the whole thing was held in place vertically by a couple of dozen threaded bolts with metal pads at the end, like the leveling feet on a washing machine. This hardware, and the gaps along the floor and ceiling, were concealed behind moldings and skirt boards. The completed unit, from the living-room side, looked like a real wall with a bank of built-in bookcases in front of it.

Our original plan was to install our baby inside this new subdivision, as various Manhattan acquaintances of ours had done already with their own babies in their own transformed dining alcoves in their own tiny one-bedroom apartments. As Ann's due date drew near, though, I began to worry. Our unborn daughter already owned more bedroom furniture than we did; how would we fit all her things into a space that had scarcely been large enough for our dining table?

Then I realized that there was an easy solution: we could give the baby our bedroom, which was significantly larger than the alcove, and move ourselves behind the books. This idea appalled most of the friends I mentioned it to, because it seemed spineless—as though we were pre-spoiling our child, by capitulating in advance to some outrageous infantile demand. Older adults, in particular, viewed it as a dangerous act of trans-generational appeasement. My father-in-law chuckled knowingly, as though this were merely the latest in a series of my follies. But the more Ann and I thought about the idea, the more we liked it. Children need lots of room in their rooms; grown-ups don't. By giving our daughter our bedroom, we were actually carving out more adult space for ourselves in the rest of our apartment, since we would now not be forced to let the nursery overflow into the living room. And because the baby's big bedroom was situated at the far end of a (short) hall, on the other side of the kitchen, we would still be able to stay up late, carousing in the living room with our friends—something that would have been impossible with an infant sleeping just a few feet away, on the other side of our significant collection of heavily underlined books from college English courses. (This was at a time when we believed that our social life would survive the birth of our child.)

Living in a tiny bedroom turned out not to be the imposition that Ann and I had feared it might be. We discovered that compactness can be a genuinely appealing bedroom feature, as long as the occupants have outgrown any need to keep toys and diapers and bouncy chairs on the floor. In most supersized master bedrooms, the surplus square footage serves no useful purpose. Why waste interior acreage on a room in which you spend most of your time unconscious?

Home improvement is an ongoing collaboration between a dwelling and its residents. Changing our apartment changed Ann and me, too, because remodeling works in two directions: as we shaped our living space, our living space shaped our lives. Walling off our dining alcove to create a new room provided our first real experience, as a married couple, of the transformative power of renovation. Remodeling and construction are human processes as well as structural ones, and they leave all the parties altered, just as marriages and lawsuits do. Ann and I set out to turn our apartment into the kind of place that we thought we wanted to live in, and we ended up meeting it halfway, by becoming the kind of people who, it turned out, would live in a place like ours.

NOTWITHSTANDING OUR fortuitous discovery of the appeal of claustrophobic sleeping spaces, when our daughter was almost a year old we decided that we now absolutely had to have more space, plus a yard, and that to acquire these things at a price we could afford we would need to move fairly far from New York City. One Wednesday in June, I rented a car and went shopping for a house in a small Connecticut town about ninety miles north of Grand Central Station—a town that we had selected essentially at random. (My parents had friends who had a son I'd never met who lived there; Ann's step-grandmother had graduated from a boarding school there in 1921.) The town had a postcard-quality New England village green and fewer than four thousand residents. The first house the real estate agent showed me seemed too small and too new, and I told her so. (Ann and I had decided that we didn't have many strong opinions about what our house should be like, except that it should be "big" and "old.") The second, which was near the village green, was much bigger and much older. It was a two-hundred-year-old white box with black shutters, and its asking price was only about 25 percent more than the absolute maximum that we had figured we could spend. The house had a colorful history. During the previous two centuries it had been a private home, a social club, a prep-school dormitory, and a private home again. In 1970, after being decommissioned by the prep school, it had been sold to a local teacher for a dollar, sawed in two, moved by truck (in two trips) to its present location, and put back together on top of a new foundation. There was a seam in the floor in the hall where the two parts had been shoved back together, and the floorboards at the seam were a half-inch out of alignment. The owner had converted the attic into a rental apartment, which was now occupied by a second-grade teacher and her husband, a recently married couple a little younger than Ann and me. The shingles on the roof were worn out, the exterior paint was cracked and peeling, the interior walls were covered with at least a dozen mutually contradictory patterns of garish wallpaper, and the garage, which theoretically had room for three cars, was falling down and was filled with leaves, trash cans, and squirrels.

But there was a tantalizing abundance of floor area inside the house: eleven rooms that I had never seen before, each of them a blank slate. Shortly after Ann and I had moved into our apartment, I'd had a dream in which I opened a door I'd never noticed before and found a staircase leading to our apartment's unsuspected second floor, which was filled with comfortable antique furniture and Oriental rugs, and had windows that looked not onto Second Avenue but far across a rolling expanse of generic countryside. Exploring this two-hundred-year-old house in Connecticut made me almost as happy as I had been in that dream. After walking from room to room for a while, I stood in the yard and tried to imagine myself living here with my little family. I realized that I could. I counted the rooms on my fingers; there seemed to be more than enough. Then I told the real estate agent, "I think I'd like to buy it." Her jaw dropped. This was only the second house she had shown me, and we had spent just a few minutes inside it, and I hadn't asked her anything about (for example) the quality of the local schools—because how could a one-year-old ever become old enough to go to school?

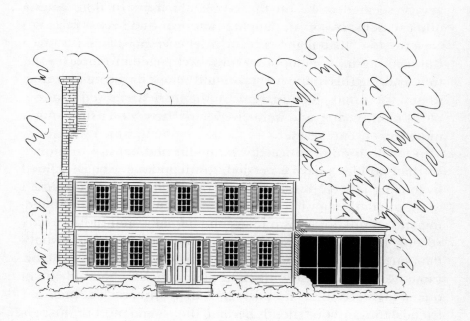

Our house.

When I took Ann and our daughter to see the house, a few weeks later, I couldn't find it; in fact, I couldn't find the town. And when Ann finally did see the house she didn't like it: the wallpaper depressed her, the kitchen was too dark, and the garage seemed to be on the verge of self-destruction, among other reasons. (Also, our daughter was crying and it was raining.) Nevertheless, that night, after a brief, gloomy discussion in a Burger King in a neighboring town, we decided to look no further. Finding this house had taken me almost an entire morning; what was I supposed to do, rent another car? We moved in a couple of months later, and we've lived here happily ever since—now more than twenty years.

Our decision to proceed was uneducated but not irrational. We had no idea what we needed, so what could we have gained by looking longer? By electing to complete the deal, Ann and I were, in effect, allowing a dilapidated eighteenth-century building and an unknown town to assume partial responsibility for directing the course of the rest of our lives. And that's what's happened. The lawyer who handled the closing and his wife became two of our best friends, and their daughter became one of our daughter's best friends, and their friends became our friends, too, and our friends became theirs, and most of the people we hang around with now are people we met through them, or met through other people whom we had met through them, or met on our own and later introduced to them, and so on. One thing led to another. Our lives brachiated and complexified, as lives always do, so that our accidental network of friendship and acquaintance eventually came to seem far too intricate, convoluted, and inevitable to have been the product of anything but intelligent design.

The house, on the other hand, had all the usual problems. One day, when I was out doing errands, Ann smelled something burning and called the volunteer fire department. When the firemen arrived, one of them opened the basement door and shouted, "It's down here!" Ann's reaction, naturally, was not dismay but relief—the same relief one feels when one's child vomits in the waiting room of the pediatrician: it wasn't a false alarm. The firemen quickly found the smell's source, a smoldering electronic control box connected to the submersible pump in the well that supplied our drinking water.*

I had been vaguely aware that we owned a well. I knew, for example, that we had running water and that the water must run from somewhere. I also knew that the purpose of the small, ugly barrel standing in the yard not far from the backdoor was to conceal the uppermost end of the well's pipe-like casing, which protruded about a foot and a half above the lawn. But I had never bothered to wonder how water got from the well into our house, or to consider that anything might ever go wrong with that process, whatever it was. That afternoon, a plumber removed the ugly barrel, opened the top of the casing, and used a contraption that looked like a huge fishing reel to raise the pump from the well's lower reaches, two hundred feet underground. The pump—which was cylindrical, a couple of feet long, and a few inches in diameter—had been zapped by lightning, or, rather, it had been zapped by a subterranean electric current related to a nearby lightning strike, a common problem with submersible well pumps, the plumber told me. Replacing the pump and the controller, and adding a "lightning arrester" to the well, cost roughly a thousand dollars, a sum I soon began to think of, in connection with home-repair disasters, as a "unit." A unit was a depressingly large amount of money to surrender to solve a problem that I hadn't known I needed to worry about, yet a unit, I noticed, seemed to be pretty much the minimum charge for anything that went wrong with a house. If, the day before the well disaster, my closest friend had asked to borrow a thousand dollars to pay for emergency medical care for his child, I would have explained, in desolation, that I just didn't

---

* My friend Don had a smell-related emergency a few years ago. He told me, "Wednesday night we had to go to a hotel at 3:30 A.M. because our house filled with smoke from the furnace. It had just had its annual maintenance, and the guy had un-maintained it, by putting in a faulty nozzle. Thursday night, there was still a burned-oil smell blowing out of the vents, so they sent another guy, who said he didn't smell anything. This guy personally reeked of oil. I said, 'Let me ask you something. Do you think you smell?'" A FedEx employee with powerful body odor once delivered a package to me. Ann came home two hours later and said, "The back step smells like B.O."

have the money. Yet here I was, giving that same thousand dollars to a plumber. Our house was somehow able to find money we didn't know we had, and suck it from its hiding place before we'd had a chance to recognize it as ours. You buy a house for more than you can afford; then, almost immediately, the house forces you to spend even more money, generally on parts of it you didn't know it had. As my friend Jim, who also owns an old house, told me once, "If I'd known I could afford to spend this much on a house, I'd have bought a nice one to begin with."

Somewhat surprisingly, incidents like this, rather than making me yearn to move back to the city, increased my determination to become a proud, confident homeowner, and inflamed my curiosity about my house and how it worked. I ordered the entire Time-Life series of home-improvement books, and when its successor series came out, a year or two later, I ordered that, too. When tool-bearing men arrived at our house to fix things that had broken, I used their presence as an excuse to stop doing my own work and stand around observing them—self-defeating behavior, since, in truth, I needed to work even harder to earn money to pay them. Under my cheerful supervision they replaced the leaky roof, expanded a cramped screened porch, and remodeled a bedroom. These improvements occurred whenever Ann and I were in funds and couldn't recall what a nuisance the previous round of improvements had been—the same forgetting process that enables parents to have more than one child.

Sometimes, the workmen seemed to enjoy having me around while they measured and hammered and drilled; other times, they didn't. One carpenter devised a passive-aggressive technique for getting rid of me: whenever I asked him a question, he stopped what he was doing, turned to face me, and amiably provided a thorough, thoughtful answer—for which, I finally realized, I was paying him the same frighteningly high hourly rate that I was paying him for his carpentry. After that, I learned to learn mainly by watching. I also began to buy tools of my own. When we lived in New York, I owned a hammer, a couple of screwdrivers, and an electric drill, but I seldom used any of them for any task more complicated than hanging a picture or reattaching a towel rack to the bathroom wall. Now that we lived in the country and didn't have a superintendent, what was stopping me?

The first new power tool I bought was a saw that I ordered over the telephone, after seeing it demonstrated on TV. It was the answer to all my cutting needs, according to the commercial. Its gleaming saber blade could handle the most delicate scrollwork, yet was stout enough to fell young trees. I would never need to buy another saw.

My first doubts arose when the UPS man handed me my purchase: how could a box containing the world's most versatile cutting implement weigh less than a family-size loaf of bread? The blade, buried deep in packing popcorn, turned out to be flimsy, dull, and nearly impossible to attach. When I flicked it with a finger, it twanged. Nevertheless, I hurried to the basement and attacked a large plywood scrap, which the house's previous owner had bequeathed to me. The blade noisily chewed into the wood for a foot or so, throwing inch-long splinters in all directions, before being seized by its own meandering kerf. Then the saw performed a trick that I hadn't seen on television: it used its now immobilized blade to hold the plywood steady while pounding its base plate furiously against the surface. An acrid odor ascended from the motor housing. After five or ten seconds of deafening percussion, I released the trigger. I never used my new saw again.

Later that day, I had my first inkling of a profound truth about power tools: instead of buying a single, inexpensive device that is intended to perform many functions, one should buy a large number of costly devices whose purpose is narrowly defined. In fact, the costlier and narrower the better. I now own several saws, and the price of each was a significant multiple of the price of the first. None of my saws is capable of doing everything, but each can do one thing better than the saw that I bought over the phone.

Of course, mere use isn't the only point of owning a fabulous tool. I love my saws in part because they, unlike the projects that I undertake with them, are beautiful and enduring and brilliantly engineered. As with all good tools, their power lies partly in their promise. Buying them, and proudly exhibiting them on the shelves above my workbench, is itself an act of home improvement.

_____

AS THE MONTHS went by, I found opportunities to attempt small remodeling projects of my own. One of my first successful attempts at actual construction was building an enclosure for the baseboard hot-water radiator near the toilet in our downstairs bathroom. Years of heavy use by the previous occupants had turned the radiator into a sort of low-tech factory for converting splattered urine into odor and rust. (If men did all the world's bathroom-cleaning, they would sit down to pee.) Using discarded boards and some perforated-sheet-metal grillwork, I devised a decent-looking built-in cover, which also served as a shelf for magazines. I cut the joints with a twenty-dollar handyman miter box and backsaw, which I had purchased at my local hardware store. Few of the joints were tight, and none of the corners were perfectly square, but in an old house concepts like *plumb* and *level* are relative rather than absolute, and by artfully arranging the magazines on the shelf I could conceal most of the worst flaws. (A few weeks later, I bought an expensive electric miter saw—my favorite power tool ever.)

Results aside, I found wearing a tool belt to be so much more fun than doing my actual job that I began to look for ways to combine the two activities. In 1987, after spending many months dealing with crumbly old plaster walls in our living room, dining room, front hall, and bedrooms, I wrote an (appreciative) essay about Sheetrock, for *The Atlantic Monthly.* That essay later became part of a book about home improvement, called *The Walls Around Us,* which was a compendium of slightly more than everything I knew at that time about how a house works.

Researching that book and working on my house taught me two powerful lessons. The first is that the knowledge one gains in undertaking a major home-improvement project is inevitably the knowledge one ought to have had before attempting it in the first place. The second is that a house is far less complicated than the average ignorant homeowner usually assumes. The seldom-seen spaces inside walls, floors, and ceilings aren't filled with circuit boards, laser beams, and liquid helium; for the most part, they contain nothing but insulation, mouse nests, and stale-smelling air. The difficult parts of a house are relatively few and compact, and they fit together in a logical way, and when they malfunction they do so for reasons that can almost always be discovered, understood, and dealt with. Every time I learned something new about my house, my anxiety about it lessened.

Fairly quickly, I became truly adventurous in my renovation efforts—which I began to think of as an exalted, adult form of play. I built a stone wall and rebuilt a patio. I made some bookcases. I tore open a 140-year-old wall, in the dining room; found a 200-year-old wall behind it; took samples of ancient wallpaper, plaster, lath strips, and nails; made a cursory, futile search for clay tobacco pipes, gold coins, and arrowheads; and closed up the wall again. I successfully reproduced some century-and-a-half-old paneling. I helped a friend do a poor job installing Sheetrock in his guestroom. I hung a door—after trimming one side of the door on my new table saw, a very, very bad idea. I replaced a broken light switch, then wired a room. I joined some other volunteers in helping to complete the unfinished new house of a woman whose husband had recently died in a farming accident. I built an entire room on our third floor, and another in our basement. I gave an old wood-burning furnace to some plumbers, who, in return, taught me to join copper pipes—and as soon as I'd gotten the hang of the technique I realized that there wasn't a room in our house which wouldn't be improved by the addition of hot and cold running water (an idea vetoed by Ann).

MY DEEPENING immersion in remodeling inspired me to become surprisingly thoughtful on the subject of home improvement. When Ann and I moved into our house, it was still the shell of the previous owners, even though they'd legally signed it over to us and moved to another part of town. The stove, the wallpaper, and the flaking powder-blue toilet seat in the upstairs bathroom were still entirely theirs. So powerful was their presence that for months we felt like intruders—like imposters only pretending to be at home.

Then, gradually, we displaced our predecessors. We patched, we scraped, we painted, we moved things around. We removed their low-hanging chandeliers and replaced them with fixtures that were less likely to crack our foreheads and were also, to some extent, expressions of us, not them. Room by room, we got rid of the sandy, textured finish that they had applied to all the ceilings. Living for an extended period in any house in which someone else used to live is an act of personal superimposition. This is especially true if reciprocating saws are involved, but even physically unchanged parts of our house underwent a transformation. The ugly slate-tile floor in the kitchen—which the previous owners had installed and then, in a masterstroke of poor judgment, coated with polyurethane—stopped seeming like a holdover from the prior regime and began seeming like an unfortunate decorating decision for which we ourselves were somehow solely to blame: time had made it ours.

Shortly after we moved in, we attended a party given by a couple our age who also lived in an old house. They said that fixing up their place had taken six years and that they weren't finished—even though their living room, unlike ours, didn't have bare walls that nobody had gotten around to painting. I scoffed inwardly, figuring that putting Ann's and my transplanted former dormitory into the sort of condition that a self-respecting grown-up's home ought to be in would probably take two or three years, at the most.

Well, it has taken twenty so far, and we aren't finished, and there have been many surprises. When we moved in, we agreed that the first room to be gutted and remodeled would be the upstairs bathroom, which was huge (it had been a bedroom originally) and almost comically unattractive. Back during our house's dormitory days, there had been a walk-in shower and several urinals; those fixtures were long gone, but other horrors had taken their place. The walls were covered with lush floral wallpaper, which had been hung upside down. The floor was covered with light-blue vinyl sheet flooring with a fake-pebble pattern that made people think of *The Flintstones.* The toilet seat and the tub enclosure were the same pale blue as the floor.

The bathroom was an embarrassment, and Ann and I agreed that it would have to go. But the house knew better than we did. We first began to suspect that we were wrong when we noticed that our daughter liked to play there. The floor on one side of the room was raised about four inches, to accommodate the plumbing, and she liked to walk up and down the small step between the two levels. (Real steps frightened her, but this one she could handle.) She also liked arranging toy animals on the fake pebbles and squeezing herself under the bottom shelf in the closet.

When we saw that the bathroom was temporarily too useful to gut, we began to decorate it. We had an old green couch that didn't go with any of our other furniture, so we moved it in, along with an old sewing-machine table, a rocking chair, a couple of bookcases, and a whatnot that had belonged to one of my grandmothers. On the wall above the couch we hung a large picture of some sheep, and on another wall we hung a small picture of some other sheep. When my parents cleaned out their attic and found an old gilt-framed oil painting of a barefoot peasant girl walking through a mountain pass, they sent it to us and we hung it over the toilet. When the old refrigerator in the third-floor apartment died, I put it next to the sink (after first removing the power cord and the doors). For years, we stored towels, toilet paper, and bath toys on the shelves, and we kept books in the freezer.

On winter evenings, that bathroom was often the warmest room in the house. The windows would steam up, and our dachshund would lean into the blast of the heater and fall asleep standing up. One of us would bathe our daughter, while the other read a magazine on the couch. Occasionally, we stretched bath time from dinner until bed. When we had company, we sometimes served cocktails in the bathroom while our daughter had her bath, so that neither of us would have to miss the party.

If we had had the money at the outset, we would have fully remodeled that bathroom before moving in, and we never would have guessed what we had lost by forgoing an opportunity to store towels and toilet paper in an old refrigerator. Instead, the ugly bathroom survived for fifteen years, until our kids were shower-dependent teens, and it generated many happy memories. Those memories should be considered a joint production of the bathroom and ourselves.

————————

A REPORTER FROM USA Today once asked me which remodeling task I had found to be the most difficult. I said, "The last 10 percent of anything I start." I used to feel bad about that, but now I think that it is inevitable, and even desirable. Home improvement is not an onerous chore to be finished once and for all, like paying down a mortgage. It's an ongoing relationship between a dwelling and its dwellers, and when it's done right it doesn't end. My renovation role model (after Don Blanding and Jim Blandings) is Thomas Jefferson, who spent most of his life working on Monticello and felt no overwhelming need to drive the final nail. Jefferson took "a very long time maturing his projects," according to one acquaintance, who also observed (in a diary entry), "Mr. J. has been 27 years engaged in improving the plans, but he has pulled down and built up again so often, that nothing is completed, nor do I think ever will be." Jefferson began the site work for Monticello when he was in his twenties; he was still cooking up ideas for changes and additions when he died, nearly sixty years later.

Truly completing almost any big project is always a little unnerving: it reeks of mortality. As long as I haven't installed the shoe molding under the vanity in the kids' new bathroom, I don't have to step back in final judgment and I can preserve the fantasy that the end result will be the masterpiece that I imagined when the project began. When I look at an unfinished room, I see only its possibilities; once the final coat of paint has dried, though, I begin to brood about shortcomings. It's always better to leave a few ends dangling.

Besides, completion isn't the real goal of home improvement; you might as well yearn to be finished with your life. Ann and I have lived in our impulsively purchased former dormitory for more than two decades, and fixing it up has followed a course that neither of us could have predicted at the outset, when we thought that all we needed was a little less wallpaper, a little more paint, and a significantly less ridiculous bathroom. The fact that we're still at least 10 percent away from being finished is a good sign, not a bad one: it's life-affirming. Every so often, I will run down a mental inventory of projects that I've either not finished or not begun, and feel comforted, rather than dismayed, that there is so much left to do.

2

OUTSIDE, INSIDE

WHEN MY LITTLE FAMILY and I moved from Manhattan to our new home in Connecticut, we felt uprooted and unsettled. The most severely affected member of the family was probably our daughter, who was fifteen months old. In New York, one of her favorite activities was being taken for walks along the city's chaotically busy avenues. I would load her into her backpack and give her a bagel to gnaw on, and we would walk thirty or forty or fifty blocks, sometimes doing errands or exercising the dog but often just wandering around. I checked on her constantly, by looking back at her reflection in a big store window to make sure she hadn't gagged on her bagel. When she found the urban panorama particularly stimulating, she would kick my back or grab my hair, or she would twist her body to get a better look at something we had just passed, causing the backpack's straps to torque my shoulders. I talked to her about what we saw. As she learned to talk, she made efforts to hold up her end of the conversation. There was always something to watch, to investigate, to discuss.

How I looked forward to the walks we would soon be taking in the infinitely more pleasant Connecticut countryside! And when we finally did move out of the city, in mid-October, that countryside was staggeringly beautiful, in full New England autumn mode. The first walk my daughter and I took together was up the one-lane road that bends past our house, along a succession of old stone walls, under a canopy of red and orange and

yellow leaves. I couldn't believe how lucky we were to have transplanted ourselves into this picture book.

Yet the walk clearly disappointed my daughter. She rocked in
her backpack and pushed against my neck, and I could tell that
she was squirming out of boredom, not fascination. As far as she
was concerned, there was nothing interesting to look at: no
pedestrians, no dogs, no cars, no buses, no store windows. Squirrels were about the best the place had to offer, and there were
nowhere near enough of those to hold her attention for very
long.

To me, my new hometown's almost corny beauty, both natural and man-made, was one of its most appealing features. But I
could also see my daughter's point. New York City, whatever else
it may be, is extraordinarily visually engaging. When we lived in
the city, I especially liked leaning out of our fourteenth-floor window and looking down on people walking past our building, because their feet, when viewed from directly overhead, comically
appeared to dart out simultaneously behind and in front. The
apartment building across the street from ours was like a television set with a hundred tiny screens. Watching was easy, because
most people in that building kept their curtains open most of the
time, as Manhattanites tend to do. The crush of big-city life creates a paradoxical form of privacy: in an apartment, you hide not
behind drapery but behind the near certainty that no one who
might be watching you from across the street would ever be able
to connect the figure in your window with you, in the unlikely
event that the two of you should ever meet.

My daughter's disappointment in the vistas of exurbia made
me think more deeply about what I could see from the property
that Ann and I now owned. After our new house began to seem
less strange to me—as the thrill of buying something huge began
to dissolve into the terror of owning a two-hundred-year-old box
sitting in a hole in the ground—I became susceptible to an ail-
ment that's fairly common among homeowners in certain parts
of the country: view envy. Our house was surrounded by trees. In
the winter, when the leaves were gone, I could look all the way
down a steep hill to a pair of creeks, and then up another hill,
which was stitched with old stone walls. When the trees were bare

and there was snow on the ground, the second hill looked a little like the scalp of a man with thinning hair. I liked studying that hill through the bare trees, but the view was one that most people wouldn't think of as a view, and, besides, it was distinctly seasonal. When Ann and I visited friends whose houses surveyed more magnificent vistas than our house did, I ruminated covetously. If I hadn't been so quick to buy our house, I brooded, then I, too, might now own property from which I could gaze into neighboring states.

Eventually, I was able to deal with my view envy—at first, by rationalizing. There is a powerful bias in favor of long views over short ones, but why is a distant mountain peak necessarily more stirring than a geranium growing on a windowsill? I couldn't see the Southern Hemisphere from my house, but I could see some pretty darned interesting trees at certain times of the year, and our bird feeder attracted the occasional non-sparrow. And what better view could there possibly be than the sight of your own child playing in her sandbox?

Then rationalization ceased to be enough, and I decided to be proactive. I realized that I could lengthen the view from one side of the house by cutting down a row of tall, half-dead red pine trees, which had been planted along the property line during the nineteen-thirties and were now succumbing to a blight that was killing red pines everywhere in my part of the country. I knew that my friend Rex Swain—an independent software consultant, who also owns an old house in my town and shares my infatuation with power tools—had recently purchased a chain saw and was now spending his spare time felling superfluous trees on his property and converting them into logs. I bought a chain saw of my own, a handyman model that was on sale at my local hardware store, for something like a hundred and fifty dollars, and invited Rex to come over for a play date. He was in my driveway almost before I'd hung up the phone.

IF AMERICA'S EUROPEAN settlers had possessed chain saws, the continent would have been treeless by 1800. As it was, those early settlers managed to level state-size forests with astounding efficiency—a remarkable feat, considering how much torturous labor was involved. In the seventeenth and eighteenth centuries, trees in my part of the country grew thickly everywhere and were enormous. (The deck boards on the roof of our house are local chestnut, and some of them are the width of a sheet of plywood.) Yet before any settler could plant crops or raise sheep, these giants had to come down, and their stumps had to be pulled out of the ground, by oxen, and the glacial boulders that riddled the topsoil had to be pried out of the dirt and disposed of, usually by dragging them on sledges and then piling them into walls. Many of these stones weighed hundreds of pounds; some were so massive that they could be moved only during the winter, when the ground was covered with snow or ice. Fully clearing an entire farm's worth of New England forest could take generations.

American settlers' principal implement of arboreal destruction, beginning in the early seventeen hundreds, was a tool that they themselves had created: the American chopping ax. This is the tool that you and I picture when we picture an ax. It has a curved handle, a wedge-shaped blade, and a heavy head, or poll; there's also a "double-bitted" version, with a blade on both sides of the head and a straight handle. Locally unique versions evolved in different parts of the country, their heads as subtly varied as the beaks of Darwin's finches. In all its forms, the American ax was a far more effective cutting tool than its European predecessor, a heavy, square-headed implement unchanged since Roman times. The European ax looked like something that a gladiator might have used to fend off a lion, and it was poorly suited to hacking the robust primeval vegetation of the New World. The curved handle of the American ax increased a woodsman's leverage, and the weight distribution in the head increased his cutting power. A skillful user—holding the handle lightly and using it almost as a sling, to throw the blade at the tree—could convert a first-growth oak into fuel and building materials before soft-bellied twenty-first-century city slickers like us would have been able to close our gaping mouths. An ax was the first tool that any settler owned, and it was cared for and respected. Abraham Lincoln once said, in a different context (emancipation), "If

I had eight hours to chop down a tree, I'd spend six hours sharpening my ax."

Modern Americans tend to think of forest-leveling as an inexorable, ongoing, cumulative process, but many parts of the United States are far more heavily wooded today than they were a hundred or two hundred years ago. By the early twentieth century, my little town had been stripped almost bare, not only because farmers had cleared thousands of acres for marginally productive agriculture but also because the most important local industry, other than farming, was charcoal-making, which insatiably consumed trees, as well as fouling the air. The charcoal was used mainly in iron-smelting, another heavy polluter. Subsistence farming, sheep-raising, charcoal-making, iron-smelting, and heating houses by burning wood all declined or became extinct during the early decades of the twentieth century, and as they did the forests began to grow back. In 1900, somebody standing in what is now my front yard would have had unobstructed miles-long views in three directions; now, during the summer, I can't see my neighbors.

Well, Rex and I were determined to turn back the clock on at least part of my view. We started with the smallest, deadest trees, which came down easily. In fact, for some of those trees the chain saw was not, strictly speaking, necessary, since Rex and I probably could have felled them by leaning heavily against them. We used the saw, though, of course. Then, as the pine corpses piled up on the slope below the house, we became more ambitious.

The world's first mechanical chain saw was a medical instrument. It was called an osteotome, and it looked a little like an egg beater and a little like a medieval torture device. It was used to amputate human limbs. Bernard Heine, a German "master of prosthetics," invented it around 1830 and was hailed throughout Europe as a medical pioneer. (Amputation was the standard treatment for more maladies in the nineteenth century than it is today; wounded soldiers being carried into field hospitals during the Civil War usually had to pass tall piles of the fingers, hands, feet, arms, and legs of earlier patients.) To use an osteotome, a surgeon braced its wooden stock against his stomach, held the device steady with his left hand and, with his right hand, turned a crank that caused a serrated chain to rotate rapidly around a guide blade, as in a modern chain saw. "The osteotome made it easy to cut through hard bone without the impact of hammer and chisel or the jolts of a reciprocating saw," Wolf Seufert, a Canadian medical professor, has written. "The surgeon skilled in its use could now resect bone without splintering it, perform craniotomies with smooth-edged holes, and cut in topographies that did not permit access to a circular saw—without damage to surrounding tissue, all by himself, and with a minimum of force and time." Time was the main consideration. In the dark era before anesthesia, no one wanted a surgeon to linger over an amputation.

The modern tree-felling chain saw was invented by another German, Andreas Stihl, of Stuttgart, in 1926. Stihl's device, which was electric, weighed a hundred and forty pounds and required two operators. It wasn't the first power saw used in tree-cutting— various industrial-strength machines, some of them the size of miniature lumber mills, had preceded it—but it was the first to have the same general form and method of operation as the tool we know today. Stihl followed it three years later with a gasoline-powered version, and in 1950 he introduced the first model that could be handled by a single user. At around the same time, a Portland, Oregon, logger named Joseph Buford Cox invented an especially efficacious chain, whose cutting elements resembled the interlocking C-shaped jaws of a timber-beetle larva that he had observed one day while chopping firewood. Many other innovations followed, among them numerous safety features: chain brakes, throttle interlocks, front and back hand guards, anti-kickback chains, chain catchers, and heavy, protective chaps filled with sprocket-clogging fibers. These and other innovations have made today's chain saws less likely than yesterday's chain saws to accidentally mimic (or necessitate) the function of an osteotome. Nevertheless, timber cutting is the most dangerous occupation in the United States, and a chain saw is probably the deadliest hand tool that you can simply walk into Sears and buy— both because it is inherently lethal and because it can induce seemingly rational users, mostly men, to behave with moronic disregard for the safety of themselves and others. In the Delta terminal at LaGuardia Airport not long ago, I saw a display of items that passengers are not allowed to carry onto airplanes anymore. Among them was a Stihl chain saw—an item whose inappropriateness for modern air travel should be self-evident, even to men, you would think. But maybe not.

AFTER REX AND I had warmed up our equipment by removing the weaker members of my red-pine herd, we moved to the heartier specimens. Among these was a very tall tree that measured perhaps a foot and a half in diameter and that, though clearly infected, appeared to be somewhat more alive than most of the others. This particular tree also seemed to be leaning not toward the bottom of the slope on which all the trees stood but in the opposite direction, toward my house. However, Rex and I soon decided that the tree's apparent inclination was most likely an optical illusion, and that even if it wasn't an optical illusion it was probably something that we could overcome with brute force. We tied a heavy rope as high up the trunk as we could reach. "You cut," Rex said. "I'll pull." He took the end of the rope, walked away a safe distance at an angle to the desired fall line, and pulled the rope taut.

The classic technique for bringing down a tree with a chain saw has several steps. The first is to cut a wedge-shaped notch about a third of the way into the trunk on the side toward which you want the tree to fall. Once the wedge has fallen away, you make another cut, called the back cut, from the opposite side. This cut is made toward the notch and, usually, at a level an inch or two above the bottom of the notch. You don't go all the way through to the other side, but leave intact (for the moment) a slender, board-thick section of inner tree trunk, called the hinge. When you cut down a tree, you essentially high-low it: making the face cut is like sticking your leg out in front of it; making the back cut is like giving it a shove from behind. If all goes well, the tree starts to lean while the back cut is under way. You then remove the saw, kill the motor, and evacuate the area in a calm, orderly manner, leaving gravity to handle the rest.

Well. I successfully removed a fragrant wedge from the downhill side of the tree trunk, then started my back cut. As expected, the tree soon began to lean—but in the wrong direction. That is, it began to lean toward the house. For that matter, it began to lean toward me. It didn't fall, but it did pinch the blade of my saw, gripping it as tightly as Excalibur and, eventually, stopping the chain. After making a futile effort to cut my way out of this difficulty—the average man's instinctive, off-the-shelf response to a power-tool crisis—I stepped back to consider my options. (If cutting down trees came with an instruction booklet, this is the moment when I would have opened it for the first time.)

Although Rex wasn't strong enough or heavy enough to pull the tree down in the desired direction, he was apparently able to prevent it from falling in the undesired one. We conferred. "You pull, too," he said. Even together, though, we couldn't budge the tree. Foolishly, I tried pushing the trunk directly while Rex pulled on the rope. Still nothing.

Most home improvement disasters occur so quickly that you can't be sure what's happened until later, if then. This one occurred so slowly that I had time to mull the permutations as they unfolded. While Rex held the rope, I did some quick mental trigonometry, hoping to assure myself that the tree, when it finally did fall, wouldn't hit my house—or, at least, wouldn't hit the roof, which had just been re-shingled, in cedar, at numbing expense. I estimated the tree's height, paced off the distance between the base of the trunk and my dining room, compared the two figures with dismay, and held the rope while Rex reworked my calculations. Then I gave the rope back to Rex, strode calmly into the house, and told Ann, who was in the playroom with our daughter and a couple of our daughter's friends, to keep everyone away from the front of the house for the next fifteen minutes and to ignore any sounds of breaking glass, rending timber, or cursing men that might reach their ears. This warning, naturally, sent everyone running into the living room for a closer look.

At last, there seemed to be nothing to do but allow the tree to fall. Of course, that didn't work either. When we let go of the rope, the tree seemed unperturbed, although it did groan a little. Rex and I, with considerable trepidation, then approached the trunk from the downhill side and, on the count of three, gave it a push. More groans, then nothing. Then Rex took the rope up toward the house. "I'll pull, you push," he said. That, finally, was enough.

The tree fell like a slain giant, and its trip to the ground seemed to take whole minutes. I watched its highest branch draw an agonizingly slow quarter-circle toward my dwelling. Semi-miraculously, the tree missed the new shingles, missed the new gutter, missed an upstairs window, missed the dining-room window, missed the house entirely—and by a good twelve inches. Shock waves ruffled the pachysandra when it landed. Various branches speared the lawn. After a moment, I walked down to the stump and saw that my new chain saw—whose blade had been the fulcrum over which the falling trunk had teetered—was pretty much done for.

The next day, chastened, I hired a guy to take down the remaining dead trees and to clean up the mess that Rex and I had made. He cut the felled trunks into long logs—useless as firewood, since burning pine coats chimney flues with creosote, which is flammable and is the main cause of chimney fires—and left them strewn among the pricker bushes that covered the lower portions of the hill. There the logs remained, undisturbed except by vines and rot, for the next five years. Finally, I hired two other guys to get rid of them. They had a tractor with a scoop on the front and a sort of prongy thing on the back. My son, who was two, asked me what the prongy thing was, and I said I wasn't sure but that it was probably some kind of rake. The next day, my daughter, who was six, asked the same question and I said I wasn't sure, and then my son—whose faith in the wisdom of his father was mildly unsettling, given the provenance of those logs—told her, "Pobby kind yake."

ALMOST ALL OF my other direct attempts to beautify our new yard were similarly disappointing. Our house stands on the side of a hill, and the slope above it is covered with weeds, miscellaneous large growing things that aren't quite weeds, but almost, and several orderly rows of white pines and blue spruces. In a burst of misguided home pride one afternoon, I used a pair of heavy-duty loppers to annihilate a great deal of untidy underbrush—including what I later learned had been a couple of dozen large rhododendrons and mountain laurels. (Fortunately, the rhododendrons and mountain laurels all grew back, even though I had cut them virtually to the ground.) I also pulled down many thick vines, which had appeared to me to be throttling the pines and spruces. These vines—some of which were inches thick—turned out to be poison ivy, as I discovered when my hands and arms broke out in a painful, oozy rash.*

Among my first purchases at our local hardware store were two fifty-foot hoses and a lawn sprinkler. The weather had been hot and rainless, and much of our lawn looked parched to the verge of spontaneous combustion. I had spent a summer in college working on the grounds crew at a condominium complex in Colorado, and I figured that I knew a thing or two about watering grass. (One night that summer, I dreamed that one of my housemates had set up a sprinkler on the floor of my room, so that water repeatedly swept across my bed as I was trying to sleep; when I woke up, I was filled with dream fury.) I placed my new sprinkler in a particularly forlorn-looking patch and turned on the water, then moved the sprinkler every twenty or thirty minutes, intending to gradually cover the entire lawn—and so on, for the rest of my life, I guess. After a couple of hours, though, I noticed that the sprinkler's arms were no longer turning, and that what had once been powerful jets of water were now feeble dribbles. I searched the hose for a kink, without success, then realized that the fault was not in my equipment but in the ground: I had run our well dry. Ever since that moment, our grass has been on its own.

---

* I had always thought that I was immune to poison ivy, and had rolled around in a patch of it at camp one summer, years before, to impress my tent mates. But very few people are truly immune to urushiol, the irritant in poison ivy and its relatives, and an individual's susceptibility may increase with exposure—a good reason to keep your distance even if you've never broken out. American Indians were supposedly able to handle urushiol-bearing plants without ill effect, and they may have made themselves immune through contact or by regularly ingesting the plants, but no one has succeeded in creating a medication that safely does the same thing. The extremely unpleasant side effects of one experimental formulation include "severe anal itching."

And what a relief. When we moved in, I had assumed, without thinking about it very hard, that keeping my lawn green was simply an unshirkable grown-up responsibility, which I had taken on by signing my mortgage—and now I was permanently off the hook. As I looked around town, too, I noticed that virtually none of my new neighbors ever watered their own lawns, presumably for the same reason. At first, I did worry that their lawns appeared to be more robust than ours, and seemed to consist of actual grass, while ours looked suspiciously like the stuff at the far end of the produce counter in the grocery store—not turf, exactly; more like bok choy. Later, though, I decided that this was mainly a trick of perspective: any lawn looks better when you view it obliquely and from a distance, as you do when you study it covetously from a passing car.

During our first weeks in residence, I also bought a power lawn mower, which Ann and I took turns pushing around the yard for several years, before handing that job over to other people: first a local teenager, then a man with a Gravely, who now knocks off the entire yard in less time than it used to take me to do the tricky parts under the trees. For a while, I had tried to make myself think of mowing the lawn as a convenient form of semi-aerobic exercise, but in the end I couldn't get past its essential futility: you mow your lawn only because if you don't mow it your grass will soon become so long that you won't be able to mow it anymore.

A few years later, when I took up golf, I got interested in my lawn again, as a place where I could work on my swing. I bought a non-motorized reel mower, set its blades to their lowest setting, and used it to create three target greens, each of them circular and roughly twenty feet in diameter, in the grass that our lawn-care man had already mowed with his Gravely. I enjoyed hitting golf balls at these circles, and I congratulated myself for giving my property an interesting new dimension. But a couple of days later all my target greens turned brown: I had cut them so short that they couldn't withstand the summer heat. So I gave away my reel mower and went back to hitting my practice balls in random directions, mainly into the trees.

Occasionally, Ann—whose father is an accomplished gardener—feels guilty about her lack of interest in our yard and decides to do something about it, such as hiring someone to stick little thyme plants between the stones in the patio, or hiring someone else to pull the weeds from our foundation plantings, almost all of which were planted by the previous owners. But these moments of enthusiasm seldom last very long, and they are sometimes self-canceling, as when the young couple she hired to pull the weeds from our foundation plantings also pulled out all the little thyme plants in the patio. Mostly, though, Ann is an un-apologetic non-gardener. As she herself once wrote, in *Smithsonian,* "Being out in the sun is only one of the things I don't like about gardening. I also don't like digging (too dirty), dragging hoses around (too twisty), seeing leaves close up (too veiny) and accidentally cutting worms in half with a trowel (too messy). If I ever get more money than I can bear, I'll hire a gardener. Until then, I'm fine with a tattered lawn and a border of shrubs that my father once euphemistically called 'primitive.'"

All of us, at some level, want to please our parents. In the long run, though, who cares? Despite occasional pangs of con-science, I don't think that lawn neglect is a bad thing. You can travel for miles through suburbia and see no one doing anything in a yard except working on the yard itself (often with the help of a riding lawn mower, one of the few four-wheeled passenger vehi-cles that get worse gas mileage than a Hummer). The modern American lawn is perfectly, perversely self-justifying: its purpose is to be taken care of. If you decide that you don't care about your yard very much, you free up time and money that you can then invest in more productive activities. Such as working on your wreck of a house.

———————————

THE MOST DISCOURAGING interior feature of our new house was its acres—no, hectares—of unattractive wallpaper, which covered virtually every vertical surface. The previous owner had pasted wallpaper even across the bare studs alongside the stairs leading to the basement, and when we moved in he gave me his extensive collection of spare rolls, in case I should suc-ceed where he had failed, by finding a wall somewhere that hadn't already been covered, perhaps inside a closet. When I first saw the house, with the real estate agent, I hadn't been bothered. I realized that most of the wallpaper was ugly, and that some of it was extremely ugly, but I figured that if there were rooms that Ann and I couldn't stand we could just pull the stuff off or slap some paint over it, and that would be that. Ann was gloomier, viewing the wallpaper as a permanent problem. I accused her of being distracted by appearances, and said that if the walls had been truly beautiful someone else would have bought the house before we did, and for a lot more money. I wouldn't want to live in a purple house (I told her), but if I were shopping for a place to live I'd love to find one on the market, because the color would keep away bidders who couldn't see past the surface.

In the end, we were both right, sort of. Wallpaper really is just a cosmetic problem—but in our case it turned out to be a cosmetic problem in the same sense that basal cell carcinoma is. In many of the rooms, the wallpaper served almost a structural function, since it had been hung on top of cracked and crumbling old plaster walls, and, like a huge Band-Aid, was helping to keep them intact. In other rooms, the wallpaper was stuck to unpainted, unsized gypsum wallboard—Sheetrock—and couldn't be removed without damaging the wallboard's unprotected outer layer, which was itself made of paper.

Our old apartment building had received a makeover shortly before we moved out, and one day I had watched workmen removing old wallpaper from our hallway. They used a putty knife to loosen a corner or an edge of each sheet, then pulled the whole thing away, with a satisfying rip, like removing the waxed-paper backing from an adhesive label. When I tried the same technique in our new house, though, I got nowhere. I could loosen a few corners and edges here and there, but when I pulled I got little flecks, not whole sheets. Eventually, I realized that the wallpaper in our old building must have been some kind of industrial-strength vinyl wall covering, which could be tugged without tearing.

The recommended approach to removing wallpaper made of paper, according to the books in my burgeoning home-improvement library, was to rent (or buy) a wallpaper steamer, a machine that loosens wallpaper by softening the paste that holds it to a wall. A heavy-duty model is about the same size, and has roughly the same general anatomy, as a jumbo workshop vacuum cleaner. It consists of a large water reservoir, an electric heating element, a long hose, and a perforated metal plate, which you hold against one small section of the wall at a time until the paper beneath it has come free. When I asked about steaming wallpaper at my hardware store, though, the head of the paint department told me to forget it. He said that the machines were hard to handle, that the steam would condense and make a mess everywhere, possibly harming my nice old floors, and that I would quickly tire of holding the plate to the walls. He suggested taking a low-tech approach instead: roughening the surface of the wallpaper with heavy-grit sandpaper, then soaking the roughened surface with a wet sponge and letting it sit for a while before scraping it with a paint scraper or a wide-blade putty knife. He said that I could add wallpaper-removal solvent to the water (or a little vinegar or dishwashing soap), but that he wasn't convinced that doing so would make much difference. The most important tools, he said, were water and patience.*

The hardware-store man's method worked fine on the old plaster walls, although it was more time-consuming than I had imagined it would be. The most effective technique, I discovered, was to roughen one wall area with sandpaper, dampen the scuffed paper with a sponge, do something else for fifteen minutes, dampen the wall again, do something else for fifteen more minutes, dampen it again, and make a few tentative scrapes with my putty knife. Attacking prematurely was pointless; until the paste had given up, brute force was counterproductive. Some patches surrendered sooner than others, and working on them made it easier to remove neighboring patches, because scraping created new entries for the water. I bought a small hand tool that was supposed to speed up the soaking process—it was a roller

---

* Several manufacturers now make small, handyman versions of wallpaper steamers. A popular example is the Wagner Power Steamer, which sells for about fifty dollars. Handyman steamers are less messy than the big old rental machines, because they produce less steam, but they require far more tedious effort than the sponge-and-bucket method, in my opinion.

with lots of small, sharp teeth, which poked tiny, shallow holes through the paper as I rolled it across the wall—but I found that it was less effective than sanding, because the perforations were so small and so widely separated. A similar tool, called a Paper-Tiger, is widely available today, and it may work better than the one I used. (I finally have no wallpaper left to test-drive one on, thank goodness.)

Soaking and scraping was possible only on the plaster walls; on the unprimed Sheetrock walls, nothing worked. No matter how gentle I tried to be, I inevitably made a mess of the wallboard underneath, sometimes by gouging it with my putty knife, sometimes by pulling away small sections of the surface paper, sometimes by partially dissolving and mangling a taped joint. If you are getting ready to hang wallpaper on new wallboard, you should do future generations (and your own fickle self) a major favor by preparing the wallboard first—ideally by coating it with: a primer/sealer recommended for use under wallpaper (such as Benjamin Moore's Universal Wall-Grip 203); an ordinary acrylic primer followed by a coat of semi-gloss paint; or a coat of acrylic primer followed by a coat of size, which is a glue-like, gelatinous substance that is also used to prepare new plaster walls for wallpaper (and to stiffen fabrics). The wallpaper will stick well to all these finishes, and will be vastly easier to remove later on.

For a time, I thought that I might be able to hide recalcitrant wallpaper simply by painting over it, but when I tried this approach in one room the result was disappointing. The paint made all the wallpaper's seams, bumps, and other surface imperfections almost ludicrously obvious; the paper's loud pattern showed through even two coats of paint; and in some places the paint soaked under the seams, loosening the edges slightly and causing them to lift and harden when the paint dried. On one wall, before painting, I tried attacking the seams with a paint scraper, tearing the coated surface of the wallpaper back as far as I could in both directions, and then filling the rough gap between sheets with joint compound. That didn't work perfectly, either, although it did produce a result that seemed almost acceptable. If you are determined to paint a wallpapered room without completely removing the wallpaper first, something like this may be worth trying—although the water in the joint compound (and in the paint) may cause some of the wallpaper to lift away from the wall, creating an unsightly bubble.

In the old days, plaster walls were often "lined" before being wallpapered or painted. That is, they were covered with canvas, muslin, or unprinted paper, which was installed just like wallpaper, using paste. Lining prevented small cracks in the plaster from showing through the finished surface, hid minor plaster blemishes, improved the adhesion of decorative wall coverings, and simplified remodeling. The painted walls in the living room and dining room of the house I grew up in, which was built in the nineteen-twenties, were lined, with paper. Today, wall-lining is mostly a lost art, and is used mainly in fancy restoration projects, often as a way of holding crumbly old plaster in place. But it's a sound old idea, and it might be worth pursuing—although I myself never got around to looking into it.

Finally, when I could think of nothing else, I asked for advice from a local building contractor. He suggested covering my troublesome wallboard with more wallboard—that is, burying the wallpaper-covered Sheetrock beneath a layer of pristine Sheetrock—and getting on with my life. He said that this would be easy to do in the most troublesome areas of my house, the living room and the central hall, because the nice old trim on the windows and the main doors (which had been installed during an earlier renovation, in the mid-1800s) stood almost two inches from the surface of the walls, leaving plenty of room for half-inch or three-eighths-inch wallboard to be laminated right on top. The cornice moldings would have to be replaced, but that wasn't a problem, because they weren't old. (For more on wallboard, see Chapter 7.)

Placing new walls on top of old ones was not an innovation in my house. I had already discovered that two of the very old plaster walls in the dining room had been erected on top of an extremely old plaster wall. I took an exploratory core sample in another room and found even more strata, reaching back more than two hundred years. The oldest layer was eighteenth-century wood lath and plaster, followed by: very old paint or whitewash, ugly wallpaper, a thin veneer of plaster (presumably intended to hide the wallpaper), more ugly wallpaper, mid-twentieth-century wallboard, and more ugly wallpaper.

Hiring the contractor to bury the wallpaper in our living room and front hall was the first major elective home-improvement investment that Ann and I made in our new house. Some of the work was done when we weren't there, during a brief period when we were just visiting from the city for a few days at a time. Arriving one Friday afternoon to find that absolutely no trace remained of the ugly glue-green-and-white floral wallpaper in the hall or the ugly ivory-and-gold wallpaper in the living room was extraordinarily exciting. The living room—which had been created many decades before by combining two parlors, and which during the house's dormitory days had been partitioned to form two bedrooms—looked beautiful to me. The soft gray of the new Sheetrock set off the fall foliage outside the windows, enlivening the room and somehow humanizing its scale. Savoring the happy result of this first important project proved to Ann and me that our house could be made to obey our will, at least until we ran out of money. The finished room looked absolutely nothing like the one whose place it had taken. Indisputably, it belonged to us.

As things turned out, we had plenty of time to contemplate this transformation, because a little over two years went by before I got around to painting either the living room or the hall, and bare Sheetrock is plainly visible in the background of the photographs I took on successive Christmas mornings. When you begin a home-improvement project, any urgency you may feel to be finished is a rapidly diminishing commodity, with a half-life that can be measured in months, if not in weeks. After a very brief period, our unpainted living room stopped seeming quite so unpainted to either Ann or me; the taped joints on the smooth new walls lost their ability to remind us of how much remained to be done. I have often noticed similarly stalled renovations in the houses of friends—a dining room ceiling from which a large section had been missing for many months, kitchen cabinets without doors, a sink-less bathroom in which the sink was standing in the shower. An unfinished home-improvement project quickly dissolves into near invisibility. If you want to finish before other people begin to make pointed remarks, you have to act while you can still see what needs to be done.

———————

THE SUMMER AFTER the new Sheetrock went up in the living room, Ann and I hired the same contractor to remodel a small sitting room in the back of the house, across the hall from the playroom. The previous owners had told us, when we bought the place, that this had always been their favorite room. It measured twelve feet by fifteen feet, and it had two windows and a French door, which opened into the backyard. It also had a few ugly built-in bookcases; an expanse of fake brick on one wall, against which the previous owners had kept a wood stove; and, everywhere else, red-and-white wallpaper. The wallpaper had a rectangular grid pattern, like oversized graph paper, and the pattern made it easy for anyone in the room to see how severely the ceiling sloped from one side to the other. The room's entrance, from the back hall, was just two feet wide—narrower than a standard doorway—and it was tucked into a corner. When you entered the room you felt almost that you were squeezing into a gap in the wall which someone had pried open, and the room itself seemed like an afterthought, a little dead end in the back of the house.

Shortly after we moved in, Ann and I visited the house of some new friends and saw a room that we both loved immediately. It was about the same size as our odd sitting room, and it had built-in floor-to-ceiling bookcases on the walls, and it was painted dark, dark green—an ancient-looking green, which was almost the color of an old Army Jeep and which seemed nearly black when the lights were turned off. As soon as we saw those bookcases and that green paint, we knew that we wanted to have the same kind of room. We would turn our ugly little sitting room into a dark-green sanctuary filled with books.

Storing books had been one of the great joint endeavors of Ann's and my marriage from the beginning. We had both been English majors in college, we both now worked in publishing, and we both loved bookstores and secondhand-book sales. By the time we moved out of New York, we had acquired and filled a half-dozen freestanding bookcases, plus the four-section wall unit with which we had turned our dining alcove into our bedroom. Having a lot of books around is nice, even when you aren't reading. Books emit knowledge molecules into the air, and when you display your collection in great shelved expanses it has the same stimulating visual impact as an Oriental rug. We had brought our bookcases with us when we moved, but they looked all wrong in our old, old house—they were too modern and too insubstantial—so we banished them to the basement and the third floor, where we used them for storing things like nails, extra rolls of toilet paper, and old wedding presents. The playroom already had some built-in shelves, on which we parked our daughter's growing supply of picture books, along with various toys and the odd hamster cage, but most of our own books were still in boxes piled on the floor of our (unpainted) living room.*

I knew so little about construction at that point that I had a hard time telling the contractor what to do. I said that we wanted floor-to-ceiling bookcases on the two long walls of our little sitting room, and that we wanted some sort of built-in bookcase-and-cabinet arrangement on one of the short walls, so that we would have room for our TV and our stereo, and that we wanted to replace the fake brick on the opposite wall with old-looking raised paneling. Initially, I think, I imagined that he would simply be able to extend the existing bookcases. Fortunately, he had a clearer understanding of what we wanted than we did. He asked, first of all, whether we thought we really needed the existing big French doors—which, he pointed out, were made redundant by the house's real backdoor, just a few feet away. If we got rid of those doors and put a single double-hung window in roughly the same location, he said, the new built-in bookcases would work better, and we would be able to fit in more of them. He also suggested that we replace the two existing double-hung windows, which were in lousy shape and were positioned slightly asymmet-

---

* Some New York friends of ours moved to Chicago, stayed three years, then moved back to New York. The second move was easier than the first because they had never gotten around to unpacking their many boxes of books, which they had stacked on their living room floor.

rically in the wall that we wanted to cover with raised paneling—a problem from a design point of view. If we replaced those two windows, he said, the paneling would look better, and we would spare ourselves the trouble and expense of stripping paint from the sashes; we would also end up with windows that would keep out winter winds and, during the summer, wouldn't have to be propped open with books. He also said that the tiny interior doorway was a problem, both because it was tiny and because it was in a corner, where it would interfere with the placement of the cabinetry on two of the walls. The cabinetry would work better, he said, and the room itself would seem like less of a backwater, if people didn't have to enter it from the back hall. He suggested reorienting the room by giving it a wider, more formal entrance, in the end wall of the living room, and getting rid of the existing doorway altogether.

It's lucky for us that he knew what he was talking about, because we pretty much left him alone, except for occasionally asking questions and offering impractical suggestions. The room came out great, and it cost roughly what he had said it would before he began. I didn't quite grasp the scale of what we had undertaken until the men showed up on the first day with sledgehammers and a dump truck, and gutted the old room, right down to the studs and ceiling joists. I don't know what I had expected; you obviously can't remove a double door, two windows, three walls' worth of wallpaper-covered Sheetrock and one of fake brick, a sloping ceiling, and a bank of ugly bookcases without creating a little rubble. But the logic of the project gradually revealed itself to me, and after just a few weeks of dust and noise Ann and I had a beautiful (though still unpainted) new room of our own—a room that, even more than the de-wallpapered living room and hallway, betrayed no trace of the previous owners. We had already begun referring to it as "the library."

Watching the contractor and his men as they worked was both exciting and educational for me. The demolition of the old walls and ceiling allowed me, for the first time, to closely examine my house's ancient, uninsulated skeleton. Replacing the windows involved replacing some of the cedar-clapboard siding, so I got to see how that was done, too. The cabinetry began as a dozen simple plywood boxes, which the men assembled off-site, in the contractor's woodworking shop, and brought to the house in the back of a pickup truck. When these boxes were first fitted into place around the perimeter of the room, I was alarmed at how crude they looked, and I worried secretly that I had somehow failed to communicate to the contractor that Ann and I wanted a formal, grown-up living space, not a garage-like storage room. But then the men began to tie the boxes together with trim pieces and moldings, concealing the raw edges of the plywood and gradually transforming the plywood into finished, unified cabinetry. They fabricated the raised panels in the shop as well, and when the panels were installed they annihilated my memory of the fake brick that they had replaced. Ann found the perfect shade of dark-green paint, and I painted the room during the week of the World Series—which, miraculously, was being broadcast on the only channel that our helicopter-size roof antenna was able to receive. (Cable hadn't reached us yet.)

The transformation of that room made me realize that construction is a sequence of logical steps. You cut this board, then you cut that board, then you join the two boards together. Some of the steps are more complicated than others, but all of them can be described and understood, and they happen one at a time, and they can be performed by human beings. Snooping on the contractor and his men as they built the library was like watching an illusionist reveal, move by move, the secret of a card trick.

Two years later, inspired by what I had observed, I built myself an office, in the master bedroom of the former apartment on the third floor. (The second-grade teacher and her husband had moved out shortly before we moved in, and we had decided not to rent the apartment to anyone else.) I vividly remember the moment when I started that project. It was late at night and I was watching TV. Suddenly, my desire to build something serious became overpowering. For several months, I had been thinking that I ought to move my office out of the third bedroom on the second floor and into the second bedroom on the third floor—to make room for our son, who had just been born. I put down my

drink, loaded my tools into a canvas bag, carried the bag up to
the third floor, and began, very quietly, to demolish an old plaster wall, in which deep cracks shaped like cartoon lightning bolts
stretched from the ceiling to the floor. Carefully, I wedged the
claw end of the hammer into one of the cracks; carefully, I pried
off a piece of plaster the size of a chocolate chip cookie; carefully,
I caught the plaster cookie in my other hand, so that it wouldn't
hit the floor. I was trying very hard not to make too much noise,
because my kids were asleep one floor below. Yet I was so excited
about building my office that before beginning I hadn't bothered
to cover the room's freshly made bed or to remove some recently
dry-cleaned clothes that were hanging in the closet. (I did take a
moment to close the closet door.)

Working on my office turned out to be as much fun as I had
hoped it would be. When I found myself with even ten spare minutes, I would run upstairs and quickly pound a few nails, then
step back to admire what I had done. The admiring was the most
satisfying activity: standing in the middle of the half-built room
and slowly turning in a circle filled me with a sense of well-being
and personal accomplishment. To gain extra work time, I would
allow my daughter to sit in a pile of sawdust in the corner and
squirt carpenter's glue onto scraps of wood and eight-penny finish nails, which she pretended were students in a nursery school.
Late in the evening, I would run upstairs before going to bed and
add a few quick touches to a bookcase, then look at my watch
and see that two hours had somehow gone by.

My office project was like an amateur version of the construction of our library. I began by gutting the room to the framing
and removing a superfluous closet. My main implements of destruction were a claw hammer—a brilliantly conceived device,
whose basic design has remained unchanged for centuries—and
a foot-long prying tool known as a Wonder Bar. As I worked, I experienced for myself the great paradox of residential demolition:
tearing the plaster off a room's walls creates more rubble than
can be contained within the room itself. I threw the old lath and
studs out the window, and I loaded the crumbled plaster into
plastic garbage bags, and lugged them down two flights of stairs

and across the yard to the garage, where I taped money to them, to entice the trash man to cart them away.

I insulated the gutted room, then installed new wallboard by myself—even on the sloping ceiling under the roof. (I had to press each panel against the rafters with my back, then drive the first screws under my left armpit and above my left shoulder, then quickly turn around while still keeping my right shoulder pressed against the panel.) I built cabinets and bookcases the same way the real carpenters had for the library, by constructing plywood boxes (in the basement), positioning the boxes on two-by-four rails around the perimeter of the room, and tying them together with trim pieces and moldings. Getting everything on the same plane required patience and ingenuity—the floor of my office slopes several inches from side to side and end to end—but I managed. A continuous countertop (which I made from birch plywood and stained chestnut color) runs above the cabinets along three walls and over the built-in desk, and the entire surface is level, even though the countertop is twenty-eight inches above the floor on one end of the room and thirty-one and a quarter inches above it on the other. I also rewired the room and added two dedicated electric circuits inside the desk, for my computer equipment.

Building my office took more than a year, and it came out great, in my opinion. In fact, as I type this sentence I'm sitting at my desk, which I built myself and is so over-engineered that removing it may require explosives. And right now—as I continue to type (though very slowly and with just my right hand)—I am extending my left arm to my left and, while keeping my eyes on the keyboard and monitor, clumsily retrieving a reference book from one of the bookcases, which I also built all by myself.

YOU NEVER KNOW when an overpowering urge to improve your house is going to hit you. Sometimes, as with my office project, it strikes late at night. Other times, the desire burns for a month or two, then goes dormant for several years, only to rekindle without warning—say, a couple of weeks before Christmas.

Shortly after I'd moved into my new office, I decided to tackle the dining room, which, like almost all our other rooms, had a serious wallpaper problem (intense, intricately figured red-and-blue pattern, like a cheap tie). I patiently stripped three of the walls, which were made of semi-solid old plaster, and buried the fourth wall, which had resisted all my efforts at eradication, under new wallboard. I repaired cracks in the plaster, and smoothed joint compound over the ugly sand finish on the ceiling. I used a heat gun to strip old paint from the windows, and on two walls I used custom-made moldings to build wainscoting that reproduced the nice old woodwork under the windows.

Then I lost interest. The room sat unfinished and unpainted for some number of years—I'm not sure how many years. This wasn't a huge imposition. Like most Americans, Ann and I hardly ever used our dining room for its intended purpose. We ate in it on Thanksgiving and Christmas, on the kids' birthdays, during the rare dinner party, and that was about it. The rest of the year, the room served mainly as a room-temperature larder, as a general storage area for construction supplies, and as a place to keep the dogs out of (they like to pee on the rug). We threw a big cocktail party at our house while my dining-room project was under way, and made a virtue of necessity by decorating the dining table with two joint-compound buckets filled with flowers. Soon, however, both of us stopped caring about the condition of the dining room, or even noticing how much work remained to be done. We went back to treating our dining room like an annex to the garage.

This state of persistent renovation amnesia lasted for a very long time—during which, nevertheless, Ann and I did occasionally discuss our dining room on a theoretical level. "We hardly ever use it," she said once. "What if we did something interesting with it, like replacing the dining table with a pool table?" Doing this would enable us to turn a seldom-used room into the scene of happy recreation. I would be able to transfer a small part of my obsession with golf into an obsession with eight-ball, and our kids would have an interesting non-electronic activity to pursue with their friends as soon as they were all tall enough to see over the edge of the table. Furthermore, we would still be able to use the dining room as a dining room—Beverly Hillbillies style—assuming that I could contrive a removable tabletop to protect the felt.

As brilliant as this idea was, we did nothing about it for several years. Then, without warning, the moment for action arrived. The holiday season was approaching, and I suddenly realized how much more festive Christmas dinner would be if we could eat it in the dining room rather than in the kitchen. I would remove all the extraneous junk, then paint the walls and the woodwork (some of which had been bare for so long that it had darkened with age). This would not only improve Christmas; it would also constitute a serious first step toward Ann's and my dream of converting our seldom-used dining room into a festive billiard hall.

At this point, however, my mind skipped several steps ahead. Before we could install a pool table in our dining room (I realized), I would have to do something about the room's floor, which was so bouncy that the windows rattled in their frames when our dogs, miniature dachshunds, entered the room to try to get at the cookies cooling on the boxes of old board games that we were storing on the table. The floor was bouncy because it, like most of the floors in our house, was held up not by modern joists or floor trusses but by two-hundred-year-old tree trunks with the bark still on them, and the tree trunks had sagged and weakened with age. Before we could buy a pool table, I would have to reinforce the floor.

This thought made me forget all about cleaning and painting the dining room. Full of redirected enthusiasm, I drove to the lumberyard and bought two dozen two-by-sixes. I tied them to the roof rack of our minivan, then drove right across the lawn. I carried my two-by-sixes into the basement two at a time, happy as an ant, and made space for them by shoving bicycles, hamster cages, and window screens out of the way. I then identified the tree trunks that served as the dining room's floor joists, and—using a plumb bob, a measuring tape, and a chalk line—made a line on the floor directly under midpoint of the joists. My plan was to build a two-by-six stud wall on top of this line, halving the span of the joists and making the bouncy dining room floor as solid as a parking lot.

Doing carpentry by yourself involves certain complexities, especially if you are too impatient to thoroughly prepare your work area before beginning. When I built my office, I often used a file box or an open window as a sawhorse, and I once had to slide my hammer across the floor toward me with my foot, since I needed to keep one hand securely on the thing that I was getting ready to nail and couldn't reach the hammer with the other. Similarly, to snap my chalk line on the basement floor I had to hold down one end of the string with a concrete block.

As I was nailing two-by-sixes into place, a new idea popped into my head: as long as I was going to have one stud wall, why not build three more, creating a complete frame for a new, finished room? I didn't know, at that time, what the purpose of such a room might be, beyond holding up the pool table. Maybe I'll use it for storage, I thought. Or maybe I'll line the walls with glass-fronted displays that have tiny light fixtures inside them, and then begin collecting electric trains. In truth, I didn't care. All I knew, suddenly, was that the room I was going to build would have Sheetrock and storage shelves and electrical outlets and wall-to-wall carpeting and anything else that might suddenly pop into my head. At that point, I more or less stopped thinking about the dining room altogether.

Building my basement room took several months and absorbed me almost as much as building my office had. Not entirely coincidentally, perhaps, I began to think that the best use of the room would be as another office, one for my children—a place where they could go to do their homework, talk on the phone, use their computers, and avoid unwanted contact with their mother and me. I loaded more supplies from the lumberyard into our minivan, which I had begun to think of as an enclosed pickup truck. I designed the room as I went along, mainly in response to various obstacles, such as a round steel lally column inconveniently situated near the door, and a much bigger column, made of fifteen-and-a-half-inch concrete blocks, a couple of feet inside my framed enclosure. I eliminated both intrusions by hiding them inside improvised built-ins—the lally column inside a floor-to-ceiling bank of shelves, and the concrete blocks inside a computer-nook-cum-gift-wrap-storage-console, which I still consider to be a masterpiece of last-minute, half-baked design. (I had recently interviewed a very rich person whose enormous house included a room devoted solely to gift-wrapping—a shameless extravagance, of course, but a pretty useful feature at certain times of the year.)

I wanted the new room to have a carpeted floor, but I didn't want to place the carpet directly on the concrete, which had a pronounced slope in that part of the basement. I used two-by-fours to create a horizontal grid of pseudo-joists, called sleepers, and I shimmed the grid in various places to compensate for the slope of the concrete. I then screwed sheets of three-quarter-inch plywood to the sleepers, creating a level platform for the carpet (which I later hired someone else to install).

The trickiest part of the project was installing a large, L-shape Formica counter, which I had ordered ready-made from a kitchen supply store at a cost of something like a hundred and fifty dollars. The ends that fit together to form the corner were pre-cut at forty-five-degree angles, and the pieces came with hardware for bolting them in place. Maneuvering the counter through the door and into position ended up involving quite a bit of cursing, because I was too impatient to take the time to find someone to help me. Luckily, I didn't have to break one of the counter segments to get it to fit, the way my friend Jim did when, a couple of years later, I helped him install a similar counter in his kitchen.

This story has two happy endings. First, my children made heavy use of their basement office during their junior-high and high-school years. (Now that they've moved on to college and adulthood, the basement office has become a sort of craft-and-hobby room for Ann. That is to say, we use it as a place to pile junk that we don't have room for anywhere else.)

Second, the dining room eventually did get finished. I had to hire a professional to paint the woodwork, and I had to hire another professional, our friend Polly Roberts, to decorate the room and paint the walls. Polly—whose husband is my chainsaw buddy Rex Swain—graduated from the Rhode Island School of

Design, has worked as a writer, editor, and Web-site creator, and now makes her living partly as an interior decorator and design consultant. Some of her clients are so famous that you would gasp if I told you their names; others are just regular neighbors and friends, like Ann and me.

One of Polly's many useful contributions was teaching Ann and me that walls don't have to be white. All by ourselves, we had chosen an interesting color for our library, but that room was all woodwork and cabinetry. Regular walls, we had both believed, are always white, as they had been in our old apartment and in the houses we had grown up in. Choosing an actual color for the walls of an ordinary room seemed far too daring and compli-cated—especially after I had realized how problematic even plain old white was. When I went to the hardware store to buy my first gallon of flat interior latex, shortly after we moved in, I was ap-palled to discover that white isn't a single neutral entity, as I had assumed, but is subdivided into dozens, if not millions, of minutely gradated tones. Paralyzed by indecision, I finally asked the head of the paint department which shade he had chosen for the walls in his own house, and bought that.

I was going to use the same thing in the dining room until Polly intervened. She painted the walls a shade of brownish red that's a bit darker and richer than the color of tomato soup. She painted a base coat and then sponged on four subtly different shades, in successive layers. You don't notice the sponging as sponging; it just makes the red look subtly three-dimensional. Polly also picked out a rug for the room, designed valances for the windows, found fabric for the chairs, and chose burgundy-colored felt for the pool table—which we really did buy. The table is a Brunswick from the late eighteen-hundreds; I found it at an antique-pool-table store a couple of towns away. I also bought a made-to-fit vinyl-covered foam-core insert, which fits in-side the bumpers and drapes over the sides, and allows us to use the pool table as a dining table. We don't push bowls around with pool cues, the way the Clampetts did, but we really do eat meals on it.

I should admit, however, that we don't use our dining room as a dining room any more than we used to. We eat in there on

Thanksgiving and Christmas, on the kids' birthdays, during the rare dinner party, and that's about it. We also don't play pool in it all that often, either—perhaps in part because old habits are hard to break. Mostly, we use our pool table the same way we used our old dining table: as a place to store stuff that we can't find room for anywhere else.

3

THE BIG KITCHEN PROJECT

THE KITCHEN IN Ann's and my Manhattan apartment was the size of a closet. Along one wall was a sink and enough counter space to park two or three bags of groceries; along the opposite wall was a range and another small counter. The two counters had cabinets underneath them. The refrigerator stood at one end of the room, and at the other end was a window through which we occasionally saw a neighbor in another part of the building doing something interesting, alarming, or embarrassing. There was no dishwasher, except the human kind. Ann and I created an additional work surface by permanently closing the door to the dining area and placing a small enamel-top table in front of it. The dog's bed went under the table. There was also a stool, which we had to remove if two people needed to be in the kitchen at the same time.

That tiny kitchen was actually a good place to prepare meals, because the cook could reach almost everything without having to take more than a step or two in any direction. Instead of a work triangle it had a work circle, with a diameter of just a few feet.* You could fill a big pot with water at the sink, then move

---

* The work triangle is a kitchen-design concept that grew out of time-and-motion studies conducted in the nineteen-fifties. In its simplest version, it says that the most

the pot to the stove by turning on your heel, and you could grab a stick of butter from the fridge on your way back around to the sink. Kibitzers had to stand in the hall, next to the bathroom, and wait for a pause in the action before darting in to grab more ice.

The kitchen in our new house seemed like Grand Central Station by comparison, although it was measly by modern standards—about twelve feet by thirteen and a half feet, with a dining table, another table, a high chair, and a two-story prairie-dog cage taking up most of the maneuvering space in the middle of the room. (Two prairie dogs lived in our kitchen for a number of years, and they would sometimes pull cloth napkins from a nearby shelf and shred them, to make bedding.) Instead of a work triangle or a work circle it had a work line: fridge, counter, sink, counter, and stove, arranged in a row along one wall. Meal preparation involved a lot of inefficient lateral shuffling, with occasional excursions around the table to retrieve a roasting pan or a cookbook from the shelves on the opposite wall. On the positive side, the kitchen had a built-in feature found only in very old houses: a sagging floor that sloped five inches from one end of the room to the other. The incline made the refrigerator door open all by itself, once you got it started, and it caused dropped grapes, cherry tomatoes, olives, and other round objects to roll to a single, convenient collection point under the baseboard radiator near the table on which we kept the microwave. This was also good for the dog, whose bed was under the table and who was able to snap up dainties as they rolled by.

That kitchen had another unusual feature: a window-like pass-through over the sink. The pass-through opened into the adjacent room, which we used as a playroom. There was no door connecting those rooms; to get from the kitchen to the playroom you had to go out into the main hall and then down an odd, narrow corridor whose floor sloped almost as severely as the one in

---

efficient placement of a sink, a refrigerator, and a cooking surface is at the vertices of a triangle whose sides have a total length of between twelve and twenty-two feet. The work triangle isn't a law of nature, but it's a useful guide to appliance arrangement, and it can be extended to offices, basement workshops, large laundry rooms, and other confined areas in which people continually move from one task to another.

the kitchen. (Years of running up and down that corridor in just socks made our children and their friends unusually sure-footed.) When we moved into our house, I thought the lack of a direct passageway would be a problem. If our tiny daughter needed us while she was in the playroom and we were in the kitchen, what would we do? Why, we would have to run all the way out to the hall and around the corner to come to her aid! Later, though, I realized that separation was a good thing. The pass-through prevented playing children from feeling entirely abandoned by their parents, who were drinking wine and howling with laughter at the kitchen table, while the lack of a direct path to authority made the children marginally more likely to settle disputes by themselves. You could lean over the sink and yell, "Don't make me come in there!" or you could crouch down and eavesdrop. One winter afternoon, I listened as my daughter entertained her dolls with a long, complicated version of the Christmas story, in which the baby Jesus wore "long pants, a royal coat, shoes made of wood, and long, straight socks."

A playroom, incidentally, is not the same thing as a family room. Grown-ups watch TV, read books, and take naps in family rooms; they usually set foot in playrooms only when they have reached their wits' end. A playroom is where children go to escape the values that a family room is meant to enshrine. When furniture in the family room wears out, it moves to the playroom; when furniture in the playroom wears out, it moves to the dump. My sister, my brother, and I had a playroom when we were growing up, and it was the most important room in our house, as far as we were concerned. I used my blocks to build a hamster prison there, and my sister made a movie theater for her dolls, and my brother created a Fortress of Solitude out of blankets, cardboard packing boxes, and our bunk beds, which we ordinarily used just for sleepovers and platform-diving competitions. Our playroom was our sanctuary. When some friends of mine and I semi-accidentally broke a window in an empty house down the street (by throwing a homemade javelin, which we had fashioned by sharpening and then charring one end of a mop handle), I hid in the playroom with all the curtains drawn until I was certain that my trail had grown cold.

The playroom in our Connecticut house was a useful amenity when our kids were little. It had the kind of rug that you are allowed to spill things on, and it had a beat-up old couch, which, during a dozen years of hard use, served as a boat, a car, a submarine, a fort, a garbage truck, an airplane, a trampoline, and a daytime sickbed, among a great many other things. There were dark spots on the ceiling, from a contest that our son and a friend of his held to see which of them could shoot a shaken-up can of orange soda higher into the air. There was a rocking horse named Emily, which had two baby-bottle nipples taped to its stomach, for colt-nursing. The floor was often ankle deep in Lego bricks, Barbie clothes, and stuffed animals covered with Band-Aids and rubber bands. At various times, real animals lived in cages on the shelves—among them a black-and-white rat named Blaze, which had enormous testicles but was a girl, according to our daughter. There was a metal wastebasket into which Ann one day threw something small and brown that she had found on the rug. She told our son, who was two and a half, "One of Blaze's poops must have fallen onto the floor when Daddy cleaned his cage last night." The thing made a clanging noise when it hit the side of the waste basket. Our son looked puzzled. "It dry out?" he asked. Then he said, "It can be coffee peanut." And, indeed, it turned out to be a coffee bean.

A room full of happy memories, in other words. Nevertheless, Ann and I had always eyed it covetously. As soon as our kids were too old to need it for actual playing, we would claim it for ourselves and merge it with the kitchen, remodeling the combined space to the maximum extent we could afford. Our existing kitchen was falling apart and was entirely unworthy of Ann, who has written cookbooks and is therefore a professional chef in the same sense that I am a professional builder.* And while we were at it, we would remodel all three bathrooms and the laundry room, replace the furnace, add a couple of closets, and change the light over the front door.

---

* Ann's books about food and related subjects are *Beat This!*, *Beat That!*, *One Bite Won't Kill You*, and *I Saw Mommy Kicking Santa Claus*.

IT IS A SIGN of the essential depravity of the American psyche that kitchens have become more important in people's minds as cooking has become less. When I was in high school, in the late sixties and early seventies, the mother of only one of my friends had a kitchen that was remotely comparable to the go-to-hell kitchens that people have nowadays, or dream of having. The friend's mother's kitchen was very large, by the standards of the time, and it had a feature that impressed even me and my friends: some shallow drawers whose bottoms had little ribs affixed to them so that cans of mandarin oranges and tomato sauce could be stored on their sides without rolling around. Drawers with a specialized function—now, that was extravagance. I think there may also have been two ovens.

My own mother's kitchen was small, I now realize, although I never thought of it that way. It was also poorly designed. Its work triangle had a very long hypotenuse, which was intersected by the line of foot traffic from the back door, making the refrigerator nearly as easy to get at from the driveway as it was from the sink— a convenience for anyone playing outside, but an inconvenience for my mother, who was constantly jostling with poorly behaved intruders. Along one wall was a white Formica counter, at which my brother, my sister, and I sat on barstools to eat breakfast, and to eat dinner when my parents were going out. That kitchen's most modern feature, beginning a year or two before or after 1970, was a microwave oven, which my father brought home one day. I was very interested in it, initially, because my father had said that you could use it to cook a hamburger on a paper plate—like something from the Jetsons. But then my mother actually tried to cook a hamburger on a paper plate, and the result wasn't what any of us had imagined: the microwaved patty was gray and wet, as though it had been poached, and grease had dripped and spattered everywhere. Nobody dared to eat the hamburger, and cleaning the inside of the oven took forever. Later, my mother tried to microwave a whole chicken, with a similar result. We ended up using our microwave the way most early adopters did: to heat small amounts of water and, occasionally, to thaw things.

The microwave oven is a good example of a high-technology invention that didn't acquire a truly useful purpose until after it had been around for a while. People at first thought of microwaves simply as speedier versions of regular ovens—futuristic tools for rapidly cooking traditional meals. Only later did people discover their true primary function: heating prepared foods that had been manufactured specifically to be heated in microwaves. The machine came first; the use arose later. Something similar happened with videocassette recorders, which were introduced in the early seventies. The movie industry initially viewed the VCR as a threat to itself and tried to kill it, not anticipating that the VCR would eventually save the movie industry, by creating a profitable secondary market for lousy movies.

Microwave ovens didn't just change the way people cook; they changed the way people eat. That's not what anyone would have guessed in 1946, when Percy Spencer—an engineer at Raytheon Company, who, during the Second World War, had played a big role in the development of radar systems—noticed that electromagnetic radiation emitted by an experimental vacuum tube had melted a candy bar in his pocket. Subsequent experimentation by him and others showed that high-frequency radio waves excite the molecules in water, fats, sugars, and certain other substances, causing them to heat up, but have little or no effect on plastic, glass, paper, or air, and are reflected by metal. In 1947, Raytheon introduced the first microwave oven, a commercial model, which weighed nearly eight hundred pounds, was the size of a refrigerator, and cost several thousand dollars. Raytheon called it the Radarange, a name submitted by an employee in a company contest. The oven was used mainly in restaurants, railroad dining cars, and the galleys of oceangoing steamships, and it was not an immediate success. Eleven years later, an admiring article about Percy in *Reader's Digest* cited two applications that no sensible microwave user would ever try twice, suggesting that the article's author had never seen Percy's invention in operation: "The new device will cook a sirloin steak in one minute, a plump Thanksgiving turkey in little more than half an hour."

The first relatively affordable microwave ovens for home use were introduced in the late sixties; today more than ninety percent of American kitchens have at least one. Paradoxically, the rise of the microwave and the consequent decline of actual cooking has been paralleled by the fetishization of traditional cooking equipment. Back in the pre-microwave era, when people really cooked the food they ate, almost everybody got along fine with a four-burner gas or electric range from Sears. Today, when much family meal preparation is little more than high-order thawing, people sometimes feel poor if they don't own a stove that could be used in a restaurant. Like SUVs, commercial-style ranges usually have less to do with the lives their owners actually lead than with the idealized lives they lead in their imaginations.

The most unlikely object of modern kitchen lust is the four-oven Aga cooker, a furnace-like device that was invented more than eighty years ago, is made of cast iron, has a single 15,000-Btu gas burner that stays on all the time, has no heat controls, weighs almost 1,300 pounds, has to be imported from Britain, and costs more than $15,000. Agas are fearsomely industrial in appearance, with oven doors that look as though you should shovel coal into them. In this country, Agas seem to be particularly irresistible to the sort of people who do most of their eating in restaurants, among them Billy Joel and Sharon Stone. Why anyone else would imitate the British, of all people, in any area related to cooking is a mystery. The main source of the Aga's appeal must be that it costs a fortune. There's a nice house on my town's village green which was renovated and expanded at staggering expense, five or ten years ago, by someone who moved out shortly after the job was completed. The finished house has a roof made of slate—a costly material that you don't see in my area very often. Why slate? My best guess is that the owner, before construction began, asked his architect, "Isn't there a kind of shingle that's more expensive than cedar?" I once asked a manufacturer of golf equipment why some of his company's irons were made of an exotic alloy called beryllium copper. He said, "Some golfers feel more confident looking down at a more expensive club."

It could probably be a renovation rule of thumb that the cost of almost any new kitchen will be inversely proportional to the amount of actual cooking that will go on in inside it. One of the biggest, most expensive kitchens I've ever seen belonged to a woman who surely can't bone a chicken breast or separate an egg. She has a huge commercial range, two dishwashers, three sinks, an enormous rack of expensive pots and pans, and every conceivable implement for slicing, chopping, mixing, pureeing, and anything else that can be done to an ingredient. Yet she seldom cooks and, from all appearances, doesn't really like to cook. The main use she makes of her kitchen is showing it off. (The people who cater her parties love it.)

All this is dumb, of course. Still, the impulse to use a kitchen renovation as a means of putting one's friends to shame is a human one and is therefore comprehensible. When Ann and I decided that the time had finally come to do something about our own kitchen—which hadn't been in great shape when we moved, and had deteriorated steadily during fourteen years of hard use by adults, children, and animals—we tried to be sensible, but we did include at least a couple of features that were not strictly necessary, except in some dark psychological sense.

———

IN THE FALL of 1998, Ann and I made an appointment with a local kitchen-and-bathroom company, called Ducci Kitchens, Inc., whose trucks we had often seen in our neighborhood and whose crews, we knew, had worked in the houses of several friends. (I had also interviewed one of Ducci's co-owners a dozen years earlier, while doing research about kitchen design.) At Ducci, we met with Peter Roth, a certified kitchen designer, who asked us a lot of questions about what we were looking for and what we liked and didn't like about our current kitchen. Ann had some very specific ideas, because she had been thinking about kitchens for most of her life. (When she was fourteen, she won *Mademoiselle*'s annual cooking contest; when she was thirty-five, she sampled dog food and cat food on *The Tonight Show*, with Jay Leno, after writing a cooking column about pet food in *Spy*.) Ann knew that she wanted food-preparation surfaces that were adapted to certain specific uses and were easy to keep clean; that she wanted at least one of those surfaces to be Corian, because she had always liked the way Corian looked and felt; that she didn't want a commercial range; that she wanted two ovens; that she wanted two sinks, both of them seamlessly attached to the counters surrounding them so that crumbs and spills could be swept into them easily; that she wanted lots and lots of electrical outlets; that she wanted some serious storage space for her cookbooks, of which she owns several hundred; and that she didn't mind if other people in the kitchen were able talk to her when she was cooking but that she didn't want to face them as she worked and didn't want them to be able to get in her way.

We wandered around the showroom, commenting on what we liked and didn't like about the various models. Peter made notes, and a few days later he visited our house and measured everything. He discovered that, by combining the spaces occupied by the current kitchen and playroom, eliminating two unnecessary closets (currently used for storing outgrown toys), reconfiguring the back hall and the downstairs bathroom, and moving the washer and dryer upstairs, he could create an L-shape space measuring a little over four hundred square feet—plenty of room for both a kitchen and a sitting-and-eating area. He asked more questions and looked around at the rest of the house. (During my visit to Ducci a decade before, one of the company's owners' had told me that a kitchen designer can usually learn a lot about clients' probable taste in kitchen cabinets by looking at their living room furniture.) He also took measurements for our upstairs bathroom renovation, which would take place at the same time. Then he went back to his office and his drafting board.

A week or two later, Ann and I returned to Ducci to look at some kitchen drawings that Peter had made. We liked the first one immediately; in fact, with very few modifications it became the final plan. I marveled at how neatly Peter had solved certain layout conundrums that I had been wrestling with for years. I think I'm pretty good at imagining different ways in which living spaces can be arranged, but Peter, in just a few days, had found good solutions to problems that had stumped me during a decade or more of architectural daydreaming—like where to put the refrigerator, and what to do about the bathroom near the back door. I decided, upon further reflection, that knowing a house or a room too well can be a disadvantage when it comes to

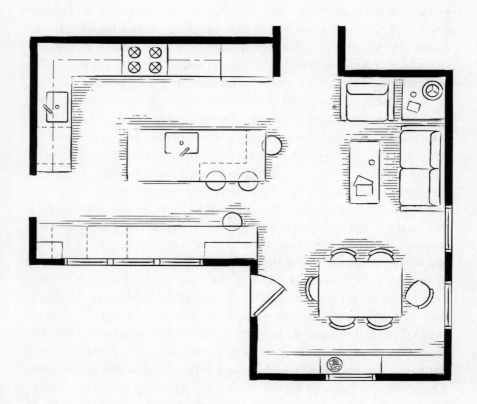

New kitchen, floor plan.

thinking of new ways in which the same spaces might be used: concrete images acquired through long familiarity can impede abstraction. Peter made his design on a blank outline of the available space, whereas I had been trying to mentally superimpose a new arrangement over one that I knew well. My ideas had always ended up being variations of the existing layout; Peter's reoriented the room.*

At any rate, we loved the design. We spent the rest of the meeting looking at samples and talking about details. At the end of the meeting, full of excitement, we shook hands with Peter, and Ann said, "Isn't it funny to think that in six months we'll all hate each other."

———

THERE ARE SEVERAL ways to go about a major kitchen-and-bath renovation. You can do all the conceptual and physical work yourself; you can devise a plan and hire carpenters and others to execute it for you; you can hire an architect to create the plan and then help you find contractors; or you can work with a company that does nothing but kitchens and bathrooms. Having snooped around a lot of people's houses over the years, I had decided that, for a kitchen project as ambitious as this one, hiring a specialist made sense. I've seen architect-designed kitchens that looked breathtaking at first glance but gradually revealed what struck me as significant design flaws: too much distance between appliances, a central island so huge that you almost couldn't reach the center from any of the sides, built-in wastebaskets in inconvenient locations, a refrigerator in the wrong place. We all learn mainly by trial and error. In any field, a specialist usually

———

* I own a potentially useful book called *Planning the Perfect Kitchen,* by Bo Niles and Juta Ristsoo, which was published in 1988 but is still available. The inside of the book's back cover is a scaled grid on which you can arrange two hundred and sixty Colorforms-like peel-and-stick templates for appliances, counters, cabinets, furniture, and so on. (Today, there are a number of software packages that let you do the same thing.) Five or ten years ago, I used the grid and the stickers to try to make a rough design for our new kitchen, which at that point was hypothetical in the extreme. The layout I came up with is still preserved in the book. It looks absolutely nothing like the one that Peter created, and it would have made for a terrible kitchen.

has more opportunities than a generalist to make instructive mistakes.

As is the case with many kitchen-and-bathroom specialists, Ducci has its own crew of installers and a stable of favorite subcontractors who are accustomed to working with them. The money that Ducci earned from our job was built into the price of the cabinetry, appliances, and other fixtures we ordered through them—like the markup on furniture which pays for the services of an interior decorator. We also received design help from Polly Roberts, who had decorated our dining room and several other parts of the house. The only parts of the project Ducci and Polly didn't manage were the demolition and rough construction that had to take place before the nice new cabinets could be installed, plus various odds and ends. For these, the people at Ducci led me to a carpenter and general contractor, Rudy Bascetta, who had often worked with them in the past.

Rudy came to our house a few days later, to meet Ann and me and look over the job. I liked him immediately. He was briskly efficient as he walked through the rooms, comparing them with Peter's drawings and asking me a few questions. His verdict: "no problem." I learned later that Rudy had been born in a larger town about an hour away, that his father had worked in a wire factory, and that Rudy had learned carpentry in trade school, as a teenager, in the late fifties. After graduation, he worked for a local homebuilder for a year, then spent three years in the Army, in the early sixties, mostly doing carpentry on a military base in California. When he got out, he went back to work with the same builder. He married a woman he had known since grammar school. He built their house, with help from his father, in three months and ten days, working nights and weekends. He spent ten years working for another contractor, then established his own business. He told me that he preferred remodeling to homebuilding because every job was different and the challenges were more varied. For our job, he would have a crew of two: his son, Mark, who had spent sixteen years as an automobile mechanic and had recently decided that he was ready for a change, and Joe, who had come to carpentry from photography, which he still worked at part time.

One of the things I like best about Rudy is his low threshold of boredom. One day a few months later, when he had knocked off for lunch, I watched him eat his sandwich in about five minutes, then look fidgety. His eyes scanned the room. His hand drifted to his hammer. He lifted his hammer from his belt and began sort of idly swinging it back and forth at his side, eyes still scanning. The little swings got bigger. Suddenly, he spotted a protruding nail in the framing on the opposite side of the room, strode over to it, and pounded it in. Then he pulled another nail from his pouch and pounded it in, too. Then he got a saw. He had more than twenty minutes left to go on his theoretical lunch break, but he was clearly happier to be working than he had been sitting on an overturned joint-compound bucket.

At some point during Rudy's first visit, I mentioned that I was pretty handy and was looking forward to making myself useful on the job. His face fell, of course, but I've always felt that part of what I'm paying for in any household construction project is entertainment for myself. As things turned out, though, I don't think Rudy minded having me around. I limited my contributions to two relatively unskilled areas: getting the house ready before the men began, and cleaning up after them as they worked and at the end of the day. By doing these things, I actually did save myself real money, yet I didn't take on more than I could handle.

I also didn't deceive myself into thinking I could act as my own general contractor—something that ordinary homeowners are sometimes tempted to do in the hope of saving money. It's almost always a bad idea. Finding subcontractors and tacking surcharges onto their bills doesn't sound like real work to someone who's never done it before, but it's almost impossible for an amateur to do it well. An amateur doesn't have experience scheduling the complex sequence of activities that go into a construction project and is unlikely to be good at doing things like judging prices and estimating quantities of raw materials. Most important of all, an amateur doesn't have an existing network of capable subcontractors who know they depend on his good opinion for future work. An amateur ends up asking friends for recommendations and flipping through the Yellow Pages, and he has no leverage when subs don't show up on time.

I knew all this, and yet I told Rudy and Ducci that I wanted them to use my own regular electrician and plumber. I explained that I liked both of them, that they already knew our house well, and that I often saw them around town. Rudy urged me to let him use his own subs, saying that things would go more smoothly if he did, but I insisted. It turned out that Rudy was right. During the entire project, the only guys we waited on were my own regular electrician and plumber. They weren't trying to screw me; they're my pals. But my town, like much of the rest of the country, was undergoing a construction boom at that time, and my electrician and plumber were deeply involved elsewhere, in big projects with big builders. In any scheduling conflict between me and a big builder, the big builder always won, for obvious reasons. Making me wait might cause me to call someone else the next time a buzzing light fixture needed to be replaced or my furnace needed cleaning, but making a big builder wait could mean not being called for big jobs in the future. And Rudy didn't have any more leverage with them than I did, since he didn't know them and since he would have been unlikely ever to use them again even if they had shown up when they were supposed to. It all worked out in the end, but I had to relearn a lesson that I already knew.

GETTING THE HOUSE ready for Rudy had two main phases: removing everything that could be removed from the rooms that were going to be gutted, a project that I performed a little at a time, over the course of about a month; and fully isolating the work area from rooms that were going to remain untouched. The second of these was especially important. I knew that no one else would be as careful as I would be at protecting my house from construction trauma, and because I wasn't paying myself by the hour I could be as obsessive as I wanted to be. I had two goals: to confine the mess to the renovation area, and to spare myself having to refinish any floors. Contractors tend to act as though refinishing all the floors in a house were just the normal final step in any significant renovation project, but I was determined to preserve as much as I could.* The floor that I was the most concerned about was the one in the long downstairs hall, which runs past the kitchen and which, I knew, would be a principal thoroughfare and staging area during demolition and construction. That floor is a hundred and fifty years old, and it's made of caramel-colored quarter-sawn tight-grained three-and-a-quarter-inch-wide tongue-and-groove pine boards, and the same floor runs through the living room, the dining room, and the library. Refinishing the hall floor would almost certainly mean refinishing all those other floors, too, so that they would look the same—a nightmare of furniture moving and sanding and finishing and expense. Rudy was skeptical that I would really be able to protect the hall floor from carpenters, plasterers, plumbers, electricians, and everyone else, but I insisted on trying.

Here's what I did in the downstairs hall, the upstairs hall, and in a little room at the top of the hall which has an ancient chestnut floor and which Ann and I were turning into a dressing room:

- I removed all rugs and furniture.

- I cleaned the floors and paste-waxed them (with Butcher's Boston Polish).

- I covered each bare, clean, waxed floor with red rosin paper—a pinkish, heavy building paper that lumberyards sell in long, three-foot-wide rolls. I covered every inch of each floor, trying to be as exacting as if I were laying vinyl sheet flooring, and I used big scissors and a sharp utility knife to trim the rosin paper to fit various nooks and crannies. Doing this was surprisingly satisfying—a fulfilling hobby in itself. I used duct tape on the seams, but I always taped only paper to

---

* Traditionally, each building trade ignores the needs of all the others. Framers put studs where plumbers will have to chop them apart, finish carpenters put moldings where flooring installers will have to remove them. And each contractor in the great chain of construction assumes that some later contractor will undo any damage that he himself does, and that the painter and the floor finisher will make everything look nice when they're finished.

paper, not paper to woodwork. (I didn't want the tape to pull off the paint a few months later, when I finally disassembled my protective carapace.)

- Looking ahead to the plasterer and his water hose, I put plastic sheeting on top of the rosin paper. I used 6-mil plastic sheeting, which I bought in a large roll at the lumber yard— the kind of heavy-gauge stuff you might use to make a vapor barrier on top of the dirt floor of the crawl space in your basement. (It's also sold in folded sheets.) Six-mil poly is more expensive than the flimsy plastic drop cloths that you often see for sale in the paint departments of hardware stores, but it's worth the money. Those little handyman drop cloths cost almost nothing, but they are usually too small to cover anything important, and they are so thin that they tear easily and don't stay put. The only time I ever tried to use one, during an early painting project shortly after we moved in, the plastic stuck to my feet and came with me when I walked across the room. I might as well have tried to cover the floor with Saran Wrap.

- On top of the plastic I put sheets of Masonite, smooth side up, and used duct tape to seal the seams. Masonite sheets are eight feet long and four feet wide, and the halls in my house are a shade over four feet wide, so in most places I was able to lay down whole pieces, without trimming. The main purpose of the Masonite was to prevent things like ladders, dropped tools, and falling ceiling joists from making dents in the floor. It also held the plastic sheeting in place, and provided a significant additional line of defense against spilled water, plaster, and paint. (When the project was over, I stored my Masonite sheets in my basement, for reuse during future projects. They're useful boogers.)

- On top of the Masonite I put another layer of rosin paper, once again using duct tape on the seams. I also used blue painter's masking tape to join the edges of this layer of rosin paper to the baseboards. Blue masking tape is more expensive than regular beige masking tape, but it is made with an adhesive that is less likely to leave an annoying, irremovable residue on surfaces it's stuck to. (The adhesive in regular masking tape hardens and becomes nearly impossible to remove if the tape is left in place for any length of time. This is a lesson I learned the hard way, during an early painting job in my daughter's bedroom, whose wood floor is still blemished by a foot-long strip of what looks like caramelized sugar.)

When my project was complete, I had a virtual second floor floating on top of the first. The surface of the second floor was tough enough to endure heavy equipment being dragged across it, and the smooth rosin paper was easy to vacuum. Once demolition and construction began, I inspected my defenses every evening, after the men had gone home, and I repaired or replaced sections that had been damaged by the activities of the day.

This may seem like a crazy amount of effort to protect a few floors, but the materials didn't cost very much, and my outlay was trivial in comparison with the potential inconvenience of sanding and refinishing. Protecting those floors consumed just a day or two of my time and maybe two hundred dollars' worth of materials. If I had left the job to the contractors themselves, they would have been far less thorough, no matter how careful they thought they were being. The guys who built our library, the summer after we moved in, put down a single layer of rosin paper on the floor before they began. I was impressed, at the time, because the paper, with its neatly taped seams, looked extraordinarily prim and protective—but that was before the sledge hammers started flying. The library floor survived the experience with just a few nicks, which a rug has concealed ever since, but the contractor told me later that he had simply assumed I was planning to refinish the floor and that he hadn't needed to worry about things like crumbled plaster being ground into the polyurethane. If you would prefer to keep parts of the construction area intact, you have to speak up at the outset. You probably also have to pitch in.

My protective measures were effective, I'm happy to say. The hallway floor survived demolition, booted foot traffic, the reconstruction of one wall, many days of plastering, the installation of raised-panel wainscoting along its entire length, and painting.

When the project was finished, I was lazy about taking up the masonite, which was much easier to vacuum than the old rug had been, and which we all enjoyed sliding on in our socks. When I finally did remove it, though, the underlying floor was pristine.

Paranoid precaution is also useful when dealing with ordinary repairmen. The guys who fix broken household items often act as though scraping paint off walls and leaving deep gouges in kitchen floors were just unavoidable consequences of what they do for a living. Before the guy from Sears comes to wrestle with our misbehaving washing machine, I cover the laundry-room floor with a canvas drop cloth, and when he arrives I offer to help him move anything that needs to be moved. I don't come right out and say, "By the way, I'm not planning to remodel this room after you've left," but that's the message. A spread-out drop cloth is like a note saying "Don't screw up my house."

IN ADDITION TO protecting key floors, I also sealed off all parts of the house adjacent to the demolition and construction areas. I used half-inch plywood to cover the two most vulnerable doorways: the one connecting the kitchen and the dining room, and the one connecting the back hall and the living room. These sheets of plywood I actually screwed to the door casings, which were going to have to be repainted anyway. To prevent dust from sneaking around the edges, I stapled some old carpet padding (which was headed for the Dumpster) on top of each sheet of plywood, on the side facing the construction. I cut the padding about a foot wider and a foot taller than each doorway, then overlapped it six inches onto the walls, floor, and ceiling, so that it functioned almost like weather-stripping. Dust could not get past it.*

For doorways into rooms that had to remain accessible, I made dust curtains out of 6-mil plastic sheeting. For each open-

---

* You can do something similar with a product called ZipWall. It uses spring-loaded poles (and optional foam-edged rails) to hold plastic sheets or canvas tarps tight against ceilings and floors, making it possible to create a temporary dust barrier around an indoor construction area. A ZipWall might be especially useful if you had to isolate part of a room, rather than sealing off doorways, as I had to do.

ing, I cut two pieces of plastic, each about a foot taller and a foot wider than the doorway it would cover. I installed these two pieces one on top of the other, stapling the first to the door casing along its uppermost edge and left side, the second along its uppermost edge and right side. To enter a room thus protected, you had to lift the top flap, bend down, and sort of squeeze through sideways—an inconvenience but not a huge one, since we were moving out for the duration. The barrier was less impregnable than plywood and carpet padding, but it worked pretty well. Very little dust got into the protected rooms, and what did get in I was able to take care with the vacuum cleaner.

The only semi-disaster occurred upstairs one day, when the plasterer's young assistant decided to investigate my son's room during his lunch break. He squeezed through the plastic barrier over the doorway, and left a faint trail of plaster-y footprints across the rug. I didn't find the footprints until after they had dried, and because this was real plaster, not joint compound, I couldn't just wipe up the mess with a wet rag. (Plaster sets, in essentially the way that concrete does; ordinary joint compound can be cleaned up with water.) Removing all traces of those plaster footprints required fifteen minutes of aggressive rubbing and spot vacuuming, plus a few months' worth of ordinary foot traffic; now everything looks fine.

During demolition, I showed up on the site most days, eager to help out, but I confined my contributions hauling junk out to the Dumpster and cleaning up at the end of the day. This was the best kind of sweat equity, since every hour I spent doing those things was as valuable as any hour that Rudy, Joe, or Mark spend doing something complicated and skillful. I did require a little instruction in Dumpster-loading. If you simply throw stuff into a Dumpster, as I did at first, the Dumpster fills far too quickly. Instead, Joe showed me, you should pack it almost as carefully as you would pack the trunk of your car for a long vacation, leaving as few empty spaces as possible.*

---

* The Dumpster was invented in the nineteen-thirties by George Roby Dempster, who was born in 1887, helped to dig the Panama Canal in the early nineteen hundreds,

I also handled some of the cleanup in the evenings—a time-consuming chore that forces carpenters to stop carpenting, and disperses dust and debris into the farthest corners of a house. Many nights, I went over the entire worksite myself with a push broom and my shop vac. Doing this allowed the people with actual skills to stay productive longer, and to start more efficiently the following morning. It also gave me a daily opportunity to study what they'd been up to, to notice details that looked different in reality from the way they had in the drawings, and to identify and correct misunderstandings before they'd become irreparable. While cleaning up the kitchen and the back hall one weekend, for example, I realized that one part of the planned layout wasn't going to work very well, and that we could simplify everything by sliding the powder room about four feet to the left. Doing so would create a useful space for coat hanging, right next to the back door, and would eliminate a flooring problem that had been gnawing at me. I never would have thought of moving the powder room if I hadn't been boredly vacuuming sawdust out of stud cavities and letting my eyes wander around the room.

The very best thing about handling the cleanup is that it enables you to hang around the job site without being hated by your contractors. Why, sometimes when I showed up on the site, Rudy and the other guys seemed almost glad to see me.

————————

RUDY'S FIRST JOB was to gut the old kitchen, playroom, upstairs bathroom, and rear entry hall—an area comprising perhaps 15 or 20 percent of the house's interior volume. Following this demolition, there was a brief period when I could stand near my office on the third floor, look down through what had once been a back stairway, and see all the way into the basement. Gazing into this vacuity was both fascinating and unnerving; the view was like something from a dream. I could orient myself by using

————————

and served as the mayor of Knoxville, Tennessee, from 1951 to 1955. The Navy used many Dempster Dumpsters during the Second World War, and the idea caught on widely afterwards. Dempster died in 1964.

familiar windows as landmarks: the double bathroom sink used to be over there, the shower over here, the kitchen stove down below. Having the house partially eviscerated also provided an opportunity to seal gaps in the house's skin and to add insulation to walls that had never had it. Before the insulation was installed, I vacuumed dust, old mouse nests, gnawed acorns, and broken chunks of plaster from the wall cavities. I found some scraps of ugly old wallpaper and a couple of empty cigarette packs, which students in our house's dormitory days must have stuffed into a crack, hiding evidence from a proctor. The plumber found a charred beam in a wall above the kitchen, the remnant of a long-forgotten fire. Rudy discovered that another beam, in a bearing wall, had broken in two many years before and wasn't holding up anything important. Everything else was in reasonably good shape.

When that corner of the house had been stripped to the framing, I somehow had the foresight to ask the electrician to install an empty conduit between the third floor and the basement, since a day might come when I would want to run a cable or wire of some kind between the top of the house and the bottom and I would never again have such easy access to the cavities inside the walls. The electrician installed two conduits, of a type called annular convoluted tubing. The tubes are an inch in diameter, are made of blue plastic, and are flexible, within limits. Their upper ends poke through a corner of the floor in what used to be the kitchen of the third-floor apartment; their lower ends dangle from the basement ceiling.

For two years after the completion of the renovation, those conduits had no function, unless mice were using them as an inter-story transportation system—a possibility, since mouse-edible items stored in the basement often appear mysteriously inside cabinets on the third floor. Then our cable-television provider began offering broadband Internet service. I upgraded my own computer first, naturally—then realized that I could hook up all the computers in the house if I networked the cable connection through a router. Adding Ann to the network was easy; all I had to do was make a small hole in the wall between my office and hers and feed an Ethernet cable through it. Hooking up the kids, whose computers were in their hideaway in the basement, seemed like more of a challenge—until I remembered my unused conduits.*

My son and I ordered a hundred feet of Ethernet cable from an electronic supply company. We plugged one end into the router in my office, then ran the other end through and under my desk, behind a file cabinet, through a hole in the wall, behind a bookcase, around a door, along a baseboard, behind a couch, and into the old kitchen. My first thought was that we would be able to simply feed the cable down to the basement through the conduit. But the tubing follows a meandering, opportunistic route through the walls, and the cable wasn't rigid enough for me to be able to push it past the first bend.

If we couldn't push the cable from above, maybe we could pull it from below. I found a roll of fishing line, attached some lead sinkers to the end, and lowered the line into the tube. I was thinking that the weight of the sinkers would quickly drag the line all the way to the basement, and that we could then tie the upper end of the line to the Ethernet cable and pull it down. But the sinkers got stuck, too, in about the same place the cable had. Hmmm. Now what?

Suddenly, I thought of my Craftsman six-horsepower sixteen-gallon wet-dry vac, the same machine I had been using to clean up after Rudy, Joe, and Mark. My son and I went down to the basement, lifted the vac onto a workbench, and duct-taped the end of the vac's hose to the basement end of the conduit. I then returned to the third floor. I made several knots in one end of roll of twine, fed the twine into the conduit, and put my mouth next to the opening and shouted, "Let her rip!" My son turned on the vac, and the twine pulled through my fingers, like an anchor chain sliding over the side of a ship. When the line had unspooled itself, my son turned off the vac. I tied my end to the Ethernet cable, and my son, when I gave him the signal, pulled it through.

---

* Nowadays, I have a wireless router, which I love, but most of the computers in our house are still networked by Ethernet cable, which is faster and more reliable.

I learned later that real electricians do the same thing, more or less, in similar situations, although instead of knotting the end of the string to increase their sucking power, they typically attach a small foam plug intended for that exact purpose. When I learned this, I felt as proud as if my son and I had independently reinvented the wheel.

My wet-dry vac is one of the most useful tools I own. About ten years ago, I bought a second one, for the garage, on the theory that I would clean the interior of my car more often if the necessary equipment were always right at hand. My theory turned out to be correct. I also use that vac to clean the garage, which, if left on its own, would gradually fill to the roof with dirt from our dirt road. The other vac, which lives in the basement, is used mainly by Ann, who keeps a small menagerie of caged birds, rodents, rabbits, and other creatures back by the oil tanks. Her collection at one point included a dozen rats—the unexpected offspring of a store-bought pet that belonged to one of our children. Occasionally, one of the many wild mice who winter inside our walls would venture into the rats' cage to share their corn—"We are all rodent brothers!"—and end up as a meal for the rats. We knew this was happening because we would find leftovers.

Until a couple of years ago, surprisingly, I had never used either of my wet-dry vacs to suck up anything wet. Then, an extraordinarily heavy rainstorm (in combination with a clogged gutter and a broken bulkhead door) created several half-inch-deep puddles on the floor of the basement. After ignoring the problem for several days (while the relative humidity in the house rose to rain-forest levels), Ann and I attacked the puddles with sponge mops—a very tedious activity, even though working together toward a common goal in this way was arguably a marriage-strengthener. Suddenly, while I was wringing my mop for what seemed like the ten millionth time, yet making no discernible progress with the puddle, I thought of my Craftsman six-horsepower sixteen-gallon wet-dry vac! Getting rid of the remaining puddles with the vac took about five minutes, and doing it was so much fun that I didn't let Ann have a turn. If I could earn my living doing any job in the world, I now know what it would be: vacuuming up water.

MOST OF THE WORK that Rudy, Joe, Mark, and the subcontractors did in my house is not directly observable today. They
stripped the renovation area to its frame, replaced broken framing members and braced inadequate ones, built new partitions,
replaced and repositioned windows and doors, ran wires and
pipes inside the walls, added insulation, covered the joists with
plywood subflooring, and enclosed the walls behind a Sheetrock-
like plaster system, about which I'll have more to say in Chapter
7. The final product of their efforts was a series of connected
empty boxes, inside which the visible elements of our new
kitchen, bathrooms, laundry room, and hall would be arranged.
In most kitchen renovations, four such elements get most of the
attention (and most of the money): cabinets, counters, appliances, and floors. In Ann's and my meetings with Peter, these
four items had always been the main topics of discussion.

The most conspicuous and expensive feature in most new
kitchens and kitchen renovations is usually the cabinetry. Cabinets can be built entirely from scratch—as the built-in bookcases
and storage cabinets in our library had been—or they can be ordered, with varying levels of customization, from a cabinet manufacturer, or they can be selected from a set menu of stock sizes,
styles, and finishes. The cost usually rises with the degree of customization, although an efficient solo cabinetmaker may be able
to compete on price with larger manufacturers. The cabinets that
Ann and I chose were made by Wood-Mode, a company whose
advertisements you have surely seen if you've spent any time
thumbing through home-decorating magazines. Our cabinets
would be classified as semi-custom, since we selected the sizes
and features from the lengthy list of standard ones that Wood-
Mode offers but had the visible parts finished in a particular Benjamin Moore paint color that we specified and Wood-Mode
reproduced.

Kitchen cabinets nowadays are available with an astounding
variety of functional options: drawers designed specifically to
hold silverware, knives, cans, or potatoes; pullout pantries, wine
racks, spice racks, towel racks, recycling centers, and ironing

boards; cabinets that turn into tables or rolling service carts; cabinets inside which you can store a mixer or a food processor on a platform that can be swung up to counter height; countertop "garages," in which appliances can be hidden when they're not in use; shallow tilt-out trays for storing sponges and scrub brushes; built-in dog houses (honest—I saw one in a magazine).

Ann and I resisted most of these and similar features, although we did order one that Peter recommended strongly and that has turned out to be very useful: drawer-like rollout trays, instead of ordinary shelves, for the large double cabinet under the cooktop. These trays hold what seems to be an impossible number of sauce pans, frying pans, omelet pans, double boilers, casseroles, colanders, and other bulky items, and they pull all the way out so that you never have to get down on your hands and knees to find the screen thing that keeps bacon grease from spattering the walls. We also sprung for a two-level lazy Susan cabinet for the blind corner at the elbow of the main counter, which is L-shaped. The lazy Susan is more accessible than ordinary fixed shelves would be, although any item that falls from it disappears more or less forever into the virtually inaccessible space beyond and below.

One feature that Ann and I both wanted in our kitchen was a built-in desk for doing things like making shopping lists and scheduling doctors' appointments—a once-exotic feature that has become almost standard in modern kitchen design. Ours is at the end of a counter. It's a bit less than three feet wide and a bit less than two feet deep, and it has a shallow drawer called a pencil drawer (in which we actually do keep pencils, along with paper clips, ChapStick, nail scissors, unopenable tubes of Krazy Glue, and other small, flattish items), and it has three built-in shelves above it (on which we keep phone directories, paper, envelopes, a few books, and a stereo speaker). There's a phone jack above the writing surface, and there's an electrical outlet that we use mainly for charging cell phones. We keep the main family calendar on the desk.

Our kitchen desk is quite handy, in other words. However, in the six years since the project was completed, I don't think that anyone has ever actually sat down to use it. (My idea of menu planning, on the fortunately few days when that responsibility falls to me, is to run to the grocery store fifteen minutes before it closes and wander around until I've thought of something—usually one of those already-roasted chickens.) Virtually all of the work that anyone ever does at that desk is done while standing, usually on the fly. The large space beneath the pencil drawer is therefore wasted, except as a parking place for a stool that no one ever sits on. Far more useful to Ann and me, and maybe to other people as well, would have been a stand-up desk of some kind, with storage rather than empty space underneath—the kind of thing that Thomas Jefferson might build for his kitchen if he were still around.

The only serious problem we have had with our cabinets occurred a couple of years after they were installed, when I noticed that the recessed panels in many of the cabinet doors were crazed with tiny, wrinkly cracks, all running in the same direction. I recognized these cracks as veneer checking, a furniture malady that is well known to woodworkers. The panels in the cabinet doors, like the panels in almost all modern doors, were made of plywood, which is manufactured by gluing together thin layers of wood veneer, sometimes in a sandwich with other wood products, under tremendous pressure. Every sheet of plywood has an odd number of layers—called "plies"—and these layers are always arranged so that the grain of the wood in any of them runs at a 90-degree angle to the grain of the wood in any adjacent one. All wood shrinks and expands as local moisture and humidity levels fall and rise, and most of that shrinking and expanding takes place across the wood's grain. Plywood is more dimensionally stable than solid lumber because the shrinkage or expansion of each ply is resisted by the adjacent plies, which are shrinking or expanding mainly along opposite axes. (I'll have more to say about moisture and wood movement in Chapter 7.) But the wood in plywood still tries to move, and as it does it exerts stresses on neighboring plies.

In some kinds of plywood, including the plywood often used to make door panels, only the outermost plies are made of wood veneer, while the central core is made of particleboard or something similar. If panels of this type are not manufactured under carefully controlled conditions, significantly different rates of shrinkage and expansion between the inner and outer layers can create stronger-than-usual stresses, which can cause the outer veneers to crack in a characteristic way. This is veneer checking. The cracks are usually most apparent during the winter, when the air is very dry and the wood has shrunk to the maximum extent, and they sometimes disappear entirely during the summer, when humidity is high.

Veneer checking is exacerbated by lathe checking, a similar defect, which is an unavoidable consequence of the plywood manufacturing process. Most plywood veneers are produced by a method called rotary cutting, which consists of turning a peeled log against a very sharp blade—like turning a pencil inside a pencil sharpener, or dragging a cheese slicer around the rim of a wheel of cheese. Doing this introduces stresses that can result in cracks, called lathe checks, on the inside surface of each veneer. Woodworkers usually arrange veneers so that the unchecked surface faces out, but even if they do this the cracks are weak points and they can spread, especially in the presence of other stresses.

I told Ducci about my veneer checking problem, and a representative from Wood-Mode came to look at my cabinets. He agreed with my diagnosis, and said that the doors would all have to be replaced, under warranty. He took a cabinet door with him, as a color sample. I heard nothing for a while, then discovered that the representative had left the company and that my sample cabinet door had been lost. I had to do a little hollering at that point, both at Ducci and at Wood-Mode, but everyone came around, eventually, and the cabinet doors were all replaced at no cost to me. The new doors, I am happy to say, do not seem to have the same problem.

CHOOSING KITCHEN cabinetry is mainly a stylistic decision moderated by money: people pick a look they like at whatever price level they've decided they can afford or tolerate. Choosing countertops—the second most conspicuous element in most kitchens—is trickier because the correlation between price and functionality isn't as close as it is with cabinets, since the options are bewilderingly numerous, and since the costliest materials go in and out of fashion very quickly. Ann did something that most people planning new kitchens don't do: she chose a different countertop material for each of the three principal surfaces: stainless steel, a sort of grayish-green Corian with tiny brown, tan, and white speckles in it, and slate. She selected each for a different reason, and uses each in a different way. A friend of ours warned Ann before the counters were installed that using three dissimilar materials might be visually jarring, but it's not, somehow. The colors are close enough that they don't register as different unless you study them—and even then the combination is not disharmonious. A home-decorating magazine ran an article about Ann and her most recent cookbook shortly after the kitchen was completed, and I would bet that most of the readers who looked at the very large color photograph accompanying the article didn't notice that the counters were not made of the same material.

During the seven years Ann and I lived in New York City, I thought so little about building materials that I never consciously noticed what our countertops were made of, and I recently had to look through an old scrapbook to find out. Those countertops, I discovered, were made of plastic laminate. Seeing the photograph made me recall the design as well: a dark-gray background with little boomerang shapes all over it.

Plastic laminate is the most popular countertop material in the United States; its best known brand name is Formica. It was invented in 1913 for use as an electrical insulator—in which capacity it was a replacement "for mica"—and it began to be used in kitchens a couple of decades after that. It is manufactured by impregnating multiple layers of kraft paper with phenolic resin, then compressing the layers, under high heat, into a thin, durable sandwich. (Kraft paper is what grocery bags are made of. Phenolic resin is a synthetic adhesive that permanently hardens when it's heated; it's typically made from phenol—a derivative of coal tar—and formaldehyde.) The color and decorative pattern of a sheet of plastic laminate comes from the sandwich's uppermost layer, which is almost always a fancier type of paper than kraft paper. This top layer is coated with melamine resin, a tough, transparent material that's made from formaldehyde and a relative of cyanide. (I guess it might be better not to know this.)

A sheet of plastic laminate is quite thin. To turn it into a countertop, you glue it to a thicker, stiffer substrate, such as a sheet of plywood or some form of particleboard, then glue more laminate to the substrate's edges, which are often built up to make the countertop look more substantial than it really is. The brown line you often see at the junction of these two planes is the inner layers of resin-impregnated kraft paper peeking through. Some fancier forms of plastic laminate are made with colored paper in all the layers, eliminating the brown line—a product sometimes known as color-through laminate. The edges of the countertops in our New York apartment were covered not with more laminate but with beaded metal strips, a treatment that was popular in the fifties and that you may have seen on the edges of the tables in the booths of old diners. Today, there are lots of other popular edge treatments, too, and most of them are more stylish than the old ninety-degree corners.

During the long middle decades of the twentieth century, before kitchens and bathrooms became objects of longing and ostentation, even rich people had countertops made of plastic laminate. The material's only real drawbacks, as a countertop surface, are that the melamine coating erodes with use; that the substrate is vulnerable to attack by water; and that you can't set down a hot pan for more than a moment without discoloring the surface or destroying the glue bond that holds everything together. (Cigarette burns, an old problem, are less troublesome now that fewer cooks habitually stand over the stove with a smoldering Lucky hanging from their lips.) I grew up in a house whose kitchen had plastic laminate counters, and I never once felt ashamed of them, or of myself. In fact, I thought that our counters looked kind of swanky, to the extent that I thought about them at all.

One of the greatest advantages of a plastic laminate counter is that by the time you get sick of the way it looks it is usually worn and fully amortized—something that is seldom true of marble. In the meantime, the material's physical vulnerabilities can be overcome through the judicious use of cutting boards and hot pads and by preventing water from soaking into the seams. The counters in our New York apartment were probably twenty-five years old when we moved in, and they still had plenty of miles left on them when we moved out. In fact, they were very nearly old enough to have come back into style.

Plastic laminate counters are especially inexpensive if you buy them ready-made and install them yourself. The L-shaped work surface in the basement hideaway I built for my kids is made of so-called post-formed plastic laminate—a factory-made counter material that I ordered to size from my town's hardware store. Post-formed counters usually come in a relatively limited selection of colors and styles, but they are available with two features that are virtually impossible to produce by hand: seamless, curved leading edges and back splashes, created in the factory by bending the laminate around the substrate as the counter is being made.

The single counter in the kitchen of our house, at the time we moved in, was a disaster. It was made of butcher block—strips of maple or some other hardwood glued together edgewise to form a thick, strong slab. Butcher block works well for some kitchen applications, and butchers probably swear by it, but wood of any kind is a poor choice for a surface that's going to be wet a lot of the time. Our counter had a standard stainless steel kitchen sink set into it, and the wood around the sink's rim had become black and slimy after many years of contact with water. Trying to scrape away the crud only made the problem worse, since aggressive cleaning created depressions in which water was even more likely to collect. Wood is also a poor choice for any surface on which a cook might want, or suddenly need, to set down something very hot.

Butcher block looks terrific when it's first installed, and it stays terrific-looking if you maintain it carefully and never use it, but Ann cursed our counter from the moment we moved in, and after five years of heavy use the wood had deteriorated to the point where neither of us could stand it anymore. I replaced it myself, with a post-formed plastic laminate counter for which I paid about a hundred dollars. We viewed that counter as a stopgap, and it turned out to be a very economical one, since it was still in place when we began our big renovation, nine years later.

CERAMIC TILE CAN be an inexpensive choice for kitchen countertops. The range of colors and designs is essentially unlimited, and tiles are tough, stain-proof, and extremely heat-resistant. Their main significant drawback is the grout-filled spaces between them. The grout inevitably discolors over time, as it also does on bathroom floors. Epoxy-based grouts are more stain-resistant than traditional grouts, but they're not impermeable. The spaces between tiles also create an uneven surface on which you can't do things like roll out (flat) Christmas cookies, and they make it difficult to create a truly waterproof seam between the sink and the counter, since water always finds ways to sneak through gaps. The tiles closest to counter edges tend to detach themselves over time, especially if there are people in your family who like to sit on kitchen counters. Ceramic tiles are often used to cover the narrow strip of wall between the top of the counters and the bottom of the cabinets above, a use to which they are better suited. Ann and I chose 2.5-inch-by-5.75-inch slate tiles for this space in our renovated kitchen—pretty much the same idea.

Among the most popular countertop choices in recent years have been solid surfacing materials, the best-known examples of which are Corian, which is made by DuPont, and Avonite. These and their many competitors are usually manufactured by combining a synthetic resin (such as acrylic or a combination of acrylic and polyester) with a mineral filler (such as alumina trihydrate, which is refined from the same ore that yields aluminum), along with various pigments and additives. The earliest versions tended either to be plain white or to look vaguely like imitation marble; current versions come in a huge and growing variety of colors and patterns. My own favorite colors and patterns, generally speaking, are the ones that don't try to look like other things. Corian is a cool material in its own right; it should be allowed to look like Corian.

One of the best features of solid surfacing materials is that they can be worked with woodworking tools and joined without visible seams. This makes it possible for trained fabricators to create complex countertops that seem to have been formed from a single chunk of material—a major advantage in a work environment that is often wet. Ann chose Corian for the countertop of the rectangular island in the middle of the work area of our new kitchen. The island measures forty inches by a hundred inches and has a seamlessly integrated Corian sink at one end. There is no joint between the sink and the counter, so there is no gap for water to seep into. Ann keeps her mixer next to that sink, and when she spills flour or some other ingredient she just sweeps it into the sink with a sponge—no problem.

Solid surfacing materials are usually described as impervious, but they aren't quite. While our Corian countertop was being installed, someone placed a wet bag at one end, and part of the bag's blue label bled into the countertop. I thought the marks would wipe right up, since I had read that solid surfacing materials were stain-proof, but they didn't. I complained to the countertop installer, who showed how to gently rub out the discoloration with a Scotch-Brite pad or a mildly abrasive cleanser, such as Soft Scrub. Ann and I learned subsequently, through experience, that stains in Corian need to be rubbed out right away, before they have penetrated deeper than mild abrasion (or bleach) can reach. The bottom of our otherwise wonderful integrated Corian sink is now permanently dingy—the result of too many cast-iron skillets, used tea bags, and grounds-filled coffee filters being left to sit overnight. The discoloration is slight, though, and the advantage of having no seams outweighs the small annoyance of the Corian's susceptibility to staining.

Custom-made countertops made of solid surfacing materials are very expensive. You can save a considerable amount of money by ordering stock sizes and colors, or by choosing ready-made configurations. You can also save money by using so-called solid surfacing veneers, in which the expensive stuff is a relatively thin layer applied to a thicker supporting substrate, like plywood or particleboard. Only you will know that you have cheated.

The counters in extremely expensive kitchens are usually made of some form of stone, typically granite or marble. Both are available in a bewildering variety of types, colors, figures, textures, and grades, and from quarries all over the world. Costs vary, but all are high. Stone counters are great for rolling out dough, and they can easily tolerate hot pans and other kitchen insults. Granite is harder and more chip-resistant than marble, and it is more dense and therefore less likely to stain, although both granite and marble need to be sealed and (periodically) re-sealed. Stains, if they do occur, can be impossible to get rid of. My favorite granite countertop is in the kitchen of my friends Ken and Gina. It is almost dead black, and it has a honed rather than a polished surface, giving it a dull appearance that I like. (Shiny/not shiny is one of the absolute divides in home-decorating taste.) Black countertops are a little like black cars: no color looks better when clean or worse when dirty.

If a kitchen has lots of counter space, highly polished, heavily figured granite or marble may begin to seem visually exhausting after a while—like a patterned dress or sport coat that's a big hit the first time you wear it but gradually gets on people's nerves. I once saw a huge new kitchen with acres and acres of very shiny red-and-white granite countertops and wondered whether the cook had begun to hate them yet. The best advice I've heard re-garding stone countertops is to look at a full slab before order-ing, since sample-size pieces are difficult to extrapolate from. A stone countertop, unlike a plastic-laminate one, is both costly and virtually indestructible. Before writing the check, you ought to be confident you can stand to live with it until you no longer feel that it owes you anything, or until you've sold your house to someone else.

Ann wanted one stone surface in our kitchen, on the long counter above the pair of ovens, so that she could place a hot cookie sheet or roasting pan directly on it without having to look around for a hot pad or a trivet. Neither of us liked the granite and marble samples that Peter showed us; we ended up choosing slate, mainly because its mottled gray color seemed subdued but interesting, with occasional dark swirls that looked like spilled ink. Best of all, it wasn't shiny. Our slate countertop consists of two pieces. One is about ten and a half feet long and twenty-eight inches deep, and the other is about three feet long and twenty-three inches deep. (The second piece forms the writing surface of the kitchen desk.) These stones were cut and honed at a quarry in Vermont, and they arrived in an enormous wooden crate, which was carried into the house by six large men taking tiny, shuffling steps. I was one of the six large men, and as we moved slowly toward the back door we looked like pall bearers. Lifting the big piece into place on top of the ovens and the cabinets next to them involved lots of nervous jostling and the barking of many orders.

Slate is nowhere near as hard as granite is. It scratches easily—a problem for some people—but the scratches disappear when you wipe the surface with a wet paper towel, and the remnants of the scratches are detectable only if you look very, very closely. I actually like them, and think of them as patina. Good quality, tight-grained slate countertops (such as ones from quarries in Maine, New York State, and Vermont) don't need to be sealed; ours usually gets cleaned with Windex or something like it, and every year or two I wipe it down, for no real reason, with a little lemon oil. The seam between the two pieces is visible and therefore vulnerable—as seams always are in stone countertops. The usual method of making such a seam is to run a bead of clear silicone caulk along the edges of the adjoining pieces and then butt them together. The end of one of the slate slabs had to be shimmed, to make the two slabs level. I suggested using a couple of single-edge razor blades, of which I had a large surplus, but the installer laughed at my idea, which he said sounded dangerous; he used some wood slivers instead. The weight of the slate eventually compressed the wood, however, and the slivers fell out. I *still* think the razor blades would have been a good idea.

In recent years, a number of manufacturers have introduced countertops made of synthetic stone—usually, small bits of quartz in a resin matrix, along with various pigments. These materials perform about the same way that natural stone does but are more uniform in appearance and require less fussy maintenance. Engineered stone is typically less heat resistant than natural stone (because of the resins) but is more impervious to stains (and therefore doesn't require sealing). Trade names of popular versions include Caesarstone, Cambria, Legacy, Silestone, Technistone, and Zodiac. Engineered stone occupies what could almost be thought of as an intermediate phase of countertop matter between solid surfacing and real stone. It's a wonderful material, and it's less temperamental than real stone, although it's every bit as expensive—a good thing or a bad thing, depending on your point of view.

I REMEMBER THE first time I saw a concrete countertop, in a photograph in a home-decoration magazine. (It seems like five or ten years ago, so it must have been ten or fifteen. Whenever I meet someone who seems to be about my age, I have learned to assume that he or she must be five or ten years younger.) I immediately wanted a countertop just like the one in the magazine, although I never did anything about my desire. Since that time, concrete has become increasingly popular in kitchens, bathrooms, and elsewhere, and my (hypothetical) ardor for it has cooled.

To me, the most appealing feature of that first concrete countertop I saw was that it looked exactly like what it was. The subsequent trend has been away from concreteness, however. Several years ago, at a trade show, I spoke with a representative of a concrete-related trade association, who told me, "Decorative is the rage in concrete now, and that includes countertops, fireplace surrounds, decorative interior floors. With countertops, you've got Corian, you've got granite—and then there's that one person in ten who goes, 'I want something different.' Those are the buyers for concrete countertops. In many cases they're involved in creating their own top, maybe by having personal items embedded in it. One of the things that is huge right now is toppings—dyes and tints—and you're starting to have non-concrete people coming in who are adding their own twist. Maybe they've never poured any concrete in their life, but they're able to do this outrageous stuff, so we have a lot of artists and designers in the business. And now they're making furniture. It's started, I feel, to take on a life of its own." At the same trade show, I saw concrete countertops whose main selling point, their creators said, was that they looked nothing like concrete. Well, what's the point?

Today, I would be very hesitant to use concrete countertops unless I could be sure that I was ordering them from a company with lots of experience and an ironclad guarantee. Most of the printed and online promotional literature I've read concerning concrete countertops contains misinformation, including a near-total misunderstanding of the purpose of reinforcement. Reinforcing concrete—by adding steel bars, plastic fibers, expanded metal lath, woven metal wire, or anything else—does not make the concrete stronger and does not prevent it from cracking. The purpose of reinforcement, in a concrete countertop or any other concrete structure, is to hold it together after it has cracked and to take over and dissipate the tensile load that caused the cracking to occur. (For a fuller explanation of how concrete works, see Chapter 5.) A contractor who tells you that your standard-size concrete kitchen countertop requires steel reinforcing rods, six-inch wire mesh, polypropylene fibers, or a combination of these is almost certainly leading you far, far astray, and may be increasing the likelihood that your countertop will fail, whether during fabrication or at some time in the future. An engineer on the staff of the Portland Cement Association told me that the best reinforcing material for an ordinary concrete kitchen countertop is nineteen-gauge galvanized hardware cloth with a half-inch-by-half-inch mesh—available at almost any hardware store for around thirty cents a square foot. The hardware cloth should be placed so that it will end up in the bottom third of the slab, and it serves no purpose unless the concrete cracks, at which point it helps to keep the slab from collapsing into the cabinetry. If possible, concrete countertops should be precast and cured under controlled conditions, and installed a month or two after pouring. Openings for things like sinks, faucets, and cooktops need to be made a very slightly larger than their desired finished size, because concrete shrinks a little as it sets and will crack if its contraction is resisted by an unyielding penetration like a steel sink. (Concrete shrinks very little—just three-quarters of an inch per hundred feet—so the openings don't have to be enormous.)

After installation, concrete countertops also require more care than people usually assume. They stain easily and permanently unless they are sealed, and once they've been sealed they don't react well to hot frying pans or to knives. They are nice and expensive, though.

Our new kitchen's main work surface—the one that contains

the cooktop and the principal sink—is made of stainless steel. It is a single, L-shaped unit whose outside edges are eight feet and eleven feet long. The sink, a sloping drainboard, and a four-inch-tall backsplash are all seamlessly integrated. There are no joints or gaps except for the rectangular cutout in which the cooktop is mounted.

Stainless steel is often described, usually negatively, as having a "commercial" or "industrial" appearance, but our counter has never struck me that way, perhaps because stainless steel is so well suited to withstanding what goes on in a kitchen. It is highly resistant to bacterial contamination. Water doesn't hurt it. (You can even have your countertops fabricated with a so-called marine edge, a integral lip that contains spilled liquids.) Foods don't stain it. Hot cookware can be placed directly on top of it. Stainless steel does scratch fairly easily, so you shouldn't use steel wool or abrasive cleansers on it. There are two methods of dealing with the scratching that does occur: embrace it, as a sign of character; remove it periodically by regraining or repolishing the surface, or, better, by hiring someone with experience in stainless steel to do it for you. Modern stainless steel countertops come in a variety of finishes, and some of them are trickier to restore than others.

WHEN I NEED to buy a new computer, computer program, piece of electronic equipment, TV, appliance, or power tool, I don't consult *Consumer Reports* or go comparison shopping. I just call my chain-saw buddy Rex and ask him what kind he owns. Rex has certain endearing obsessive-compulsive qualities—his basement floor is clean enough to nap on; for many years, he has used an Excel spreadsheet to track the longevity of particular light bulbs in his house; all the wires connecting his stereo components are labeled—and he is almost frighteningly thorough at analyzing major purchases before making them. If Rex buys a new vacuum cleaner (for example), I know that I can blindly buy the same model with absolute confidence, because I know that Rex will have devoted days, if not months, to due diligence and complex cost-benefit analysis.

When Rex is no help—either because he doesn't own the item I need or because he bought his too long ago—I sometimes use a methodology devised by Ann: buy the third most expensive model in a line whose manufacturer you trust. The most expensive version of anything is almost always loaded with unnecessary features and is intended just for spendthrift suckers; the least expensive is usually stripped to the point of being ineffective or inconvenient. The sweet spot lies somewhere near the median. Rather than exhausting yourself by trying to evaluate criteria you don't understand, why not throw a dart?

But this method doesn't always work. When it came time to buy appliances for the new kitchen, Ann, who wanted two ovens side by side, simply ordered two of KitchenAid's not-quite top-of-line convection ovens without doing a lot of research or brooding about her choice. (Rex is no help in the kitchen.) Her ancient KitchenAid mixer had been the most reliable kitchen appliance she'd ever owned, and she felt certain that with a brand name so well known and highly regarded she had nothing to worry about. Besides, how could anybody screw up something as simple as an oven?

But the KitchenAid ovens have been a disaster. Like many modern appliances, they have electronic controls, which are so complex that the ovens could probably be classified as small computers. The electronic controls enable you to do many things that almost no one ever needs to do—such as set an oven to automatically turn on in an hour, operate at 400 degrees with convection for thirty minutes, switch to 300 degrees without convection for an hour, and shut itself off—but make it difficult to do things you need to do all the time, such as broil a steak. The main problem is that a hot oven is a lousy environment for complex electronics. Our worst crisis occurred one day when Ann had set both ovens to self-clean at the same time, and the high heat of the cleaning routine fried all the computer chips. The ruined control boards, which cost several hundred dollars each, were covered by the warranty, but the labor required to replace them—a couple hundred more dollars—was not.

In retrospect, self-cleaning two side-by-side ovens at the same time seems potentially risky—although there's no mention of any danger in the manual, and even cleaning the ovens one at a time has caused problems. Recently, one of the ovens failed to unlock its door when its cleaning cycle had finished. The lock is a safety feature, intended to prevent the oven from being opened while its interior is still hotter than the center of the sun, but the latch is supposed to release once the oven has cooled. A customer service representative at KitchenAid suggested shutting down the household electric circuit serving the oven, letting the oven sit for ten minutes, then turning the power back on and trying again. We did, but nothing happened. Ann also tried running the cleaning cycle a second time, hoping that refrying the interior would remind the computer how to release the door. Also nothing. Finally, our trusty appliance repairman got the door open by jimmying it with a coat hanger and a screwdriver, although he had to break the latch to do it. The latch mechanism, he said, had melted during self-cleaning and would have to be replaced (no longer under warranty).

Anyway, our experience with KitchenAid ovens led Ann and me to develop a third method of shopping for large appliances: before doing anything else, ask your repairman for a recommendation. (His main advice? Never, ever self-clean an oven, no matter who manufactured it.) A corollary to this rule is to never buy an appliance, or anything else, with features that may seem attractive in the abstract but are unlikely to be truly useful. Those features, in addition to running up the price, are usually the ones that are the most likely to break down. Nowadays, many new washing machines have complicated electronic controls and dozens of possible cleaning protocols, yet most people use the same settings over and over, and would be just as happy if their machine had a dial with just two positions, hot and cold.

Not all of our appliance problems over the years have been caused by our appliances. When our dishwasher stopped working a few years ago, the repairman quickly found the culprit: four small, hard objects that had become lodged in the machinery in the bottom of the compartment. He said that he didn't know what they were—they looked like porcelain fragments—but he urged Ann and me to always rinse plates carefully before putting them into any dishwasher, despite manufacturers' claims that rinsing is unnecessary. Most dishwasher breakdowns, he said, are caused by indigestible bits of food becoming jammed in the moving parts. I nodded solemnly, even though I knew that unrinsed plates weren't responsible in this case. I had recognized those porcelain-like fragments immediately: they were coyote teeth, and I was the reason they were in the dishwasher. To make a long story short: I had bought a coyote skull on eBay (for reasons too complicated to explain) and had discovered, when it arrived, that the seller had not cleaned it as carefully as he had claimed in his listing. I left the skull sitting outside in the sun for several weeks, without having much effect. Then I had the idea of putting it in the dishwasher by itself and washing it on the hottest, most aggressive pots-and-pans setting. This turned out to be a terrible, terrible idea. Shortly after the cycle began, an overpowering odor, which was a little like the distilled essence of a hundred wet golden retrievers, filled the house. Nobody else was home, so I opened as many windows as I could and let the cycle finish. When I finally opened the dishwasher's door, the smell almost knocked me over. And the skull itself was unimproved; it fact, it may have been worse. I later soaked it in bleach overnight, then left it outside for almost a year. The house didn't take quite as long to recover, although I had olfactory hallucinations for a week: I'd be driving in my car and suddenly I'd think I could smell the skull again. Ann was furious for a while, but she got over it eventually. And after the whole dishwasher-repair thing had died down, I used a glue gun to reattach the missing teeth.

The most surprising appliance decision that Ann made about our kitchen, in the opinion of several friends of hers who are also serious cooks, was to order a glass-ceramic electric cooktop rather than a commercial-style gas range. Ann says that she would have wanted a gas range of some kind if gas service had been available in our town—to fuel a gas stove we'd have needed a propane tank in the yard, and she didn't want one—but she has cooked on commercial ranges before, and she believes that most of their supposed advantages are irrelevant for civilian cooks, even ambitious ones. Commercial-type ranges are not designed for family cooking; they are meant to accommodate harried professional chefs, frantic cooking schedules, and restaurant-size pots and pans. They're handy if you need to char peppers or quickly boil a dozen two-pound lobsters, but they are both excessive and inefficient for virtually all the meal preparation done by ordinary mortals (and even by cookbook writers). People who own huge ranges like to brag about the "heat control" allegedly provided by monstrous gas burners, but in many ways controlling heat is easier on a glass-ceramic cooktop, since you can lower the cooking temperature immediately by sliding a saucepan off the heating element. And if you accidentally tip over a bowl of pancake batter on top of a glass-ceramic, you can clean up the mess without having to disassemble the entire unit.

When it came time to choose a refrigerator, we succumbed to peer pressure and bought a huge Sub-Zero, the Hummer of refrigerators. We didn't have to reinforce the kitchen floor to support it, as some friends did with theirs, and we didn't have to dismantle an exterior wall to get it into the house, as some other friends did with theirs. A neighbor, who was renovating his own kitchen and was in the market for a new refrigerator, dropped by one day to look at ours and decided that its main compartment was surprisingly shallow for a box so huge, with upper shelves just fourteen inches deep. I said that the width of the compartment probably made the shelves look shallower than they actually were, and that, besides, truly deep shelves are undesirable in a refrigerator because they just make it easier for jars of pickles and packages of lunch meat to become permanently lost. But I'm not sure he was convinced.

Our Sub-Zero has a few genuinely appealing features, among them digital controls that make it possible to set exact temperatures for the two compartments, and a few annoying ones, among them a door shelf that is designed to hold very large items but that extends so far into the refrigeration compartment that it can prevent the door from closing completely if you don't load it very carefully. And it has one excellent feature that every large appliance ought to have: retractable wheels underneath that make it possible for a repairman to roll the unit forward, should that ever become necessary, rather than dragging it across your nice kitchen floor—although the wheels will hurt a floor, too, if you don't put down something hard for them to roll over.

KITCHEN FLOORS ARE a major challenge even if no one
drags large appliances across them. They have an important decorative function, since they are often as conspicuous as the shockingly expensive cabinets and countertops above them, but they
also have to be tough enough to withstand intense, localized
wear: chairs and stools being scraped back and forth in the same
places over and over; cooks repeatedly shuffling from sink to
stove to fridge, abrading a path along the work triangle; kids and
pets with dirty feet running in from the backyard. Kitchen floors
also have to be able to withstand major spills—an inevitability—
and, ideally, they should be resilient enough not to exhaust the
feet, legs, and backs of those shuffling cooks.

I know many people who have wood floors in their kitchens.
Such floors often look magnificent when they're new, but wood is
especially vulnerable to kitchen-related wear, even if (as is often
the case) it is drenched with polyurethane. I have a friend with
wood floors in her kitchen who wore a deep trench in front of
the sink before the floor was a year old. (She covered the eroded
area with a rug—a sensible alternative to refinishing.) Seasonal
wood movement often opens small gaps between floorboards
during heating months, and in kitchens the gaps can fill quickly
with tracked-in dirt and sand, spilled flour and maple syrup, floor
wax, and who knows what else. This is a problem that, over the
years, tends to be self-aggravating, as the filth accumulation
grows. A number of manufacturers make laminate flooring systems that tend to look either pretty much like real wood or
bizarrely unlike anything else on earth. They are generally said to
require less maintenance than real wood, but they share its vulnerability to water damage—including the gradual, relentless de-
terioration caused by wet feet, splashes from the sink, and drips
from the dishwasher. A key difference from real wood: laminate
flooring can't be refinished.

Stone and ceramic tiles are far more durable and resistant to
water damage than wood is, but they have drawbacks of their
own. Both materials can be tiring to stand on for long periods,
and both have grout lines that cause furniture to tip and are hard

to keep clean. They are also unfriendly to toddlers and wobbly old people, and they feel cold to bare feet unless they're installed over a radiant heating system (to which they are well suited). Glazed ceramic tiles resist abrasion well, but stone tiles and unglazed ceramic tiles often scratch easily, especially in dining areas, where chairs or stools are constantly in motion. Glazed ceramic tiles and highly polished stone tiles, such as those made of marble, can be slippery, especially when they're wet—as they often are in a kitchen.

The ideal kitchen flooring material, in many ways, is probably sheet vinyl, which is the modern incarnation of linoleum. Linoleum was invented in 1863 by Frederick Walton, an English manufacturer of rubber products, and it's made from linseed oil, cork, natural resins, saw dust, limestone dust, pigments, and jute or asphalt-impregnated canvas. Early customers liked it so much that they took it with them when they moved. (The first versions often weren't glued down.) You can still buy honest-to-goodness linoleum—which has become stylish again in recent years—but when most people talk about linoleum nowadays what they really mean is sheet vinyl, in the same way that when my mother talks about her "ice box" what she really means is her refrigerator, and when she talks about her "radio" what she really means is her TV.

Sheet vinyl flooring is a sandwich. The bottom layer is usually a resilient or semi-resilient backing of some kind. The middle layer consists of fused vinyl chloride resins or of a vinyl sheet onto which a decorative image has been printed. The top, or wearing, layer is made of transparent vinyl chloride and serves mainly to protect the decorative layer. Some versions have an additional protective coating, made of urethane, which acts as a wearing layer for the wearing layer. Joints between sheets are sealed with an adhesive that essentially welds the sheets together—an improvement over earlier systems, which inevitably gave way. Vinyl flooring of this type is also sold as individual tiles, which are much easier to install than the sheet version but, because they have many seams, are vulnerable to damage by water, which can seep through the seams and destroy the adhesive that holds them to the subfloor.

Sheet vinyl is appealing as a flooring material because, if it is installed properly and in the right configuration, it can create an impervious barrier between the mayhem of ordinary kitchen activity and rot-prone wood. The only problem with sheet vinyl, in my opinion, is that virtually all versions of it are shiny, if not radiant. In fact, shininess seems to be one of its main selling points, so that the costliest, most durable models also tend to look almost as though they have a quarter-inch of water standing on them. This is an issue in which I am definitely in the minority; most people like the wet look so much that they work hard to preserve and enhance it, leading to the popularity of one of the greatest ironic home-maintenance products of all time: floor wax for no-wax floors. (Nowadays, virtually all floor wax, including no-wax wax, is made not of wax but of acrylic or some other synthetic substance.) Vinyl flooring is also hard to find in colors that could honestly be described as muted or subtle. If you want fake brick, you have lots of choices; if you want a subdued, non-reflective brick color, good luck.

Ann and I—after a lengthy, aimless decision-making process that was difficult to follow at the time and would be impossible to reconstruct now—chose vinyl flooring of a different type: vinyl composition tiles, which are used mostly in commercial and institutional applications, such as the floors of supermarkets and high schools. Unlike vinyl sheet flooring, vinyl composition tiles don't have a clear wearing surface. They are made entirely of vinyl resins mixed with various fillers, and they aren't shiny. Ann and I chose a brand called Azrock, which is manufactured by a Texas company called Tarkett. We picked twelve-inch tiles in two very restrained colors: a dusty green and a khaki-like tan, both with tiny, randomly arranged black speckles (which are variably sized mineral particles that were mixed in with the vinyl resins during manufacture). The speckles look a little like cracked peppercorns and therefore provide useful camouflage if you spill cracked peppercorns on the floor.

Our Azrock tiles, which were installed in the familiar checkerboard pattern, look great, although I'm not sure we made a good choice. Vinyl composition tiles, like other vinyl tiles, are vulnerable to damage by water.* Also, the tiles' non-reflective surface, which is what attracted us to them in the first place, has turned out to be impossible to maintain. The tile material is both soft and brittle, relatively speaking, and to keep it from becoming horribly worn you have to protect it with a shiny acrylic sealer. In supermarkets and high schools, this sealer is applied in multiple coats and then polished to a urethane-like sheen, with a buffer the size of a lawn mower. Ann and I tried leaving the tiles bare for a while, then went overboard in the other direction, by repeatedly applying a popular floor finish that we bought at the grocery store; doing this produced the common kitchen-floor malady known as waxy build-up. Finally, we stripped all the yellowed, accumulated goop (using a liquid stripper sold for that purpose) and applied a single coat of an acrylic sealer that was recommended for use on vinyl composition tiles. Our kitchen floor today is shinier than it was when it was first installed, but it resists scratching better than it did when it was unsealed, and it's still nowhere near as luminous as a sheet-vinyl floor or a freshly waxed, buffed, and polished vinyl composition corridor in a hospital. For the past couple of years, I have meant to strip the sealer and apply a fresh new coat, but I've been too lazy to actually do it. The floor doesn't seem to be suffering from my neglect, however.

The conventional advice about all types of vinyl tiles is that darker colors hide wear better than lighter ones, but in my experience the opposite is true (as it also is with car finishes): in our kitchen, scratches and abrasions blend right in with khaki-colored tiles but are fairly conspicuous on the dusty green ones. To keep the scratching to a minimum, I've had to attach protective pads to the metal feet of six side chairs and four stools. The chairs are made of aluminum and were manufactured by a company called Emeco, whose founder, Wilton C. Dinges, designed them in 1944 (in collaboration with Alcoa) for use on Navy ships.

---

* We also used Azrock tiles on the floor of the kids' bathroom—something I would definitely never do again. An unnoticed toilet leak ruined that floor in just a day or two. I'll have more to say about this minor disaster in Chapter 8.

The chairs have round, flat metal feet, which probably work great on submarines but are hard on bare household floors of all kinds. I have made the feet less destructive by attaching thick felt furniture pads to them. The pads are theoretically self-adhesive, but the adhesive doesn't adhere for very long, so I supplement it with duct tape, which is the same color as the aluminum. I cut it into strips about five-sixteenths of an inch wide and wrap tightly around the outside edge of each foot so that the tape helps to hold the felt to the metal. A new pad withstands six or nine months of ordinary use before needing to be replaced.

I ordered the stools, which were designed in the mid-nineties by a California furniture-maker named Jeff Covey, from the online store of the Museum of Modern Art. They have wire legs, which look like partly unfolded paper clips, and when we first used the stools their feet left small dents in the floor tiles. I solved that problem by covering the stools' feet with inch-and-a-half-long pieces of flexible clear vinyl tubing, which I found in the plumbing department of the hardware store. The inside diameter of the tubing is the same as the outside diameter of the heavy wire from which the stools' legs and feet are made. I cut the tubing into short lengths, slit them longitudinally with a single-edged razor blade, and attached them to the stools' feet with Krazy Glue. The glue holds for about as long as the felt pads on the chairs do, and by the time it gives up the vinyl has usually become so embedded with grit that it needs to be replaced anyway.

The softness/brittleness of vinyl composition tiles causes another problem: it makes the tiles susceptible to being deformed by relatively minor subfloor irregularities, including gaps between plywood panels, soft spots caused by voids inside plywood panels, and fastener heads that are either higher or lower than the surrounding subfloor surface. There are several tiles in the kitchen that have small cracks caused by these or similar defects. Fortunately, individual vinyl composition tiles are easy to replace. I have plenty of spares piled up somewhere in the basement, and one of these days I will get around to removing the damaged tiles, repairing the trouble-causing areas beneath them, and putting brand-new tiles in their place. One of these days—but not yet.

JUST ABOUT MY favorite part of our big kitchen-and-bathroom project came at the very end, when it was time to put everything back. I told the other members of my family to stay out of my way. I suffer intermittently from an organizational mental disorder—my office filing system employs a couple of hundred color-coded three-ring binders—and I didn't want interference from the unafflicted. I had learned my lesson a few years before, when I announced to my family that the time had come to sort our exponentially growing collection of unmatched socks. My announcement led to recriminations and tears, and I discovered that the other members of my family were well satisfied with our long-established system, which consisted (and still consists) of keeping almost all our socks in a single large laundry basket, like fruit in a cafeteria. There are so many orphan socks in the basket that at any moment only about a third of the total supply is available for use. (The orphan socks are like the big pieces of lettuce under the fruit salad which you aren't supposed to eat.) I later simplified my own life by settling on a single brand of socks to wear with sneakers and a single brand to wear with non-sneakers. I store this private collection in my dresser, and I inspect the communal basket only when I suspect poaching.

Our funky old bathroom had had a storage closet whose shelves were roughly five feet, four feet, three feet, two feet, and one foot deep. (It was built into the space under a flight of stairs leading to the third floor.) The lower shelves would have been perfect for storing snow tires, but they were useless for lip balm and dental floss. All those cubic yards of shelf space defied every attempt at rational organization. Half-empty bottles of sunscreen would disappear for years behind boxes of expired pain relievers. When I finally emptied the closet, shortly before demolition began, I found scores of things I'd forgotten we owned: a hairdryer I'd been given for Christmas when I was in high school; a dust-caked bar of bikini wax; an ancient box of cotton balls, now partly filled with mouse poison, which our mice had diligently been storing for future consumption; miscellaneous Lego pieces; a hammer; four or five electric heating pads; a bucket; and a postal scale.

In Ann's and my bathroom, I had solved this problem by asking Peter to cover most of one wall with a bank of storage cabinets that had shelves just eight inches deep. Eight inches may sound skimpy, but think about what you actually store in your bathroom: backup tubes of toothpaste, bottles of shampoo, cans of shaving cream, bottles of aspirin, containers of deodorant. The largest stored items in most people's bathrooms are extra rolls of toilet paper, which are just four and a half inches tall and maybe five inches in diameter. Compact stuff like that doesn't require a walk-in closet, or even a cupboard as deep as the ones in a kitchen. The most important storage considerations for small items are visibility and access. Razor blades, swiped bottles of hotel hand lotion, eyebrow pencils, and tweezers are hard to organize and easy to lose on shelves that are more than a few inches deep. Assigning our toiletries positions on our new eight-inch shelves was an intense pleasure, and as I worked I eliminated several of Ann's more eccentric storage conventions, such as keeping bunion pads and shoe polish in the same drawer on the theory that both are related to feet. (Why not store hats and aspirin together, too?)

One of the keys to efficient household organization is to store useful items as close as possible to the place where they are used, making them easier to find and put away. Several years before our big kitchen-and-bathroom project, Ann and I hired a carpenter to cover a long blank wall in our living room with built-in bookshelves and cabinets. We quickly filled the bookshelves with books, but we couldn't decide what to keep in the cabinets, which are twice as deep as the shelves. Light bulbs? Old hats? The board games we never play? Suddenly, I realized what we should keep there: all our holiday decorations, most of which get used in the living room anyway. At that time, we were keeping them in a jumble of boxes in a room on the third floor which had been a kitchen when the third floor was an apartment. Decorating and undecorating the Christmas tree every year involved many tedious trips up and down two flights of stairs, along with much packing and unpacking of items that were believed to be too fragile to survive the journey intact if left unprotected. Inevitably, Christmas ornaments got mixed up with Halloween and Easter decorations, and you could never place your hand on any particular item except by accident. Storing everything in the living-room cabinets took care of all that. The Christmas decorations are in the cabinets on the left, and other decorations are stored in chronological order, by season, as you move to the right—easy to find, easy to return, out of the way until needed.

When I organized the new kitchen, I was brutal. Many of the cabinets and cupboards in our old kitchen had been filled with bulky items that did little but displace oxygen: a dozen shallow plastic boxes with handles, for carrying pies; three two-cup fat separators, with their price tags still affixed; an eighteen-inch cake saw, for turning one thick cake into two thin ones; a plastic ice bucket shaped like a golf ball; and our large and historically significant wok collection, which dates from our wedding. Sacrificing valuable kitchen shelf space for these and other seldom-used items was foolish. Some of them I lugged down to the basement or out to the garage; others I threw away. At my request, Rudy had left a boxcar-sized Dumpster parked outside the back door, and I filled it to the top. The stuff that remained I organized logically and unsentimentally: the dog's heartworm pills in a drawer with their food instead of on a shelf with plates, potato chips, and winter gloves; the phone book next to the phone rather than buried beneath screwdrivers and extension cords.

Deciding where to put each new item was like wrestling with a clue in a crossword puzzle. I made a few false starts, but everything worked beautifully in the end. The only problem was the wine glasses. No matter how carefully I arranged them on the shelf to which I had assigned them, I couldn't squeeze in the very last one. It rang sweetly when it hit the back of the Dumpster.

4

THE CABIN

BECAUSE WE WEREN'T willing to forgo eating, showering, and going to the bathroom during our big kitchen-and-bathroom renovation, we had to rent another house for the summer. The real estate agent who found our rental for us was the same one who had sold us our regular house almost fifteen years before—and this time we took the first house she showed us, rather than holding out for the second. The rental was on the northeast side of our town, just a ten-minute drive away, on a dirt road that I had never seen before, in a thinly settled rural area with a river running through it. A large wooded hill—the kind of hill that in New England passes for a mountain—rose directly behind it. I recognized the hill, and knew that much of it lay within the boundary of a state park. In fact, my kids and I had climbed to the top from the other side the previous fall, and had looked out over the surrounding countryside from an old stone fire tower at the summit.

The rental house was almost as old as our regular house, but was much smaller; it was a cottage. To use the only bathroom, upstairs, you had to accommodate your spine angle to the slope of the ceiling. For the past thirty years or so, the cottage had been used as a weekend retreat by a family living somewhere else. The furniture was mismatched but comfortable, and the bookshelves were filled with books we hadn't read, and there were amenities undreamed of at our regular house: a faded old vinyl-lined swimming pool, a tetherball pole, and a barn filled with bats, bat guano, and dead flies. In the evenings, we would sometimes sit among the weeds near the pool and watch the bats emerging one after another from a hole in one of the barn's gable ends, up near the peak of the roof. They looked like paratroopers leaping into action, and in the dusk we could watch them swooping over-head, gorging on mosquitoes. Ann and I could hear the river from our bed at night. There was a bridge just past the bottom of our driveway, and a smaller one a couple of hundred yards up the road in the opposite direction. Occasionally, we saw men in waders fly-fishing in the river, but usually we had the view to our-selves. After big rainstorms, water poured over some big rocks near one of the bridges and looked so smooth and deep and milky green that it seemed almost solid. A great blue heron lived somewhere near the river and would sometimes cruise along it, just a few feet above the water, looking like a special effect in a movie about dinosaurs. An abandoned railroad bed ran through the woods, and at one of its points of intersection with the river you could see the remains of an old bridge. One night, Ann and I, while sitting under a big tree near the tetherball pole, heard four different kinds of owls.

Spending the summer in our rented cottage turned out to be disorienting, but in a strangely pleasant way: we were just a few minutes from our real home, and could easily return to fill the bird feeder, say, or to spy on our contractors, yet we were far enough away that we could almost believe we were spending the summer in New Hampshire or Vermont. We could go for days without duplicating old routines. We shopped in a different gro-cery store, which was now closer than our regular one (and where the low-fat milk came in bottles with yellow tops, not blue), and we ordered our pizzas from a different pizzeria (where the crusts were actually good). We rented movies from a different video store. We bought corn and tomatoes from a different farmer. We walked our dogs on a different road, with a frog-filled ditch beside it. Yet if I suddenly yearned to wear a favorite old golf shirt, I could run back home and find it in my closet.

Experiencing a therapeutic change of scene requires less ac-tual travel than most people generally assume. One weekend when I was ten, my parents and some of their friends took my sister and me and some of our friends to a Holiday Inn. The Holiday Inn was just on the other side of town, maybe ten miles away. None of us kids had a chance to get bored or cranky in the car on the way there; fifteen minutes after leaving home, we were splashing in the pool. We played miniature golf. We ran around. The grown-ups made cocktails and glanced toward the pool occasionally, to make sure we hadn't drowned. We stayed less than twenty-four hours, but by the time I got home I felt as though I'd had a real vacation. It was the change, not the distance, that was significant.

I know a number of people who own or rent second homes—a large fraction of the population of our small Connecticut town is New Yorkers who don't live here full-time—and many of those people eventually reach a point where getting away becomes something they yearn to get away from. Often that happens when their kids have grown old enough to formulate weekend plans of their own. It also happens when the thrill of mere novelty has faded—as always happens, since novelty is evanescent by definition. Fifteen years ago, some neighbors of ours bought a cabin in the mountains in another state, a hundred and fifty miles away. They visited faithfully, for a while. Then, gradually, the commute became irksome. Do we have to go to our wonderful, expensive place in the mountains again? their kids would whine. Summers were worse, because then the kids wanted to stay home, near their friends, and the parents were left to brood about wasted property taxes and mortgage payments. After a few years of increasingly reluctant visits, our neighbors sold their cabin to someone else, and good riddance.

This kind of thing wasn't a problem with our rented cottage. Although we felt as though we were spending the summer far away, the kids could still hang out with their same friends, and I could play golf at my same little club, and Ann could play ice hockey with her regular teammates. (She's a goalie.) It was as though we had found a way to enjoy all the considerable personal benefits of travel without truly having to go anywhere. If we wanted to pretend that we were on another continent, we could, but we didn't have to spend frequent flier miles to get there. Having old friends over for dinner at our new place was unusually fun—like taking them with us on vacation but with the considerable benefit of being able to send them home after dessert.

Having to rent a house during our renovation had seemed like an imposition, but feeling so remote while being so close was such a pleasant sensation that I began to wonder about the possibility of feeling it on an ongoing basis, even after our big project was complete. A couple of years before, I had actually written an essay on a similar topic for the magazine *Home,* to which I was then a regular contributor. In my essay, I wrote that I had fantasized about owning an unusual kind of second home—one that wasn't in the mountains or near the ocean or in the country, but was "right up the street from my first home, maybe a couple of doors away." This second home wouldn't really be a place to go on vacation; it would be a place my family and I could visit "when we were tired of keeping up appearances," and where we would "live the way people would live if they didn't care what other people might think." In our second home, I wrote, our kids would be allowed to do all the things they weren't allowed to do in our first home, such as spitting watermelon seeds into the fireplace, wiping their hands on the chairs, and riding their bicycles in the living room. Our second home would be as unpretentious as a fraternity house—as unpretentious as our own house had been before we started fixing it up. It would be the place where we would hold all our family's birthday parties and poker games, and where we'd bathe the dogs, and where the kids would be allowed to dig tunnels right in the front yard, if they wanted to. It would be the home of all the messy parts of our lives, the parts that make me nervous when they take place on old wood floors or next to freshly painted walls.

All these thoughts hovered in the back of my mind during the summer we lived in the rented cottage. One day, as I was driving to our milk-with-yellow-tops grocery store, I began to fantasize about buying land in the same area and building a weekend cabin—a second home something like the one I had written about in *Home.* In the middle of this fantasy, I realized that I had just driven past a peeling FOR SALE sign. I thought, What the heck? and turned around. The FOR SALE sign was standing in a lush-looking bed of tall poison ivy, which ran along the side of the road and concealed almost all of a fallen-down stone wall. Next to the sign was a rudimentary dirt driveway with tall weeds growing in the middle and on either side. I felt nervous about driving in—what if there was a house at the other end with an annoyed hillbilly sitting on the porch?—but I did it anyway. The driveway was long. Weeds brushed the bottom of my car, and flimsy saplings scraped the sides. The driveway was mostly level for a hundred yards; then it climbed a little rise.

From the top of the rise I had a mostly unobstructed view of a big wooded hill—the same hill, I realized, that rose above our rented cottage. Between me and the hill was a valley, and at the bottom of the valley, I knew, was the same river that Ann and I could hear from our bed. I couldn't see the river through the trees, but when I got out of my car I could hear water rushing in the distance, maybe a thousand feet down the hill and two hundred feet lower in elevation. A hillside building site—the obvious place to put a cabin—had been roughly cleared from the trees near the end of the driveway. A few big trees remained in the cleared area, and weeds and saplings had grown up around them, but I could tell that whoever had done the tree-cutting had done so in the expectation that somebody, someday, would want to build a house there. I stood in the cleared area and turned slowly in a circle. I knew that there was a house somewhere to my left, on the south side of the property, and that there was a farmhouse and a barn on the north side, and that there was a house across the road that I had just come from, but I couldn't see those structures from where I was standing: I was alone in a clearing in the woods, and I was looking across a river valley to a big hill with a state park on it. I drove back to the road and wrote down the telephone number on the FOR SALE sign.

After dinner that evening, Ann and I took our kids out for ice cream, and we passed the FOR SALE sign on the way. After hesitating for a moment, I pulled in to the driveway and explained my idea to my family. Usually when I explain ideas to my family they tell me to forget them, but this time they didn't. They got out of the car and walked around. My son ran down to the tree line and disappeared into the woods. Ann said she thought the property was beautiful and that building a cabin on it might not be a terrible idea.

The next day, I called the real estate agent and found out that the asking price for the land was a lot less than I would have guessed. I found out later, by asking around, that the lot had been for sale for years, and that the owner, finally fed up, had decided a few days before to cut his asking price in half. I asked a Realtor friend of mine to come take a look at the property and tell me to forget it; he drove over with me the next day, got out of the car, and said, "I think you ought to buy it."

Owning two houses is an inexcusable extravagance, of course, so before proceeding I compiled a lengthy mental list of rationalizations—the logical first step in any large, reckless enterprise. I told myself that the place would be a sound long-term investment, and that it, unlike my IRA, would pay tangible dividends right now, in the form of appealing family activities. I told myself that having a weekend cabin so close to our regular house would make our children more likely to visit us after they'd moved away for good and started families of their own. I told myself that having a weekend cabin nearby would make it easier for friends and relatives to visit us with their children, since they could all stay over there. I told myself that Ann and I could always sell our regular house and move into the cabin when we retired or when our regular house had begun to seem too big and empty. And I told myself that we could rescue ourselves from a financial catastrophe, if we ever suffered one, by selling the cabin, or renting it to New Yorkers, or borrowing more money against it. We wouldn't really be spending our savings, I reasoned; we would be shifting our savings into a more interesting and useful form—the same thing that our veterinarian, an avid golfer, had done a few years before, when he cashed in his retirement savings and invested them in two nice condominiums at a well-known golf resort in the South. The veterinarian's investment now generates an attractive return in the form of rental fees, and golf trips for him and his friends; my investment, I told myself, would generate easy vacations and wholesome family gatherings.

The desire for a proximate second address may be genetic in my family. When my mother was a little girl, a rich bachelor relation of hers in upstate New York had a rustic retreat, called Hilltop, that was just a few miles from his regular house. Hilltop had numerous engaging features, among them elaborate plantings and rose gardens, a huge charcoal oven, a kennel filled with English and Irish setters, and a twenty-four-seat dining table made from a single piece of wood. (Unfortunately, my mother's rich bachelor relation left his fortune not to his first cousin's ninth eldest great-grandchild—me—but to various charitable causes; Hilltop is now a restaurant and lodge.) When I was growing up, my father owned a series of large motor homes, each of which we called the Bus. My parents periodically took the Bus on long trips, but what they really liked to do was to drive a bunch of their friends to a football game, say, and then hang out with them in the parking lot. Sometimes, they didn't bother to leave our driveway. Being in the Bus was like being in a different place even if the Bus was still plugged in to an outlet in our garage. More recently, my sister and her husband, who live in Kansas, bought a piece of farmland about a half hour from their house and added a pond, a barn, some sheep pens, and a small log house, which they now use as a weekend house and guest house, and which they figure they will live in full-time after they've retired. Their rationalization for buying the land was that my brother-in-law had begun to raise Australian shepherds in his spare time and needed a place to keep sheep for the dogs to practice on. He also needed a place to keep the llama that looks after the sheep when the dogs aren't practicing. Then he decided to raise ducks, too. Then one thing led to another.

I had an additional reason for being interested in building a cabin. During the long and comically eventful renovation of my two-hundred-year-old house, I had developed an almost prurient fascination with brand-new construction. What would it be like, I wondered, to watch an entire house rise from nothing, and maybe even help it along? Building a cabin—that is, hiring other people to build a cabin for me—would be a way for me to extend my home-improvement education while also learning what it's like to own a home with insulation, level floors, and walls that meet at right angles.

BUYING THE LAND on which we would build the cabin also gave me a second chance at owning a real view. Twelve or fifteen good-size trees were still growing in the cleared area, though, and they would have to come down before the cabin could go up. Even with the trees still standing, I could see that the view from the cabin was going to be extraordinary. It was the main thing that had attracted all of us to the site.

I knew enough about tree-felling at this point to know that I had to hire someone else to do it for me. The man I hired, aided by a young helper, spent a day and a half cutting down trees and running everything he could through his chipper—another tool that the average homeowner should never even think of renting. When he was finished, there was still a big pile of trunks, which were too thick to chip. A few weeks earlier, I had described the trees to someone as "about six inches in diameter"; now that they were on the ground, I could see that they were more like a foot and a half. A friend of mine who is knowledgeable in such matters told me that getting rid of the trunks could cost me as much as three thousand dollars, since someone would have to come in a big truck and pick them up with a gigantic claw thing and haul them away. I asked him if he knew anyone who might want the wood for firewood. He found a guy who did, and I told the guy he could have the trunks for nothing, as long as I didn't have to deal with them. Over the course of a couple of weeks, he cut them into smaller pieces, which he carried off in the bed of his pickup truck. I never saw him working, but every time I visited the site the pile of tree trunks was a little smaller and the pile of sawdust, left by his chain saw—mostly oak sawdust, which smells surprisingly bad—was a little larger.

Now that the cabin's building site was cleared, it was time for me to get serious about the cabin itself. I had already asked Rudy if he would be willing to build it. He told me that he hadn't built a house in more than a decade, but that he would be very interested in taking on my project, in part because he wanted show his son how a house was constructed.

I had also discussed the project with Reese Owens, a local architect. Reese and I aren't related—his last name has an *s* at the end—but people often assume that we are either brothers or cousins, and our clothes sometimes get mixed up at the dry cleaner, and I once accidentally paid his grocery-store bill. We are almost exactly the same age, we play golf together pretty often, and I occasionally play tennis with his wife.

Reese grew up in our town, in a house that was a tavern in the eighteenth and early nineteenth centuries and that was once visited by George Washington (although he didn't sleep there). Reese spent his summers as a teenager working for a local contractor named Shammy Johnson. "Shammy was a wonderful old-school small-town builder," Reese told me recently, "and he had the three characteristics of a wonderful old-school small-town builder: he was very inexpensive, all of his interior and exterior trim was made of pine, and he didn't believe in flashing." Reese studied architecture at the University of Virginia, then earned a master's degree at the Yale School of Architecture. After Yale, he worked in New York, most notably at Gwathmey Siegel & Associates, which is probably best known for its restoration and expansion, in the early nineteen-nineties, of the Guggenheim Museum.

Among the Gwathmey Siegel projects that Reese worked on was Steven Spielberg's apartment in Trump Tower. "One of our presentations was at a meeting attended by Charlie Gwathmey, me, Spielberg, Amy Irving, and George Lucas," Reese told me. "Gwathmey was a real muscleman, and most of the meeting consisted of Spielberg and Lucas showing him how many sit-ups they could do. The two of them were on the floor, and Gwathmey was saying, 'That's not enough—you've got to do a hundred more.' Amy Irving kept wanting to comment on the design. Gwathmey didn't like that, and at one point he stood up, took out his wallet, handed her a hundred-dollar bill, and said, 'There's a limo downstairs. Why don't you go shopping?' A tough-guy architect. If a builder was doing work he didn't like and refused to change it, he would send over men with chain saws and they would cut it out."

In 1984, Reese set out on his own, and eventually hooked up

with Jon Halper, another young architect, who had earned his degree at Harvard and who played in the same architecture-firm
softball league. They called their firm Halper Owens Architects,
and in 1990 they moved it to Connecticut, where they now maintain two offices, one of which is in my town. For several years
after the move, Reese, his wife, and their young son lived in a cottage next to the old tavern, and between paying projects Reese
worked on possible designs for a house of their own. This process
might have continued forever, he told me, if his wife hadn't become pregnant again, forcing them to move. "We built the house
we built because it was the one I was working on at the time," he
said. "It could have been any of them."

The house they built is one of the reasons I wanted Reese to
design the cabin. It's a great house. When I asked him how he
would characterize it, stylistically, he said, "It's a mongrel of shin-
gle-style and stick-style influences with a dash of mother of invention and a heavy dose of not-quite-finished." The house is simple,
and it was inexpensive to build, yet it's also striking and beautifully detailed—and, unlike many houses that architects design
for themselves, it's not full of oddball eccentricities. (In the
house of one architect I know, the kitchen and living room are
on the second floor, the master bedroom and a lap pool are on
the first, and there's a shower at the foot of the basement stairs;
the house of another has a twenty-foot-tall semi-conical ceiling
above one end of the garage.)

"I learned a great deal from building my own house," Reese
told me. "When I was in New York, we worked with a lot of really
good interior designers—Mark Hampton and Bunny Williams
and Colefax and Fowler and people like that—and we always
used to laugh when they would ask us for more wall space so that
they could put a 'nice little piece of furniture' there. We'd laugh
at that, but it turns out that they were right. Architects are
trained to think that the only pleasing things in a building, the
only things that are good and pleasant to see, are hard-core architectural. When you have a blank wall, your instinct is to do
something to it: add a window, add a door, connect a room. Well,
live and learn, right? My house is proof, because there really is no
good wall space, and that's a challenge. The house isn't 'mod-

ern,' and its design doesn't blaze any trails, but its organization is nevertheless pretty hard-core, architecturally. And there are compromises associated with that—like, it looks great empty, but where do you put the couch?"

REESE AND I made a nonstandard agreement for the cabin: he and his team billed me by the hour, rather than charging me a percentage of the cost of the project. Whether this was financially advantageous for either of us I don't know, but I wanted to keep the project as low-key as possible. Reese's and my agreement made it easier for me to stick my nose into things and to make changes on the fly, in consultation with Rudy. I also asked Reese to keep the drawings simple and not to specify any of the interior finish—which I was still turning over in my mind and wanted to make up as we went along.

At our first meeting, I also showed Reese a possible floor plan, which I had drawn myself. My sketch was heavily influenced by the layout of our rented cottage, but with a screened porch added on one side. The finished cabin is much different from the house I drew, but many key elements are present in that first drawing: the number of rooms and their relative size in comparison with one another, and the basic overall shape of the place—a simple rectangle. I also showed Reese a page that I had torn surreptitiously from a travel magazine I'd been reading in the dentist's office a few weeks before. The photograph was of a parlor or living room at a dude ranch in Colorado, and it included several features that were deeply appealing to me: the walls and ceiling were covered with wide boards the color of dark honey; the couch was upholstered with what looked like saddle leather; there was an animal skin draped over a balcony railing; the table lamps had parchment shades, which worked with the wood to suffuse the entire room with an amber glow, as though the sun either had just risen or was just about to set; a cowboy-type guy was striding so rapidly into the foreground that his face, right arm, and left leg were blurred. The picture was smaller than a postcard, and riding in my wallet for several weeks had veined it with hundreds of soft wrinkles, but in my

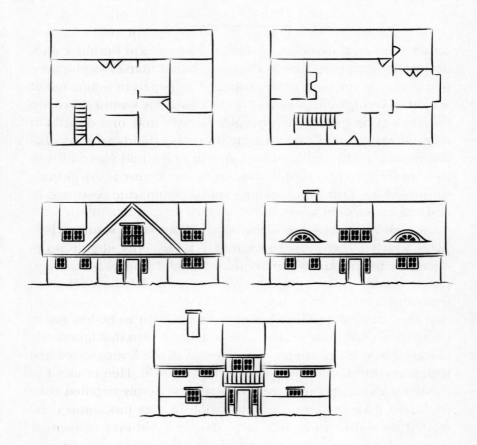

Architect's early concepts for the cabin.

mind it contained almost enough genetic information to build an entire house from. "This is pretty close to what I think I want," I said.

When I was in third or fourth grade, I had competing career aspirations. I wanted to be the owner/builder of a two-person submarine, and I wanted to be an architect. The other member of my submarine-design team was my friend John Ruth. He and I spent many rainy afternoons dreaming of undersea exploration, drawing cutaway views of the vessel we intended to build, and arguing about details: How many spear guns would we need? Would we steer with a steering wheel, a joystick, or a doorknob? How closely would our sub resemble a shark? Did it really need a ballast tank (as John Ruth contended), or could we cause it to dive or rise simply by aiming it down or up (my idea)? I had a box in my room in which I kept possible submarine parts, among them a broken wristwatch and the black top hat of a plastic snowman which to me looked like a control knob. One summer, John Ruth's parents sent him to a camp that offered scuba diving—a prerequisite for mini-sub piloting, we had both agreed—and I became almost frantically depressed, because I believed I could never catch up.

My desire to build a submarine turned out to be less enduring than my desire to design houses, an ambition that lasted until eighth grade. At Christmas when I was ten or eleven, my parents gave me a book called *Architecture,* by Donald E. Helper and Paul I. Wallach. It contained hundreds of reasonably detailed drawings and photographs, and it seemed to cover just about everything that a practicing architect in 1965 could ever conceivably need to know, including how to diffuse the light above a Formica countertop by concealing fluorescent lamps behind frosted-glass ceiling panels. My local newspaper had a weekly feature about home design, and every story included a floor plan. I cut out those floor plans and saved them in a folder, for inspiration. I did my own designing on graph paper, which I bought at the dime store, and I spent a lot of time worrying about such apparent mysteries as the difference in thickness between interior and exterior walls. I also worried about arithmetic, which my grandmother told me architects had to understand.

My house designs had a number of characteristic features, among them secret passageways, random-width doors and windows, turrets with bedrooms in them, and irregularly shaped closets (to use up leftover space). I also was a big believer in swimming pools that you could dive into from a second-story window. Most of the designs I saw in the newspaper seemed stuffy by comparison; why would anyone design a house without some kind of tunnel? Nevertheless, I'm ashamed to say, the rough sketch I showed Reese didn't include any of these elements, either—proof that adulthood is hard on the imagination.

Reese took notes as we talked, and gave me a copy when we were finished. The key points:

low maintenance
no AC
main room has low beam/plank ceiling, plank walls
1 fireplace—locate
bathrooms simple
walkout basement
casual driveway
good-quality windows are worth it
"think small"

There were some other ideas, too, including many I later abandoned. Initially, I had thought that the living room should have burgundy-colored vinyl-sheet flooring and that there should be a drain in the middle so the room could be hosed down—evidence of my early determination that the cabin should be as easy as possible to maintain, but an idea that I dropped not long afterward, as reality played an increasingly significant role in our discussions. The sketches that Reese and I talked about over the following weeks and months look to me now like the products of a logical evolutionary process, the gradual refining of an idea. The final design, though significantly different from my initial sketch, can nevertheless be traced back to it. Each new conception was an effort to solve a problem that hadn't seemed troublesome until some earlier sketch had made it unavoidable. Each iteration moved the cabin a few paces closer to reality. As I look

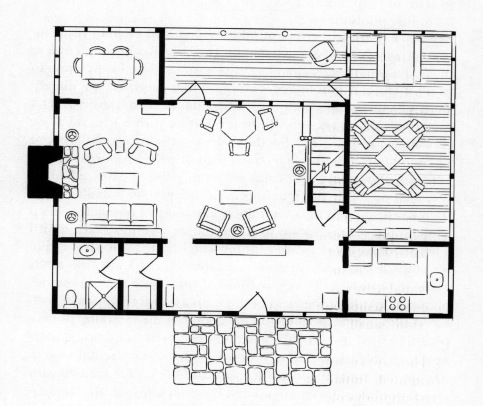

Cabin, floor plan.

back over those drawings now, I re-experience a feeling I often had at the time, which was something like this: Whoa, maybe I'm really not kidding about this thing!

———

ONE OF THE first issues on which Reese and I had to reach an accommodation was size. Generally speaking, Reese kept trying to make the cabin bigger than I wanted it to be, while I kept trying to make it smaller than was practicable. I had paced off the dimensions of our rental cottage, and had decided that everything I wanted could be squeezed into a building with a ground floor measuring twenty feet by thirty feet, plus a 150-square-foot screened porch. In the first scaled plan that Reese showed me, in contrast, the ground floor was something like thirty-five feet by fifty feet, or a little more than twice as large. I was appalled—but then Reese showed me that if the house was just twenty feet deep there would be no easy way to access the second floor, except with a ladder or with a staircase running longitudinally down the center of the living room. Because the cabin's second story was really going to be just a half-story—a finished attic—with sloping ceilings on two sides, the upper end of the staircase and the upstairs hallway couldn't stray too far from the center of the building, or people using them would have to stoop to keep from bumping their heads. In an early sketch of my own, I had placed the staircase in what struck me as the ideal location, and I felt quite pleased with myself until Reese pointed out that if we did it my way the top step would be under an eave and anyone using the stairs would have to climb the last bit on hands and knees, then crawl down the hall—something not permitted by the building code.

There were other size-related complications as well. The smaller the footprint, Reese showed me, the harder it would be to squeeze in things like closets and waste pipes, and to fit doors into places where they'd be needed. Making rooms too small can also complicate furniture placement, unless you don't mind climbing over the couch to get to the kitchen or tucking in the sheets on only one side of your bed—the same wall-space challenge that Reese had encountered in his own house, though for a different reason.

I was also aware that I had to be careful not to make the cabin so small that it would be impossible to sell to somebody else, should Ann and I decide (or be forced) to unload it at some point in the future. The two of us might be willing to get by without much storage space—almost all our clothes, after all, would stay where they were, in our regular house—but any potential buyer would probably be unwilling to rely on closets at another address. And we ourselves would want decent-sized closets, too, if we decided to move in permanently once we became empty nesters. That meant that the cabin had to be at least as big as a smallish house.

On the other hand, most people's houses, and the rooms within them, are far larger than they need to be. Fifty or sixty years ago, the average new house was about half the size that the average new house is today, and nobody felt claustrophobic. Spacious floor plans have come to seem like a necessity, but most people who have big houses actually treat them as though they were far smaller, by spending most of their time in the same few rooms—usually, the kitchen, the family room, and their bedroom. And in most cases even those few rooms could be shrunk substantially without making anyone's life less pleasant. Reese told me that the most heavily used room in his own house is one of the smallest, a study near the kitchen. People actually like small, cozy spaces, and are drawn to them. That's why you tend to find party guests huddled in the hall or your laundry room instead of spreading themselves evenly across the floor of the nice big living room that you never use when you're in the house by yourself.

The final design for the cabin represented a workable compromise on size. Although the finished footprint, at 32 feet by 42 feet, is larger than I had hoped it would be at the outset, that area is actually smaller than it seems because it includes a little over 320 square feet of screened and unscreened porches on the first floor. The first floor has just 900 square feet of heated space, the second floor has a little over 1,000—small, by modern standards. I would have been happy with somewhat less space overall, but after a certain point the problems caused by contraction overwhelmed the benefits. As it was, fitting in the staircase required adding a small landing and a 90-degree turn, which (I discovered later) made it impossible to get a king-size bed to the second floor.

THE COTTAGE WE rented while our kitchen was being remodeled had a surprisingly appealing feature: a large entrance hall, really almost a room, with a fireplace, a couple of chairs, a coat rack, and a dresser. The fireplace was one of three connected to a huge central chimney. It hadn't been used in many years, I'm sure, but it looked nice and it was a good place to keep wet boots. The dresser's drawers were filled with the sporadically useful stuff that all families accumulate over decades and have to store somewhere, usually in a drawer: screwdrivers with wooden handles, rolls of tape, old keys, a wrinkled tube of Duco Cement, water-heater instructions, bug spray, balls of twine, lawnmower parts, flashlights, orphaned winter gloves, thumbtacks, the collars of dead dogs, measuring tapes, basketball-pump needles, playing cards, and hundreds of other objects and tools and utensils—the sediment of a lifetime of household acquisition, the kinds of items that you almost never use but that seem impossible to throw away, and that eventually end up heaped together in a big box at an estate sale, the gizmo residue of your life.

This entrance hall was wasted space, technically speaking, since we never assembled there to play canasta or resolve family conflicts or build model sailboats. But it was, nevertheless, a useful, welcoming room. It was a place to take off your raincoat and kick off your shoes, a comfortable transition zone between the chaotic world on the other side of the front door and the ordered, circumscribed sub-world within. It was a decompression chamber.

New houses often have grandiloquent entrance halls, with twenty-foot ceilings, marble floors, Palladian windows above the doors, and chandeliers the size of geostationary satellites. You can drive through new suburban subdivisions in which every house looks almost as though its towering foyer came first and the rest of the house was tacked on behind: new houses often seem to have been built around their front doors in the same way that seventeenth- and eighteenth-century houses were built around their massive central chimneys. Real estate agents love soaring foyers because prospective buyers are usually impressed by all that opulent volume, but after the deal has closed most formal entrance halls become bleakly vestigial, since hardly anyone, except itinerant Jehovah's Witnesses, uses front doors anymore. Most Americans do most of their routine coming and going through the back door—or through the garage, which is often connected directly to the kitchen. I recently spent a couple of days at a house in Florida whose front door couldn't even be opened; it had a deadbolt lock to which the key had been lost years before. The owner used his garage door opener as his house key—and many Americans do the same.

For the cabin, I wanted the front door to be the main door, and I wanted it to open into a large, utilitarian entrance hall—a mudroom. In the final plans, the mudroom measures eight feet by twenty feet, with the entrance in the middle of one of the long sides. It's not as big as a basketball court, but it's the second largest room on the ground floor, after the living room. To squander a hundred and sixty square feet of a limited footprint in this way will seem extravagant to some, but I liked the room in theory and I have turned out to love it in fact. It's a room in which you can hang a dozen coats and park a couple of bicycles without making it seem crowded.

The cabin's entrance hall is almost exactly twice the size of its kitchen, which is the smallest room except for the bathrooms. My original thought about the kitchen was that it should be as primitive as possible—something like the kitchen in a friend's lake house, which has a bare concrete floor, an ancient utility sink, an old refrigerator with a microwave oven on top of it, a small table, and no other appliances or furniture. Eventually, though, I realized that there is a point at which simplicity becomes its opposite. Having no stove and virtually no food-preparation area does not make mealtime easier or more straightforward, and washing dishes in an ancient utility sink, no matter how picturesque, would be extremely unpleasant and would create an ongoing maintenance problem, since dishwater splashing over the back of the sink would end up in hard-to-reach places, which would then rot.

Cabin, mud room.

In an early sketch of the cabin, the kitchen had built-in counters most of the way around its perimeter and was spacious enough to accommodate a central island or table. I told Reese that that was far too large, and in the final design the kitchen was less than half that size—just eight feet by eleven feet, roughly the same size as the kitchen in our old apartment in New York. An early sketch also placed the kitchen on the opposite side of the layout, where it would have been closer to the dining alcove at one corner of the main room but farther from the screened porch. Gina Daniel—one of several friends to whom I showed the drawings at various stages—pointed out that during decent weather virtually all food-consumption would probably take place on the screened porch, so why not put the kitchen next to it? I agreed, and Reese flipped the layout, swapping the kitchen and a bathroom. He also added a connecting window for passing plates back and forth.

Gina made another good suggestion as well. In the original design, the little roof over the front steps is held up by two eight-inch-by-eight-inch wooden columns. Gina suggested making the columns out of fieldstone instead. Stone columns were quite a bit more expensive than wooden ones would have been, but there was a mason on the job anyway (to build the chimney, the fireplace, and the retaining walls on either side of the walkout basement) and the visual impact of the columns far exceeds their cost. The two columns are just seven feet tall, and they measure eighteen inches on a side at the base (and twelve inches at the top), but they are the first thing you notice as you look at the front of the cabin and they help to set the mood of the entire place—proving that small details can create big impressions if you put them in the right spot.

MANY NEW HOUSES don't have traditional living rooms, and if you live in an old house you probably understand why. Most living rooms defy occupancy. A living room is like the ancient tuxedo that hangs in the back of your closet: it's designed for a part of your life that exists mainly in your imagination. Even at moments when you'd think a big formal herding area would come in handy—for example, during a long-postponed payback party, with which you hope to cancel many years' worth of accumulated hospitality debt—it usually remains empty until the cramped, dark, hot, and uncomfortable parts of the house are full.

Ann and I managed to resuscitate our living room a dozen years ago by turning it into a place where people like to go to read. The design work was done by our friend Polly Roberts, who designed our dining room and chose the colors and many other details for our kitchen. The long, imposing wall opposite the fireplace is now filled with built-in bookcases, and in the middle of the bookcases (with a bookshelf running above) is a niche that was designed around a big, down-stuffed couch. The couch is the perfect size not only for reading but also for napping, and you can stretch out on either axis, because in front of the couch is a table-sized ottoman, which can accommodate two pairs of legs in addition to piles of magazines. Within the niche, in the space between the top of the back of the couch and the bottom of the bookshelf overhead, is a section of wall about the size of a sheet of plywood. That section of wall remained bare for a long time— there was something about it that resisted decoration—but then I had an idea.

I had read about itinerant mural painters, who traveled around New England in the early nineteenth century. In exchange for room and board, they provided what in those days was a thrifty alternative to wallpaper. Most of those old murals later disappeared, after mass-produced wall-coverings became available, in the mid-eighteen hundreds. Why not, I reasoned, try to help revive a lost art while we were reviving our living room? Ann and I commissioned a local painter to fill the wall above the couch with a mural depicting an idealized version of our little town. The landmarks in the mural are our personal landmarks— library, church, historical museum, Augusta National Golf Club (I was working on a golf book at the time), and the houses of our friends. The largest structure in the picture is not our house but the office of our veterinarian, who, because we have more than two dozen pets, is also over-represented in our lives. The landscape is made-up, but it evokes our real landscape. In the foreground is a river that really does run through our town.

In our house, getting people to use the living room was a matter of giving the room a purpose and then configuring the room so that using it for that purpose would seem appealing. In the cabin, the challenge was different. Since there would be no alternative indoor sitting areas (other than the bedrooms upstairs), the cabin's main room would have a captive audience. But the room would still have to accommodate the family-type activities that we hoped would take place in it: reading, talking, playing board games, playing cards, hanging around. In the earliest sketches, the main room was too small, mainly because too much floor area had been sacrificed elsewhere for the kitchen (which hadn't shrunk yet) and a separate dining room. Reese himself pointed out another problem with that first conception: it didn't have enough wall space for furniture.

In the final design, the cabin's main room measures roughly fifteen feet by twenty-six feet. That's 390 square feet, or more than 40 percent of all the heated space on the first floor. The room is big enough for a party, but it's also small enough to feel intimate when the only occupants are Ann and me, reading in front of the fire. And although the room includes two doorways into the mudroom, a wide opening into the alcove, the door that leads to the basement, two doors that open onto porches, the opening to the main staircase, and six windows, there's still plenty of wall space for furniture.

Opening off the main room, down near the fireplace, is a little dining alcove, which measures eight feet by eleven feet. This nook was one of the last elements to fall into place. Initially, I had thought that the space could be used as a small sitting area, den, or study of some kind, and that any indoor eating could be done in the main room—probably at a table that would be used for some other purpose the rest of the time. Eventually, I realized that a separate sitting area would be superfluous and that a dedicated dining area would be useful as long as it could be kept small. Reese was skeptical at first that eighty-eight square feet would be sufficient for civilized eating, but I measured the dining end of our new kitchen and found that it, too, was eleven feet wide. Since six people often eat at our kitchen table without feeling crowded, I knew we had enough space. In fact, dining is a good use for a small room, because diners, once they're seated, don't take up a lot of floor area. The cabin's dining alcove, which has two walls filled almost entirely with windows, is also a good place to read the paper, do a crossword puzzle, or attempt to reassemble a toilet valve that you never should have taken apart.

That friend of mine whose lake house doesn't have a stove keeps a Ping-Pong table in his living room, which is really the only room. I wanted a Ping-Pong table, too, but I didn't want it to be the principal piece of furniture. The walkout basement, I figured, would be just the right size, as long as the central floor space could be left unobstructed. And that's what Reese did.

WHEN WE LIVED in our apartment, Ann and I surrendered our large bedroom to our baby and moved into our former dining alcove. Now we live in a great big house, and there are four of us, and there are enough real rooms so that none of us has to sleep in a closet. But Ann and I, nevertheless, have ended up in smallest bedroom once again—also by choice. Our room measures just eleven and a half feet by a little more than fourteen feet. There's no space for couches or tables or exercise equipment, but the walls and ceilings are covered with wood the color of Grade A maple syrup, and it's the perfect place for sleeping late or taking a nap or staying up with a good book. And it has a dressing room and a good-size bathroom attached to it, so it doesn't feel crowded when two people are trying to get going at the same time in the morning.

Ann's and my preference for compact sleeping spaces is not widely shared. I know some people who built a huge new house a dozen years ago, and their bedroom is the opposite of ours: it has a soaring ceiling, windows the size of garage doors, and a vast, shiny hardwood floor, which makes their king-size bed look like a dinghy floating on a sea of polyurethane. To me, their room looks like a place to hold a ball, not a tempting lair in which to curl up for a nap.

Bedrooms in new single-family American houses have grown significantly in the past thirty or forty years; *Architecture*, the 1965 book about home design which I loved when I was a kid, used twelve feet by fifteen feet as the dimensions of a typical *large* master bedroom (equipped with twin beds, of course), and suggested one hundred to one hundred and fifty square feet as the floor area of an average bedroom. By this standard, all three bedrooms in the cabin are bigger than average—although all three sacrifice usable floor space to the slope of the roof, which intersects the rooms, and all three would strike most people with relatively new houses as somewhat on the dinky side. In the floor plan, the three bedrooms are lined up in a row and connected by a single short, straight hallway; in the actual cabin, the three rooms feel far more isolated from one another, mainly because of an optical illusion that Reese created by placing a technically superfluous door in the center of the hallway, giving the master bedroom its own mini foyer. This little bit of private hallway makes the master bedroom feel like a suite—and look like one from the top of the stairs—and creates a sense of privacy that is not detectable in the drawings. It was an inexpensive way to create a powerful feeling of separation among three closely spaced rooms.

Reese used another optical illusion to make a bath and a half feel like two full bathrooms. I had originally told him that I wanted only one bathroom in the entire house—a configuration that Americans lived with very happily during the first few decades of indoor plumbing. Reese and various friends urged me to reconsider, and someone pointed out that the first major renovation undertaken by people who purchase old houses is inevitably to add more bathrooms. These arguments were persuasive. I also realized that the incremental cost of adding a second bathroom would be far less than the construction cost of the first bathroom, because all the really expensive infrastructure (waste pipes, vent stack, septic tank) would be shared. Reese then showed me how to increase the illusion of privacy on the second floor by going a half-step further: using two small half-bathrooms connected by a small room containing a bathtub (and shower). This configuration—which Reese modeled after a similar arrangement in the house of an aunt of his—covers just eighty-five square feet. Yet to an occupant of the cabin it feels like two full bathrooms, and the central bathtub area, along with the optical illusion created by the door in the center of the hallway, makes the two sides seem fully private and separate from each other. The central bathtub, which is easily accessible from both bathrooms, acts as a buffer and creates a surprising feeling of spaciousness in what the floor plan reveals to be a very confined area.

Reese's own house contains a bathroom innovation that he did not suggest for the cabin. His master bathroom, he told me, "is the room in the house that people laugh at." It has a pair of sinks at one end, a toilet and a bidet at the other, and an open shower in the middle, with a shower curtain on either side. There is just one door, near the sinks, so that the only way to get to the toilet or the bidet is to walk through the shower. "There are three windows in the bathroom," he said, "and it's a very pleasant place to take a shower, but the floor is wet a lot of the time, and I get yelled at whenever someone has to go through it. The idea made perfect sense to me, but I have gotten nothing but grief about it from anybody who has ever seen it. And because I was both the architect and the client, there's nobody I can blame."

BEFORE CONSTRUCTION of the cabin could begin, I needed approvals from various regulatory boards. This is a process that many people dread, but I was looking forward to it because most of my involvement with local land-use boards has been in the other direction. Almost fifteen years ago, my friend Bill and I attended a local committee meeting of the major political party we belong to, for the purpose of nominating a friend of ours as the party's candidate for first selectman of our town—the equivalent of a mayor. For complicated reasons, we never got around to nominating our friend, but I did end up running for office myself. That year, it turned out, the local ballot contained more blank spaces than our party had found candidates with which to fill them, so someone suggested that each of the seven or eight people in the room should volunteer to run for something. Running for office in my town, which is the size of a large high school, has a lot in common with running for student council. Residents take democracy seriously (our voter turnout in the most recent national election was the highest in the state), but the political machinery is rudimentary. At the meeting, I looked over the list of possible positions and decided that the least time-consuming job would probably be alternate on the zoning board of appeals. I signed up to run and was elected by a flatteringly wide margin—actually, I was unopposed—and have served on my town's land-use commissions ever since. I am currently the chairman of the zoning commission, a body that is distinct from the board of appeals. (Essentially, the zoning commission creates and applies the town's zoning regulations, while the board of appeals considers individual exceptions.)

Like most small-town zoning commissions, we spend a lot of our time weighing irrelevant facts, violating our state's land-use statutes, and attempting to exceed our tightly circumscribed authority. Overall, though, I think we do a pretty good job. In a small town there aren't many abstract political issues. "The environment" is a particular river, "development" is the old Potter farm, and "affordable housing" is your neighbor's grandparents. We are our most effective not when we are trying to push forward the outer limits of land-use theory but when we are seeking simple means of helping neighbors live together in relative harmony. The best example I can think of is our regulation concerning air conditioners, generators, swimming-pool filters, and other noisy household equipment. These devices are so loud that homeowners, if left to themselves, will usually install them as far as possible from their houses, with the result that the people most likely to be bothered by them will usually be their neighbors. The commission considered many complicated remedies, including decibel limits and requirements for noise-abatement barriers. But any such measures, we eventually realized, would have overtaxed our modest powers of enforcement, and wouldn't have had much effect anyway. People can be annoyed by decibel levels far lower than any limit that could reasonably be set by law, and noise-abatement is so tricky that it can baffle even acoustic engineers.

In the end, we did something much simpler. We wrote a rule requiring people to place their generators and air conditioners within twenty-five feet of their own houses, and to place their pool filters within fifty feet of their own pools, and to situate them so that they are closer to the structures they serve than to

any building line on any adjoining property unless the applicants
can prove that installing the equipment in some more distant location would actually be less bothersome to neighbors. The new
regulation is easy to understand, and it can be enforced with a
measuring tape. Best of all, it gives the owners of the noisy equipment a natural incentive to keep down their own racket, since
they hear it first. The new regulation turns noise abatement into
naked self-interest—the most powerful force in the universe,
after water vapor.

People with a libertarian bent often grumble about zoning
ordinances, building codes, and other legal restrictions on individual autonomy, figuring that people ought to be able to use
their own property in any way they like. But regulations like this
actually represent a complex compromise among people with
disparate interests, and can be thought of as a sophisticated form
of selfishness. The basic idea is that I give up a certain amount of
control over my own property in order to gain a certain amount
of control over yours. That may mean that I can't build the six-
story house I've always dreamed of owning (my town has a resi-
dential-building height limit of forty feet), but it also means that
you can't place the rear wall of your new family room right next
to my garden (my town requires all structures to be set back at
least twenty-five feet from a backyard or side-yard property line).
Limiting the size of my patio to comply with my town's limitation
on lot coverage is the price I pay for my certainty that my neighbor's house could never be converted into a commercial dog
kennel (a use not permitted in our zone).

Land-use regulations and building codes also work to the
benefit of even grumbling anarchists whenever property changes
hands. If I were to put my house on the market tomorrow, any
potential buyer would know that a knowledgeable official had inspected the garage's footing drains before the foundation was
backfilled, and that the footing drains are therefore at least somewhat likely to function the way footing drains are supposed to
function. A buyer's confidence in my footing drains increases the
likely sale price of my house and is therefore valuable to me as
well. There is a town adjacent to mine that is unique in this region in having no zoning regulations at all, and real-estate prices

there are depressed significantly in relation to those in otherwise comparable areas nearby. Paradoxically, the things you aren't allowed to do to your own property often add more to its value than the things you are.

My first step in seeking approval for the cabin was to have the property surveyed. I gave the completed survey to a licensed engineer, who designed a septic system that would be adequate to handle the waste from the proposed structure and selected a likely site for the well. The engineer also conducted soil tests, to prove that the soil on the property could handle a septic system, and submitted an application on my behalf to the regional health department. When my septic plan had been approved, I applied for a building permit, a zoning permit, and a driveway permit. Most of these applications had to be accompanied by fees, some of them substantial, and the driveway application required a performance bond. I also notified the local power company that I would soon be needing electrical service, including a temporary hookup for Rudy, Joe, and Mark. The power company inspected the site and sent me a bill for the estimated cost of connecting me to the grid. When all of that was finally finished, and I had my permits in hand, we were ready to begin.

5

BACKHOES AND CONCRETE MIXERS

LIKE MANY LITTLE boys, my son loved backhoes, the *Tyrannosaurus rex* of trucks. When he was two or three, an inn near our house underwent a huge renovation, and I would take him to watch, always carrying a magazine in my back pocket because there was no chance that he would become bored before I did. At the local cemetery one afternoon, I let him sit inside a small excavator, a Bobcat, which was used for grave-digging; he cried and cried and cried when I said, finally, that it was time to go home. One of his favorite Christmas presents ever was a toy backhoe-loader that he could ride on. He used it to dig holes in his sandbox and around the edges of our patio, and he once asked me if I would please buy him some "toy dirt" so that he could continue his excavations indoors when it was too dark or too cold to work outside.

My son outgrew his fascination with digging machines, but I know several men who never did. My friend John once bought a piece of land, with the intention of building a house on it, and decided that a sensible way to hold down the cost of the project would be to buy his own backhoe and do all the earthmoving himself. (Don't bother to check his mental arithmetic.) He went to a huge sale of heavy equipment, in the parking lot at the fairground in another town. After wandering fearfully for an hour, he approached a salesman, hemmed and hawed, and said that he

might be interested in buying a backhoe. "Keys in 'em," the salesman said, and walked away. John, who had never driven even a
tractor, climbed into the cab of a large excavator and started it.
After a certain amount of fiddling with the levers, he managed to
lift the bucket. Further fiddling caused the bucket to drop to the
ground and gouge an enormous chunk from the parking lot. Returning that bucketful of excavated material to the hole took
John most of the rest of the afternoon. By the time he had finished, he knew something about how to operate a backhoe but
had lost all desire to own one.

My friend Bill rented a backhoe-loader for a weekend a couple of years ago. He wanted to do some grading near his house,
to clear some brush from the perimeter of his yard, and to remove some old stumps (the residue of a previous weekend adventure, with a chain saw), among other things. "Once you get
into the cockpit," Bill told me recently, "you can think of a hundred things to do." On Sunday afternoon, as his allotted time was
running out, he noticed the top of a boulder showing through
his lawn—a buried glacial erratic, a common geological feature
in our area, where most of the major landforms were shoved and
dragged into their current configurations during the Ice Age. Bill
had scraped the blade of his lawnmower on that boulder once,
or, at any rate, he had worried that he might do so someday. Also,
he had always wondered how big the boulder was—something
you can never tell just by looking at the part you can see. He happily spent the next hour or two using the backhoe to expose it
fully, and discovered that it was shaped like a potato and was the
size of a commercial freezer.

While Bill considered what to do next with his glacial erratic,
he went to work on a pile of rotting logs up near his house. He
parked the backhoe next to the logs and put on the parking
brake. He then began piling logs in the loader bucket, planning
to dump them in the woods. "While I was working," he told me,
"I heard a clank. I realized later that the clank must have been
the parking brake giving way. All of a sudden, I see the backhoe
inching backwards."

Bill's house stands at the top of a long, steep hill, and he had
parked the backhoe on a slight incline. Briefly, he considered

running after it and swinging up into the cab, but the machine picked up speed. "It was sort of bouncing along, backhoe first, and it kept going faster and faster," he told me. "I stood there and watched. I thought it was going to take out two of my apple trees, but then it did a perfect slalom between them, like an S. I was picturing the thing sailing through the trees at the bottom of the hill and crashing into the house on the other side of the road, but then it hit an embankment about a hundred yards down the hill, went airborne, tipped over on one side, and did a half gainer into the ground."

This was Sunday afternoon. The man who owned the backhoe would be returning to pick it up the next morning at eight o'clock. At seven, Bill called Mark, an old high school buddy of his and the owner of my town's gas station, and asked him if he would mind hurrying over with the big wrecker. "What'd you do?" Mark asked. "Rent another backhoe?" (Bill had rented a backhoe once before, and had gotten it stuck in a swampy area at the edge of his yard, and Mark had had to rescue him by pulling him out with the wrecker's winch.) Mark arrived a few minutes later. He got the backhoe upright and towed it to the top of the hill. The engine wouldn't turn over, though. Then, finally, it did turn over, and emitted a tremendous cloud of dense black smoke before settling down to a steady idle. The backhoe's owner pulled in to Bill's driveway with his flatbed just after Mark had pulled out.

Let's see. Bill's neighbor Art once rented a Bobcat loader to lift bundles of asphalt shingles to the roof of his house, and ended up scraping a wide swath through the cedar-clapboard siding. I could go on. Suffice it to say that when the time came to excavate the foundation for the cabin, I did not decide to do the work myself.

Instead, I hired Ray, one of my regular golf buddies, who at that time owned an excavating company. (Not long afterward, he sold the company and went back to school, to complete his bachelor's degree and earn a graduate degree, in geology.) Ray grew up operating heavy digging equipment—he took over the business from his father—and he, unlike all my other friends, actually knows what he's doing. I once had to prove to a state official that my property could accommodate a second septic leaching field, in the event that my current field should ever fail (a new requirement for all construction projects in Connecticut). Part of the test involved digging a ten-foot-deep test pit in the middle of my front yard so that the official could take soil samples, and I hired Ray to dig the hole. The official, at some point, dropped her Bic pen to the bottom of the pit, and Ray retrieved it with the backhoe bucket. He picked it up in one try, and brought up hardly any dirt with it. A mutual friend once watched him pick up a golf ball in the same way.

Ray ran his excavating business from an office at his house. One day, he realized that he had stopped receiving equipment catalogs and professional publications—something he had formerly been inundated with. He discovered that his son, who was six years old, had been intercepting them and had memorized the names, model numbers, and distinguishing characteristics of many kinds of excavators. Ray had mixed feelings about this fascination. Nevertheless, every so often he would take his son to a flat area near their house and let him spend a couple of hours digging a real hole with a real backhoe, while Ray sat on a rock and watched. This made his son one of the three or four happiest six-year-olds in the world, and made me feel like a bad father. Fortunately, my son never found out.

The object of all this male adoration is a scaled-down modern descendant of the first powered single-bucket excavating machine, the steam shovel, which was invented in 1835 in Canton, Massachusetts, by a twenty-two-year-old Philadelphian named William S. Otis. Otis worked in railroad construction, and his steam shovel looked pretty much exactly like Mary Anne, the steam shovel in the famous children's book *Mike Mulligan and His Steam Shovel*. Otis died in 1839, of typhoid, and his family protected his patents so fiercely that the machines weren't widely used until decades later.* Once mechanical digging did catch on,

---

* When the railroad reached my town, in the late nineteenth century, the builders, who didn't have a steam shovel, dealt with a very gentle slope near our little business district by erecting a miniature trestle along one side of the slope—standard practice

though, it had a huge impact. "Modern civilization, with the high standard of living we enjoy today, is largely the product of earth-moving machines," the excavation historian Keith Haddock wrote in *Giant Earthmovers*. (Haddock is also the author of the follow-up book *Colossal Earthmovers*.)

The actual excavation work for the cabin was done not by Ray but by an employee of his, Artie, whom Ray once described to me as an artist with a backhoe. As I watched Artie work, I was glad I hadn't even considered trying to tackle any part of this project on my own. Ray explained that digging a good foundation hole requires more planning than you might think. It has to be dug to an exact depth, so that the soil on which the foundation will rest is not disturbed unduly, and the operator has to think many steps ahead, so that he doesn't do the equivalent of painting himself into a corner. He also has to grade the surrounding area in such a way that concrete contractors and others will have easy access to everything they need to reach later on. A good foundation hole is really a structure in itself—a structure turned inside out and upside down. When Artie had finished, we were ready for the foundation.

———————

THE FIRST WOODEN dwellings built by America's European settlers didn't really have foundations. They were erected either directly on the ground or on top of a few large, flattish rocks placed at key points around the perimeter, and as a result they didn't stand very straight or last very long. Foundation technology improved as early American settlers developed a longer-term outlook on survival in the New World. By the time Ann's and my house was erected, around 1790, builders in my area were creating substantial foundations from slabs of quarried granite, which they stacked like building blocks. These foundations were relatively stable; they are the reason that so many eighteenth-century

———————

in the pre-steam-shovel era. Twenty or thirty years later, they simply would have regraded the bed with a big machine manufactured by Otis's descendants or their competitors, at a major savings of time, manpower, and money.

wood-frame houses in my part of the world are still standing. When our house was moved to its present location in 1970, the owner salvaged some of the original foundation stones, including one that must weigh almost as much as a small car, and used them for doorsteps. He also incorporated several dozen smaller foundation stones into a (very ugly) brick patio, which Ann and I later replaced with a handsome patio made entirely of stone. Most of those smaller foundation stones now form the walk between our backdoor and our driveway.

Before moving the house, the movers regraded the new lot and excavated a large hole near its center. They drove their truck down into this hole and deposited the uprooted building on tall cribs made of stacked railroad ties, then built a new foundation underneath it. First, they poured concrete footings—essentially, a foundation for the foundation. The footings are a bit less than two feet wide and a bit more than one foot thick, and they follow the house's perimeter, with various detours; they serve roughly the same function for the house that your feet do for you. The footings are situated "below the frost line"—that is, below the depth to which the ground freezes in cold weather. Placing the footings at this depth prevents them from shifting and cracking when the seasonal freeze-thaw cycle causes the earth to heave.

To build the main part of the foundation, the people who moved our house used concrete blocks (which are known to professionals as Concrete Masonry Units, or CMUs). The blocks in the house's foundation are mortared together in eleven staggered courses, making the finished foundation walls, which project a foot or a foot and a half above the finished grade, about eight feet high. Block foundations are easy and relatively inexpensive to build, although I wish the previous owner had splurged on poured concrete. Still, my block foundation is a big improvement over the house's original granite foundation. Unlike many owners of two-hundred-year-old houses, I have a usable, reasonably dry, full-height basement with a concrete floor. (The concrete floor was poured last, after the house had been lowered into place on top of the block walls.)

The house I grew up in, which was built in the nineteen-twenties, stands on a masonry foundation made of limestone and mortar. When I was ten or eleven, I asked my father if I could use a pickax to chop a hole through it, so that I could dig a long tunnel connecting our house and the house across the street. I planned to get rid of the excavated dirt by letting it run out through holes in my pants pockets while I walked nonchalantly around our neighborhood, and I planned to travel through the completed tunnel by lying on my skateboard and pulling myself along with a rope. (I had recently watched the movie *The Great Escape.*) When my father said no, I was deeply disappointed. I was also disappointed when he told me that he would not be willing to ask a work crew from the local electric company, which was using a backhoe to dig a big hole in the yard of one of our neighbors, if they would mind digging a big hole in our yard, too. Then my friend John Ruth and I asked the workers ourselves, planning to pay them out of our allowances. They also said no.

For the cabin, I wanted a nice modern poured-concrete foundation. Ray led me to a good foundation contractor. Shortly after Artie had finished with the excavation, the contractor and his crew arrived to build trough-like wooden forms, into which the concrete for the footings would be poured.

OF ALL THE catalysts of human progress, concrete may be the least prepossessing. If you reckon significance by cumulative mass, however, you could argue that concrete belongs at the top of the list: it's the most widely used man-made building material, and without it modern life would be inconceivable. Concrete, despite its lowly reputation, is a genuine wonder. It's a conglomerate-like artificial rock, which before it sets can be poured, pumped, spread, molded, shaped, reinforced, and manipulated in ways that no natural material can. It's fireproof, rot-proof, rat-proof, rust-proof, bullet-proof, soundproof, and antiseptic, and it can withstand compressive loads of thousands of pounds per square inch—yet it's so inexpensive to fabricate that you can have it delivered to you fresh for about two cents a pound. (Every year, American suppliers produce between three and four tons of concrete per American.)

Contrary to popular usage, "concrete" and "cement" are not synonyms. The vehicles that most people call cement mixers are actually concrete mixers; cement is transported in tank trucks. House foundations, basement floors, and sidewalks are made of concrete, not of cement—although cement is concrete's most important ingredient. The other ingredients are gravel or crushed stone, sand, water, and, optionally, various performance-enhancing additives. In concrete, the function of the cement is to fill voids between pieces of fine aggregate (the sand) and pieces of coarse aggregate (the crushed stone or gravel) and permanently bind everything to everything else.

The cement in modern concrete is called portland cement, because Joseph Aspdin, an English bricklayer who is credited with the invention of its earliest version, felt that its color was similar to that of limestone quarried on the Isle of Portland, a peninsula on England's southern coast. (The exterior of the low-slung Conference Building at United Nations Headquarters, in New York City, is made of Isle of Portland limestone, and so is St. Paul's Cathedral in London.) Aspdin received his cement patent in 1824. His process involved heating and pulverizing limestone, adding clay to the crumbled fragments and placing that mixture in a very hot kiln until parts of it had fused, then grinding the burned and desiccated result into a fine powder. Adding water to the powder yielded a workable paste and initiated a complex chemical process, called hydration, in which the water bonded with compounds of calcium, silicon, aluminum, and iron, and caused the whole thing to lock together in a rigid mass. Wet portland cement doesn't merely dry, the way mud does; hydration transforms it into a chemically distinct material, which continues to gain strength indefinitely and can't be turned back into the original paste or into the powder from which the paste was made. It also hardens as readily underwater as it does in open air—more readily, in fact—and is therefore said to be "hydraulic."

Aspdin's cement wasn't the world's first cement, or even the world's first hydraulic cement. Four or five thousand years earlier, the Chinese and the Egyptians had used lime-based mortars in various large-scale construction projects (Great Wall, pyramids). Two or three thousand years after that, the Romans made hydraulic cement by combining burned limestone with a form of volcanic ash called *pozzolana,* which abounded at the foot of Mount Vesuvius and happened to contain some of the same useful compounds also found in Aspdin's clay. The Romans used their cement both as a mortar and as the base for the world's first concrete, whose physical characteristics they sometimes described with the participle *concretus,* meaning "hardened" or "congealed." (The dome of the Pantheon, which was completed around the year 200 and is more than a hundred and forty feet in diameter, is made entirely of unreinforced Roman concrete.) When Rome fell, the secrets of cement and concrete fell with it; they remained essentially lost until various eighteenth- and nineteenth-century Europeans, most of them English, once again figured out how to make hydraulic mortars. In 1818, an upstate New Yorker named Canvass White made hydraulic cement from a local form of limestone that was naturally high in clay, and his cement was used in mortar for the locks of the Erie Canal. (The state of New York later bought White's patent, for twenty thousand dollars—a small fortune in those days.) And there were other cement pioneers as well, some of them as important as Aspdin—although it was Aspdin who thought of the name that stuck.

One of America's earliest and most vocal concrete evangelists was Thomas Edison, who built a portland-cement mill in New Village, New Jersey, in 1899, and whose lifetime list of a thousand and ninety-three U.S. patents includes forty-nine related directly to cement or concrete. For the New Village plant, Edison built gigantic rotary kilns—tumbling brick-lined steel tubes a hundred and fifty feet long and more than eight feet in diameter—and used steam shovels, rather than wheelbarrows, to feed them. Firing the kilns at peak production consumed two hundred and fifty tons of powdered coal a day and gave off fumes so intense that Edison used the waste heat to generate power for other operations at the plant. In 1903, a coal-dust explosion killed fifteen workers and destroyed much of the plant; Edison quickly rebuilt it.

Edison was ahead of his time, as usual. His mill's ability to produce cement often outran the region's capacity to absorb it, even though he worked hard to expand his market. For a few years in the early nineteen hundreds, his company circulated a monthly brochure called *The Edison Aggregate,* and in 1926 it published an effusively hortatory promotional book called *The Romance of Cement* (first chapter: "The Eternal Romance of Cement"). "Take away concrete and America would lie in ruins," the book's uncredited author wrote. "Untold acres of land would become flooded. Travel would be suspended. . . . Once again it would take 45 days or longer to go from New York to San Francisco around the Horn, for the Panama Canal would be destroyed." The book also included, as an aside, a note on the "necessity for combating high wages."

Cement manufactured at Edison's mill was used to make concrete for the original Yankee Stadium, for parts of New York City's water supply system, and for an attractive apartment building still standing at 173–5 Riverside Drive, among a great many other projects. Edison also tried, though unsuccessfully, to interest the world in concrete pianos, concrete phonograph cabinets, and concrete bedroom furniture, and he was intermittently consumed by the idea of doing for domestic shelter what Henry Ford was simultaneously doing for private transportation. He devised a system of interlocking nickel-plated iron forms, which were supposed to enable builders to cast an entire two-story concrete dwelling, including the fireplace and some of the bathroom fixtures, in a single continuous pour. He lectured on concrete houses in Manhattan and elsewhere, and he exhibited a scale model at a home show in Madison Square Garden. His casting system turned out to be both expensive and difficult to use, although dozens of Edison concrete houses were actually built. The largest surviving collection is in Newark, Ohio, where in 1915 a local businessman named Eli Hull erected eighteen Edison houses on two streets near his own home (which was not made of concrete). An associate of Edison's visited Newark at the time and praised both the project and Hull, saying, "He is today building not only for time, but time everlasting." A couple of years ago, I spoke by telephone with Barb and Bill Bowling, who at that time had lived in one of the Newark Edison houses for more than thirty years. They told me that they love their concrete home, which has two stories and four bedrooms, and that one of its few real drawbacks is that they can't drive nails into the walls.

Edison wasn't the only American to anticipate concrete's utility as a residential building material. In 1854, an indigo planter named Dennis Redmond built a concrete house in eastern Georgia; today, Redmond's house, whose walls are a foot and a half thick, serves as the clubhouse of the Augusta National Golf Club, the home of the Masters golf tournament. Twenty years later, a mechanical engineer named William E. Ward, whose wife was deathly afraid of fire, built an all-concrete house in Port Chester, New York. Neighbors referred to the house as Ward's Folly and then, after it failed to fall down, as Ward's Castle. It is still standing.

————

UNDER THE RIGHT conditions, portland cement can be transported over long distances and stored indefinitely. Until American production got going, in the early twentieth century, builders here often imported it by the barrel from England. The barrels sometimes did double duty in transit, as ballast on the ships that carried them—a tricky proposition, you would think, since cement must be kept scrupulously dry. (Portland cement practically yearns to hydrate, and will draw moisture from the unprotected skin of workers handling it.) Wet concrete, in contrast, can't be shipped very far. A standard batch must be placed—that's the preferred term, rather than *poured*—within about ninety minutes of the moment when water is first added to it, or the mix will begin to harden inside the barrel of the truck. All concrete is therefore made within a short distance of the site where it is to be used.

I didn't get to watch the cabin's concrete being made, but I did once have an opportunity to see concrete being made for other people. I did it in New York City, at Ferrara Bros. Building Materials, in Queens, on a cold day in November. The Ferrara plant is near the end of a forlorn-looking dead-end street, between a company that manufactures asphalt and a huge blue structure that belongs to the Department of Sanitation. The sign at the plant's entrance is made of cast concrete, and it hangs from a concrete beam resting on a pair of concrete posts. Ferrara Bros. was founded in 1969, when Jerome Ferrara and his five sons—the brothers—agreed to buy a modest concrete plant and masonry supply yard from a neighbor. The deal included equipment for making concrete but no trucks for delivering it, so the five brothers tracked down five twenty-year-old Autocar mixers, the only trucks they could afford, and traveled to Massachusetts to pick them up. On the company's first official day of business, the driver of one of the trucks turned sharply to avoid a car, and flipped the truck on its side. (The torque of a turning mixer barrel makes a concrete truck, which is top-heavy to begin with, especially hard to handle on corners.) No one was hurt, but the accident reduced the Ferraras' fleet by 20 percent just as their first deliveries were being made.

Joseph J. Ferrara—who is a son of the eldest of the five brothers, and is now a vice president of the company and its general counsel—remembers that accident well. "I was eleven years old and walking home from baseball practice," he told me. "I saw a big crowd and a crane up ahead, and then I saw my father and my uncles. They were trying to get the truck upright with the crane, and there was concrete all over the street. The guy who sold them the company was there, too, and he put his arm around my father and said, 'This is just the start, kid.'"

Ferrara, who was born in 1958, is an attorney (his law degree is from Fordham) and a certified public accountant. He joined the company in 1986, after working outside the concrete industry for several years. He puts in long hours—his office is almost hilariously messy—but he finds the concrete business more satisfying than either of his two previous occupations. "I tell my dad that I probably could have earned more money and had fewer headaches at night as a lawyer or an accountant," he told me, "but I discovered I had portland cement in my veins. And in my lungs."

After we'd talked in the company's small conference room for a while, Ferrara took me outside to show me part of the concrete plant—a tall, long, narrow structure comprising silos, tanks, towers, hoppers, bins, and a water-slide-size conveyer belt rising to the very top of the structure from the company's aggregate storage area, off to the right. The plant is actually two plants, side by side: a standard "dry mix" plant, which dumps concrete's dry ingredients into the barrel of a truck parked underneath, adds water, and leaves the truck to do the mixing on its way to the job; and a modern "wet mix" or "central mix" plant, which combines all the ingredients, including the water, in its own rotating barrel, and pre-mixes them at high speed before loading them into the truck. "It costs a lot of money to turn that barrel on," Ferrara said, "and the plant uses a lot of power, but you get much better hydration with the central mix, much better use of your cement, and much stronger, more consistent concrete." We climbed a steep flight of metal stairs to the batching tower, which is the plant's computerized control center. "People think that concrete is very fungible, and one-size-fits-all," he said. "But it's not."

Every load of ready-mixed concrete is made according to a specific recipe, which is known as a mix design. There are many thousands of combinations, and every one is a compromise. The ideal concrete recipe would contain just enough portland cement to uniformly coat all the pieces of fine and coarse aggregate, which would be shaped and sized so as to fit together almost like the pieces of a puzzle, with smaller particles filling the voids between larger ones. The ideal recipe would also contain only as much water as is required for complete hydration: about three gallons for every hundred pounds of cement, creating a water-to-cement ratio, by weight, of around .25. In reality, though, the ideal mix design is impossible to achieve. Aggregate particles, no matter how carefully they are screened and graded, fit together somewhat haphazardly, and a concrete mixture containing only enough water for complete hydration would be too dry and inconsistent in texture to transport, place, consolidate, or finish. (The ideal amount of water in any cement paste is "the sweat of the mason," according to an old saying; do-it-yourselfers almost always add way too much.)

For a long time, the need to maintain workability placed a limit on the maximum compressive strength of finished concrete—usually somewhere between three thousand and six thousand pounds per square inch. In recent decades, though, engineers have learned to raise the limit tremendously, producing concrete with compressive strengths above twenty thousand pounds per square inch. They have done so by adding ingredients that facilitate hydration or have other desirable effects.

Chemicals called water-reducers make it possible to create work-able concrete with a water-to-cement ratio closer to the ideal, thereby increasing finished strength. Similar chemicals, called super-plasticizers, further reduce the need for water while mak-ing the wet concrete mixture so fluid that it can be pumped to the upper floors of high-rises or spread into complicated forms. Accelerators cause concrete to gain strength faster, thus reducing curing time—an advantage in cold weather—while retarders do the opposite—an advantage in hot weather. (The pebble-surfaced concrete trash containers you see on city sidewalks are cast using forms inside which a retarder has been applied to one surface; when the forms are removed, the "retarded" surface is rinsed with water, washing away the thin layer of unhardened ce-ment and exposing the pebble-like aggregate beneath it.) Air-entraining admixtures create billions of microscopic air bubbles in hardened concrete which act like relief valves for trapped water when it freezes. Corrosion inhibitors reduce the rusting of steel reinforcing rods and other embedded hardware. Some kinds of concrete also contain additional cementitious materials, among them fly ash, blast-furnace slag, silica flume, volcanic ash, and diatomaceous earth.

In the batching tower, Ferrara and I watched Mike Graff, the company's senior batcher, preparing a load of concrete for deliv-ery to a huge sewage facility being built in Brooklyn by the city's Department of Environmental Protection. Graff was standing at a control panel in front of a large window and looking down at the back of the truck he was preparing to load. He was in contact by radio with the driver and the dispatcher, and there was a video monitor to his left, up near the ceiling, on which he was able to keep track of four different parts of the plant at one time. He was checking the digital readout from a microwave moisture probe, which sixteen times a second was measuring the percentage of water in the sand flowing past it. Immediately to his left, a printer was producing a continuous record, showing the exact composi-tion of every load and its compliance with, or variance from, the recipe dictated by the design.

Graff pointed to a digital readout on the wall. "That's the temperature of the water," he said. "About 113 degrees. We want our concrete to be over 55 degrees, so on a cold day like today we have to use hot water to achieve that. We also steam the aggregates." Ice crystals, if they're allowed to form, will destroy a load of concrete, so the ingredients have to be kept well above freezing. They can't be warmed up too much, however, because hydration itself generates a considerable amount of heat, and concrete that's too hot won't cure properly.* During the summer, Graff often has to cool his mix, usually by using ice to replace some of the liquid water. The Ferraras used to hire teenagers to break bags of ice into the barrels of the concrete mixers on hot days; they now use an automatic ice-making machine like one that Leonard Ferrara once saw being used to cool down broccoli at the Hunt's Point Market.

FERRARA BROS. HAS a fleet of more than fifty concrete trucks. I asked if I could ride along with one of them as it made a delivery. Ferrara found me a hardhat back in the main building and sent me out with Joe Mirando, who was thirty-six years old and had worked at the company for fourteen years. Mirando's job at that moment was to deliver twelve cubic yards of concrete, roughly twenty-four tons, to the Triborough Bridge, where a construction crew supervised by city inspectors was repaving an on-ramp. When Mirando's number appeared on a display on the outside of the plant, he drove into the stall under the central-mix barrel, and Graff loaded his truck with a batch of concrete prepared according to the mix design specified by the Port Authority's engineers—a design that was substantially different from the one for the job I'd watched being loaded earlier. (This one was

---

* Buried within the Hoover Dam, which was built between 1931 and 1936, is a network of pipes that were used to cool the concrete as it cured, by circulating water through it. The dam's designers had realized that a dam-size mass of concrete, during hydration, would generate and trap so much heat that without artificial cooling the structure would require a century and a quarter to cool, and would develop spectacular cracks as it did. As each section of the dam reached and maintained the desired internal temperature, measured by thermometers also buried in the concrete, the cooling pipes serving it were disconnected, drained, and filled with portland-cement grout.

formulated to have much less slump and—because cars would be driving on it before the end of the day—to achieve high strength very quickly.) On our trip to the job site, we traveled north over the Bronx Whitestone Bridge, then southwest on the Bruckner Expressway, so that we would approach the correct Triborough ramp from the correct direction. As we bounced along, I asked Mirando if the truck was hard to handle.

"You've got to be careful," he said. "These trucks are very dangerous. We're carrying forty thousand, fifty thousand pounds up in the air, so I'm going nice and easy. But if you ever come up to a stoplight just as the light is turning red, and you look in your mirror and see a truck like this right behind you—do yourself a favor and keep going. Thank God, knock on wood, nothing like that has ever happened, but it really could. If I'm doing fifty-five and somebody cuts in front of me and stops—hey, make the sign of the cross."

We arrived early; the construction workers were still eating lunch. Mirando deduced from the appearance of the excavated area that the concrete he was about to unload was not intended to become a finished road surface, but would later be covered with asphalt. (Among other clues, there were no masons in the work crew, and there were no floats or other concrete-finishing tools in sight.) He turned out to be correct. We learned from the foreman that the new pavement was meant as a stopgap, to keep the roadway usable until the entire interchange was scheduled to be rebuilt, several years in the future, at which point everything would be redone in concrete.

"Almost all the highways in the city are done in concrete," Mirando said. "Concrete highways give you better traction in the rain and better visibility, and they last a lot longer. What happens with asphalt is that it gets ruts, and it starts to stretch when trucks stop—it washboards—like on the entrance ramps to the toll plazas."

Asphalt paving material, which is also known as bituminous concrete, consists of aggregates of various sizes suspended in a thick petroleum base, along with other ingredients and fillers, sometimes including portland cement. It has many desirable qualities: it's relatively easy, fast, and inexpensive to lay down; it isn't brittle; and it forms a travel surface that initially is very smooth. But it has undesirable qualities, too: it has nowhere near the rigidity, compressive strength, or durability of concrete; it always remains in at least a semi-plastic state, as you know if you've ever walked across an asphalt parking lot on a very hot day; and the bituminous parts of it dissolve in other hydrocarbons, such as spilled gasoline. (The solubility problem is the reason that the pavement around gas pumps and at jet-refueling areas is made of concrete.) I later saw a long section of asphalt roadway not far from the Ferrara Bros. plant which had collapsed under the weight of heavy trucks passing over it, even though the road had been paved just a few years before and the asphalt was more than a foot thick.

Mirando and I chatted with another Ferrara driver until the Triborough road crew had finished lunch. The perishability of our load meant that they couldn't keep us waiting indefinitely, and a few minutes later the foreman stopped traffic temporarily and guided Mirando into position at one end of the excavated section. Mirando attached the chutes to the back of his truck and turned the rotating barrel to a higher speed, for a final stir. (The stirring is done by steel mixing blades arranged in a helical pattern on the inside surface of the barrel—"like a corkscrew in reverse," Mirando explained.) I could feel the truck rhythmically rocking sideways as the barrel went around. Mirando returned to the cab and, as the load began to dump, he moved the truck forward in response to signals from the foreman, whom he was watching in his mirrors. After a few minutes, we heard a rattle in the barrel—the sound of coarse aggregate falling from the top to the bottom. "That means the concrete's almost gone," he said. A short while after that, we were gone, too, and another Ferrara truck, which had been waiting in line behind us, took our place.

On the drive back to the plant, I asked Mirando if the ninety-minute concrete clock had ever expired on him while he was making a delivery. "No," he said. "But I did have to go inside the barrel once. It was nighttime, and I got stuck on a job, and I could tell from the way the barrel was rocking that there was a little concrete stuck on a blade. So I just jumped right in there and hit it with a hammer, and it fell off." On another occasion, he

said, the barrel on his truck stopped turning while he was driving
to a job. (A gear box had broken, he later discovered.) He
turned around immediately and returned to the plant, where he
and some other employees opened the hatch covers and removed all the concrete, which was still wet—thus saving the barrel. I asked him if it was possible to salvage a barrel after a full
load of concrete had hardened inside it.

"Well, they can drill them sometimes," he said. "And sometimes they can dynamite them a little bit. Or a couple of guys will
get in there and chip it away a little bit at a time. So, yeah, it can
be saved. But you try to prevent that. If you don't have time to get
back to the plant, you dump it where you are."

CONCRETE IS TREMENDOUSLY strong in compression,
meaning that it's very hard to crush. But it's only about 10 percent as strong in tension, meaning that it's relatively easy to pull
apart. Concrete's tensile weakness is of little consequence in a
structure like the foundation of a house, because concrete can
easily do the main thing a house foundation has to do, which is
withstand the compressive force imposed by the weight of the
building sitting on top of it. In a structure that is subjected to
other kinds of loads, though, concrete's tensile weakness can
make a difference, and, when it does, it must be compensated
for. The usual way to make that compensation is to reinforce the
concrete with steel, which is very strong in tension (as it also is in
compression). The most widely used type of reinforcing steel is
known in the trade as rebar—steel rods arranged inside the
forms, and sometimes wired together in complex cage-like as-
semblies, before the concrete is placed. Rebar's function is to resist any tensile forces that overmatch the concrete.

You will often hear people say that adding rebar to concrete
will make the concrete stronger, or that it will prevent the concrete from cracking. It can do neither. The strength of concrete
remains the same whether it contains steel or not, and the presence or absence of steel has no effect on whether it will crack.
The purpose of the steel in a reinforced concrete structure is to
take over for the concrete after the concrete has failed for some

reason—to withstand any tensile forces that the concrete was unable to handle on its own. Christian Meyer, a professor of civil engineering at Columbia University and the author of a thick textbook called *Design of Concrete Structures,* told me, "Reinforced concrete must crack. That may sound funny to the layperson, but the reason is that if it doesn't crack, you didn't need the steel." In a standard reinforced-concrete column—one holding up a corner of a building, say—the rebar does nothing as long the column is subjected only to the compressive forces imposed by the building above; the rebar doesn't come into play unless a sufficiently powerful force is applied from a different direction—as when someone crashes a car into its side. If the force of the crash creates more tension in the concrete column than the concrete can withstand, the concrete cracks and the steel takes over. "It is the challenge of the engineer to keep the cracks small," Meyer said, "so that rather than having a few big cracks we have many little cracks." Properly sized and placed reinforcement can hold cracked concrete together, and it can help prevent relatively small cracks from becoming relatively huge ones, but it can't keep concrete from cracking in the first place.

Men, especially, have an irresistible attraction to reinforcement. There is something appealing about the concept of hidden strength, as in the idea that Superman is lurking under the drab gray suit of that mild-mannered newspaper reporter over there. Perhaps grown men's infatuation with reinforcement, like little boys' infatuation with superheroes, arises from anxiety about our own strength. At any rate, it's a powerful force, and it doesn't apply just to concrete work. One of the first misguided do-it-yourself projects that I tried after we moved into our house was resurfacing and repainting a small section of wall above the pass-through opening above the kitchen sink. This section of wall, which was surrounded by wooden trim and measured about one foot by three feet, was covered with hideous wallpaper that was curling up at the edges. The wallpaper had been pasted directly to the raw wallboard and couldn't be removed entirely without damaging the wall. A good approach would have been to peel off as much wallpaper as I could, especially at the edges and at the seam near the center, and then skim the surface with joint compound or spackle before sanding, priming, and painting. Instead, I decided to cut a piece of window screening the exact size of the wall section; staple the screening to the wallboard, as "reinforcement"; and cover the section with a thick coat of joint compound, like a miniature concrete slab. My father-in-law, who was visiting, expressed skepticism, but I myself had never felt smarter. Fortunately, the bit of wall was so small that even my misguided strategy couldn't do much harm, and the entire wall was later demolished, during our big kitchen renovation.

Concrete can crack even if nobody drives a car into it. An average load of concrete is made with about twice as much water as it theoretically needs for optimum hydration, and that extra water has to go somewhere. Much of it weeps out or evaporates as the concrete hardens; as it does so, the portland cement in the concrete shrinks somewhat, often causing the concrete to crack. Terry Collins, an engineer on the staff of the Portland Cement Association, told me, "Think of a concrete slab on grade. The concrete is sitting on the ground, and there is friction between the ground and the concrete. As the concrete shrinks, that friction creates tension, and concrete doesn't like tension. If the tensile forces become high enough, the concrete cracks, taking that tensile force to zero. That's why you put control joints in sidewalks and driveways."

People often say that control joints (which are sometimes called contraction joints) keep concrete from cracking, but their actual purpose is to *cause* cracking—or, rather, to direct it. A typical control joint is a narrow groove that is cut about a quarter of the way through a slab within the first few hours after the concrete is placed. The joint is an intentional weak spot, and its function is to give way first, creating a neat, straight fissure in a specific location rather than a messy, jagged, unpredictable one. Once that cracking has occurred, the rebar holds the slab together, so that the aggregate particles on either side of the crack fit together like knuckles. "That's called aggregate interlock," Collins told me. "The steel makes the separate parts of a cracked slab move up and down together, so that you don't have a differential settlement that creates a trip hazard or a structural problem."

Cracking caused by the drying of concrete can also occur where a concrete slab is penetrated by a post, a column, or some other non-shrinking protrusion. If you pour a concrete slab or wall around a rectangular steel-framed opening, the concrete will often crack at one or more of the steel frame's corners, where the slab is the weakest. (Such cracks typically spread at roughly a forty-five degree angle from the point where they begin.) This type of cracking can often be prevented by placing a flexible isolation joint between the concrete and the penetration, to give the concrete slab something soft to push against as it shrinks.

Another common type of cracking, often seen in residential slabs, is plastic shrinkage cracking, which occurs when excess water near the surface of a new concrete slab evaporates faster than it is replaced by excess water escaping from the bottom, causing the concrete on top to shrink faster than the concrete underneath. The resulting friction between the layers can create small cracks in the top layer, which is weaker than the bottom layer because premature drying has prevented the cement within it from hydrating as completely. Plastic shrinkage cracking can often be eliminated or reduced by slowing the escape of excess water—a process known as curing. Old-time concrete contractors will sometimes cure a new concrete slab, after finishing its surface, by spreading wet burlap on top of it; more up-to-date contractors use plastic sheets or spray-on curing compounds. The purpose of curing is to hold excess water inside the hardening slab until as much cement as possible has hydrated. This allows the slab to develop more tensile strength faster, increasing its ability to resist cracking caused by its own shrinkage and by evaporation.

Contractors and others sometimes claim that cracking can be prevented by adding synthetic fibers to concrete mixture, or that such fibers can "take the place of steel." Adding synthetic fibers—usually, short lengths of polypropylene—can reduce slab cracking caused by plastic shrinkage, because the fibers bridge microscopic cracks very early in the setting process and limit their ability to turn into bigger cracks, but its effect is limited and it has no impact on drying shrinkage. Unlike rebar, furthermore, synthetic fibers won't hold a cracked slab together. Rebar and synthetic fibers have different functions; neither should be considered a replacement for the other, despite what a contractor may say.*

In certain applications, engineers can prevent reinforced concrete from cracking at all by using advanced reinforcement techniques known collectively as prestressing. The basic idea behind prestressing is that applying a constant compressive force to concrete will increase its tensile strength. Professor Meyer told me, "Imagine you have a whole bunch of books, standing in a row on a shelf. If you place one hand at each end of the row and lift, you will pick up only the first book and the last, because the tensile strength between the books individually is zero. Now, though, imagine tightly wrapping a strong rubber band or bungee cord around the row of books, and then lifting in the same way. This time, because the rubber band is pressing the books together, the entire row goes up. This is the concept of prestress. Because you have *pre*compressed the books, you can now *de*compress them—that means pull—until the precompression is back to zero, at which point the books start falling down again."

There are two methods of prestressing concrete: pretensioning and posttensioning.† Both involve reinforcing concrete with steel cables, or tendons, that have been stretched, like the strings of a piano, and then anchored to the concrete itself. As the anchored cables attempt to contract, they apply a permanent compressive force—just like the rubber band around the books—and

---

* Fiber reinforcement is often used—entirely unnecessarily—in concrete countertops. Plastic shrinkage cracking (the kind that fibers can reduce) should not be problem in a countertop, which can be cast and cured under controlled conditions. In addition, because fibers inevitably protrude through the finished surface of any concrete structure to which they are added, a fiber-reinforced countertop must be poured in two steps, with a layer of fiber-free concrete on the outside. This is a costly complication that increases the likelihood of problems in the finished countertop and adds nothing to its strength or its resistance to cracking of any kind.

† This terminology, with its confusing mix of *pre*'s and *post*'s and its use of *tensioning* to signify a force that, from the point of view of the affected concrete, is actually *compression,* is very unfortunate. There's nothing to do about it, though, I guess.

thereby enable the hardened concrete to withstand tensile forces that would otherwise crack it. (In pretensioning, the cables are stretched inside the forms and the wet concrete is poured over them; in posttensioning, the cables aren't stretched until after the concrete has hardened.) Whenever you see a long unsupported span of solid concrete, as in a bridge or in the floors of a multistory parking garage, you can be fairly certain that some form of prestressing is involved. Prestressing is also sometimes used in residential slab foundations, in which the practice can eliminate or reduce cracking caused by drying shrinkage or by movement of the underlying soil. (You probably have good examples of prestressing right in your garage: most of the remarkable strength of a bicycle wheel is created by the pretensioning of the spokes.)

Building a heavy structure, such as a house, on top of a concrete foundation has an effect similar to that of prestressing: the weight of the structure compresses the concrete, thereby increasing its tensile strength—just as pressing the ends of a row of books increases the tensile strength of the row. In addition, the house's frame (which is bolted to the top of the foundation) acts as a brace for unsupported concrete walls, and the concrete itself gains strength as hydration progresses. Until the first-floor deck is completed and the concrete has reached most of its finished strength, contractors have to be careful not to backfill the new foundation too quickly, or to pack earth around it too forcefully. They also have to avoid driving heavy equipment nearby.

BEFORE THE CABIN'S foundation could be backfilled, it had to be damp-proofed. Hardened concrete all by itself is close to waterproof—swimming pools can be made of concrete, after all—but water vapor can pass through it fairly easily, and liquid water can enter pores and cracks, which can be widened by freezing and thawing. The seam between the bottom of the foundation walls and the top of the footings is also vulnerable. To keep basements drier, builders usually treat the exterior of a new foundation with a material that at least looks as though it might keep water out. The most commonly used such material is an asphalt-based coating that is brushed, rolled, troweled, or sprayed on. Such coatings are usually at least somewhat effective, although they aren't good at bridging gaps. For the cabin, I used a more modern and (I hope) more effective version of the same idea, a bluish-green, spray-on polymer coating called Rub-R-Wall, which has a lengthy guarantee. Many other systems are also available. An architect friend of mine recently used a system, called Platon, in which the foundation is wrapped in a 24-mil-thick polyethylene blanket. The blanket is dimpled to make it stand away from the foundation, creating channels through which liquid water can drain downward. My friend said that if he had to do it all again he would have applied a Rub-R-Wall-type coating first and then installed Platon—an approach that struck me as excessively anxiety-ridden, at least for houses like his and mine, both of which sit well above the local water table. But his idea might be an immensely appealing one if you have worked yourself into a sufficiently agitated state of mind.

After the cabin's foundation walls had been sprayed, Artie installed footing drains—subterranean drainage pipes that run around the outside of the foundation's footings. The purpose of these drains, which are usually made of perforated four-inch polyvinyl chloride (PVC) pipe, is to collect excess ground water from the base of the foundation and carry it far away, relieving hydrostatic pressure in the soil adjacent to the foundation and keeping the basement drier. He then installed the septic tank—a big concrete box with two large openings on the top, protected by manhole covers. So that I wouldn't lose track of the openings in the future, I asked Artie to insert cylindrical foot-tall risers into the openings, bringing the manhole covers up to the level of the finished grade. He also dug a long, thirty-inch-deep trench down the side of the driveway and placed three conduits in it so that the cabin's utility lines could be brought from the street underground.

Closely spaced, tree-size wooden poles linked by skeins of drooping cables are such a familiar element of the human landscape that most people never really notice them: familiarity has made them invisible. If you force yourself to see them, though, you can drive yourself slightly crazy over how grotesquely ugly they are. I can do that to myself, at any rate. The largest structure on my town's village green is a Congregational church that was *re*built in 1800, after the original was destroyed in a fire. The church is austerely beautiful, a New England cliché, and people come from far away to photograph and even videotape it, especially during the fall. Whenever I see such people framing the church in a viewfinder I wonder whether they even notice the tremendous mantle of electric, telephone, and cable-TV wires festooning the side of the church nearest the main road. That part of the church is just a few feet from two huge utility poles, which lean toward the building under the weight of the transformers bolted to their uppermost spars. If those poles and wires didn't exist already and the local power company proposed to install them in their current position, the public outcry would be anguished. But we have lived with overhead wires since the invention of the telegraph, and we have blinded ourselves to their repulsiveness.

People are more likely to notice the absence of utility poles and wires—though usually without being able to identify exactly what it is that they have noticed. There's a stretch of state road near my house which seems almost primeval as you drive along it: the towering trees on either side form a canopy overhead, a green tunnel whose roof, on a sunny day, is randomly penetrated by shafts of yellow light. The road looks that way because no chain-saw-armed crews from the power company have had to prune back the trees to protect overhead power lines from winter storms, allowing the branches to meet overhead. In the neighborhood where I grew up, in Kansas City, the utility poles ran down the center of each block, rather than along the curbs, making the streets look open and airy in a way you couldn't quite put your finger on. I myself didn't understand why until many years later, after I had begun to torture myself by thinking of overhead power lines as an eyesore.

As Artie placed the utility conduits in the trench alongside the cabin's driveway, he ran a yellow nylon rope called a "pull line" through each one; the electrician would use those lines later, to draw cables from the street to the house. As Artie refilled the trench with dirt, he buried a three-inch-wide warning tape about a foot above the conduits and eight inches below the finished grade. The purpose of the tape—which is made of plastic and says CAUTION BURIED ELECTRICAL LINES in an adamant type face—is to catch the attention of anyone who, at some point in the future, might be using a rented backhoe (for example) to investigate a buried glacial erratic (let's say) that he had noticed sticking out of the ground a few feet from the edge of his driveway.

6

STUDS, WINDOWS, SCREENS, AND PORCHES

THE WATERPROOF COATING was applied to the outside of the cabin's foundation on September 4; a week later, Rudy, Joe, and Mark began framing. The day they started was thrilling—for me, at any rate. I hung around for as long as I could, taking pictures and trying not to get in the way.

The first thing the men did was to lay a strip of thin polyethylene foam on top of the foundation—a sort of whole-house weatherstrip, known as sill sealer—and on top of the sill sealer they placed the sill: a rim made of pressure-treated two-by-sixes, which they placed flat on top of the foundation walls and secured with threaded bolts that the concrete contractor had embedded before the concrete set. On top of the sill came the floor joists, for which Reese had specified not regular lumber but I-joists, an engineered-wood product. An I-joist is a little like a girder; in cross section, it resembles the letter I. Its top and bottom flanges are made of laminated veneer lumber (thin strips of wood glued together under tremendous pressure to form members that look very much like solid wood but are stronger and better behaved), and the web between the two flanges is made of oriented strand board (thin chips and flakes of wood glued together in large, multilayered sheets in such a way that the grain of all the chips and flakes runs in pretty much the same direction). I-joists are more expensive than solid-wood lumber of the same dimensions, but they are stronger and can therefore be used over longer spans. They also weigh less than regular lumber, making them easier for builders to sling around, and they are dimensionally uniform and stable, without the warps and twists that are (increasingly) common in ordinary lumber. Most important of all, they can be manufactured from small, misshapen trees and lumber-industry odds and ends— a growing necessity, now that unravaged old-growth forests full of huge trees are scarce or protected.*

In cross section, the cabin's I-joists measured one and a half inches by nine and a half inches, the same dimensions as a solid-wood two-by-ten. The men nailed them edgewise to the top of the sills, with their centers spaced sixteen inches apart. Once the I-joists were all in place, the men nailed sheets of plywood on top of them, creating a firm, level deck (on which the finished floor would eventually be laid) and making the cabin look like a concrete box with a wooden lid on it. Directly on top of this deck they began to frame the first-floor walls, using regular two-by-sixes (for the exterior walls, interior bearing walls, and some of the interior partitions). Through most of the twentieth century, house walls were framed almost exclusively with two-by-fours; modern builders (and building codes) favor two-by-sixes for exterior walls because they leave more room for insulation.

The cabin's frame is very different from our house's frame, which is an example of an ancient construction method known as post-and-girt. A post-and-girt house frame has a lot in common with the steel frame of a skyscraper: it is made of a relatively small number of relatively massive members, which are joined together at right angles to form a heavy, boxy skeleton. The posts and girts in the frame of our house were hewn from chestnut trees growing nearby, and they are held together by wooden pegs, called

---

* Low mortgage rates in recent years have helped to create a nationwide construction boom—still going strong at the time I write—which has placed additional pressure on lumber supplies and prices, making high-tech engineered-wood products more common than ever, and making almost all building materials more expensive. If the cabin had been built a few years later, Rudy might have used panels made of oriented strand board, rather than plywood, which has more than doubled in price since then and is sometimes hard to find in quantity.

trunnels, and by the kinds of hand-carved mortise-and-tenon joints that furniture makers use. There are no nails, which had to be made individually by hand and were therefore too expensive to use casually. Besides, wooden pegs work better and last longer. If our house's builders had used iron spikes rather than trunnels to join the big timbers, the iron would have rusted to powder more than a century ago.

People sometimes still build houses with post-and-girt frames. Such frames are now usually known as "timber frames," and if you do a Google search for "timber frame homes" you will find many examples. (In modern post-and-girt houses, the framing members are almost always left exposed on the inside, making the frame part of the interior decorative scheme—something that was never done in the eighteenth century by anyone who could afford to hide them behind finished woodwork and plaster.) As a standard construction method, though, post-and-girt has been extinct since the nineteenth century. It was pushed into obsolescence by stick framing, an American invention, which was first employed in 1832 by a builder in Chicago who couldn't find enough big timbers for a warehouse he wanted to build. He got around the tree shortage by using much smaller pieces of wood—two-by-fours, essentially—and he compensated for their relative flimsiness by using lots of them. The vast majority of modern American houses have stick frames of one variety or another, even if their exterior is made of something other than wood.

For the cabin, Rudy employed the most common version of stick framing, called platform framing. He, Joe, and Mark framed the walls and partitions with vertical members, called studs, spaced sixteen inches apart. On top of the studs they nailed horizontal members, called plates, and on top of the plates they nailed more joists, and on top of the joists they nailed another plywood deck. A multistory platform-framed house is a little like a stack of tables: each new story is erected independently on top of the story below.*

---

* Incidentally, the levels of a building are called stories (probably) because of a medieval practice of decorating the facades of certain buildings with rows of windows or sculptures depicting historical or legendary events—stories.

The transition from post-and-girt construction to stick construction reflected a larger evolution. A single person, working
alone with a small number of hand tools, could create all the
parts needed for a post-and-girt frame. He would hew the timbers
one at a time, when other duties weren't pressing, and label them
for eventual assembly—usually with Roman numerals, the easiest
symbols to whack with an ax. (Rafters visible in the attic of our
house are marked in this way.) Not until all the timbers had been
hewn did the builder need help from anyone else—and that help
was essential, since the framing members were too heavy for him
to raise on his own. When everything was ready, he would sum-
mon his neighbors, who, working together, would help him erect
the frame in a single day. A platform frame, in contrast, can be assembled by a single determined carpenter working alone, since
the individual pieces are small enough to be lifted by one person
and each completed part of the frame serves as the staging for
the next. But making the parts for a stick frame can't be done by
an individual. It requires the coordinated efforts of many others:
a saw mill to cut the lumber, a factory to make the nails, trucks to
deliver the pieces. The transition from post-and-girt construction
to stick framing was the transition from the Ax Age to modernity.

RUDY BEGAN FRAMING the cabin in late September, and he
wanted to enclose the building's shell before winter weather arrived. By November, he, Joe, and Mark had sheathed the outside
of the frame with plywood and had brought in a subcontractor to
put (green) asphalt shingles on the roof. They had also installed
all the exterior doors and windows.

The first American buildings didn't have windows as we know
them today. Window glass was scarce until well into the eighteenth century, and for a long time it was heavily taxed, by the
pane. What little glass there was had to be imported, usually from
England. The British had actually hoped that the American glass
trade would operate in the opposite direction, with colonists
manufacturing inexpensive glass for shipment back to the
mother country, where glassmaking was constrained by the
scarcity of firewood. The settlers who founded the Jamestown

Colony, in 1607, included several German glassmakers, who managed to build a crude glassworks the following year. They shipped a few (unpromising) samples back to England, but within a short time they had all either given up or died. In 1621, the Virginia Company tried again, sending six Italian glassmakers, but they failed, too. If you visit Jamestown today, you can watch people in period dress making glass in a manner that is probably a better representation of what British investors hoped the Jamestown colonists would do than it is of anything they actually did. At first, making glass in the New World was similar to making ball bearings on the space shuttle: its main purpose was to demonstrate to skeptics at home that the entire costly adventure had been worthwhile. Truly productive glassmaking in the colonies didn't arise until the eighteenth century.

Our word *window* comes from the Old Norse *vindauga,* which meant "wind eye"; it dates from a time before glass, when windows had as much to do with air as they did with light. Any weather that forced you to keep your door closed forced you to keep your window closed also, and when your window was closed your house was dark. If you were lucky enough to own a little glass, you protected it in foul weather by covering it completely with a solid-wood shutter, and if you were stuck indoors you burned candles by day as well as by night. Nobody in Jamestown spent a winter afternoon curled up in front of the fire with a good book, gazing dreamily out the window at a snowstorm swirling through trees on the opposite hill. A window in those days was both a luxury and a peril: it admitted breezes and sunshine in decent weather, but it was vulnerable to wind, rain, snow, animals, and armed enemies. The earliest American builders made their windows small, if they made them at all.

The world's first glass was volcanic glass—obsidian—which is formed when silica-rich lava cools so rapidly that its increasing viscosity prevents its molecules from arranging themselves neatly, into crystals; similar ingredients cooled very, very slowly become granite. Like man-made glass, obsidian resists neat scientific classification. Its non-crystalline structure makes it similar in some ways to a liquid, in which the molecules are also assembled chaotically, yet it is manifestly a solid. (Early peoples made knives and spear points from obsidian, which can easily be fractured to form an edge many times sharper than the sharpest steel edge; a few modern surgeons use obsidian scalpels for certain delicate operations.) Scientists sometimes refer to obsidian and other glasses as supercooled liquids, a term that accurately describes the process by which they are formed but is responsible for the common misconception that solid glass is *fluid.* You may have read, for example, that the window panes in very old houses are thicker at the bottom than at the top and that this difference is caused by the imperceptible but relentless downward flow of glass under the influence of gravity—an extraordinarily appealing idea, but an incorrect one. If old window panes are thicker at one end it's because old glassmakers weren't terribly good at making glass, and if the thick end is at the bottom it's because the glazier put it there. Solid glass, to the extent that it flows at all, does so over eons, not centuries. According to Edgar Zanotto, a Brazilian professor of materials science, who addressed the question in the May 1998 issue of the *American Journal of Physics,* the time required for a pane of window glass at room temperature to thicken at the bottom would be roughly a hundred million trillion years. Glass isn't a sluggish liquid; it's an amorphous solid.

Anyone who has made hard sugar candy has made glass. Heating granulated sugar to 300 degrees Fahrenheit turns the sugar from a crystalline solid into a chaotic liquid; supercooling that liquid (by pouring it onto a cookie sheet at room temperature) causes the sugar to resolidify without recrystallizing. As the melted sugar cools, it, like other glasses (and unlike water), passes through a viscous stage, during which it can be rolled, shaped, pulled, twisted, and blown, among other things. A sourball is a sphere of sucrose glass; peanut brittle is a sheet of sucrose plate glass, with peanuts embedded in it. You can see through hard candy for the same reason that you can see through a window pane: the disorganized arrangement of its molecules allows light to pass through without being deflected or absorbed.

The first human glassmakers probably lived in Mesopotamia or Egypt a few thousand years before the birth of Christ. Undoubtedly, they discovered their craft by accident, perhaps when a very hot fire used in pottery making caused sand (which is mostly silica) to melt in the presence of certain alkaline compounds, possibly supplied by ashes from the fire. Ancient Egyptians made small bottles by dipping solid cores into molten glass, then chipping out the cores. Glassblowing was invented about a thousand years later, in Syria. The Romans made glass ornaments, containers, paving materials, and wall coverings, among a great many other things, and they invented cameo glass, in which glass layers of different colors are fused and then carved to form multicolored three-dimensional designs. The Phoenicians were accomplished glassmakers. So were the Venetians, whose delicate creations dominated the luxury end of the European market for several centuries. In 1291, the Venetians moved their entire industry to the island of Murano to reduce the danger of fire in Venice itself—glassmaking furnaces are extremely hot—and to discourage local glassblowers from revealing their secrets to potential competitors. Nevertheless, those secrets did spread through Europe eventually, as Venetian glassmakers established themselves in other cities.

The most common ingredients of ordinary glass are sand, lime, and soda—silica, calcium oxide, and sodium carbonate or sodium hydroxide. The sodium compounds lower the melting point of the silica and cause it to fuse more readily. If you leave out the calcium oxide, which is better known as limestone, you get sodium silicate, which dissolves in water and is therefore known as water glass. (The main use for sodium silicate nowadays is in the manufacture of silica gel, the stuff inside those little pillow-shaped packets that come with new shoes; for many years, dissolved water glass was used as a preservative coating for eggs, but it was abandoned in favor of mineral oil, which works better.) Dozens of other materials have applications in glass production: boron increases heat resistance and is the critical ingredient of Pyrex, which was invented in 1915. Metallic oxides add color. (The glass made by those luckless Germans at Jamestown was green because the sand they used contained iron.) Lead oxide makes glass heavier, clearer, more brilliant, and easier to grind. Its utility in glassmaking was discovered in the 1670s by an Englishman named George Ravenscroft, who described his creation as "resembling rock crystal." For this reason, glass with lead in it is called crystal. Ravenscroft's discovery was actually a rediscovery: lead was first added to glass, with the same beneficial effects, in Mesopotamia.

To make window glass, an early glassmaker would blow a large blob of molten glass into a bubble, then flatten the bubble, remove the blow pipe, and attach an iron rod, called a pontil, on the opposite side. The glass was then reheated and spun, causing the mass to spread—slowly at first, then with dramatic suddenness—into a thin disk that could be five feet in diameter. This disk was slightly convex, or crowned; the panes cut from it were called crown glass. At the center of each disk, where the pontil had been attached, was a thickened nipple, called a bullion. The bullion was considered an unfortunate defect, and the section containing it was usually thrown back into the cauldron or sold at a discount to people who couldn't afford anything better. Modern old-house restorers, however, often seek out bullions, because they look extra old. As a matter of fact, modern lovers of all sorts of antique things have a tendency to esteem characteristics that old craftsmen disliked or were ashamed of: "rough-hewn" timbers would have been dismissed as amateur work by skilled eighteenth-century housebuilders, who worked hard to make their framing members smooth, and many of the dull, earth-tone paint colors that we think of as characteristically "colonial" are just the sun-faded remnants of the garishly bright colors that eighteenth-century homeowners actually loved. Early glassmakers, similarly, devoted considerable energy to eliminating the bubbles, waves, and imperfections that modern collectors prize. The four-dollar margarita glasses in last year's Pottery Barn clearance catalog would have inspired the awed admiration of thirteenth-century Venetian glassblowers; a light bulb would have flabbergasted them.

Window glass in the old days was also made by blowing molten glass inside a cylindrical wooden mold, then slitting the glass lengthwise while it was still plastic, reheating it, and flattening it into a sheet. Ten years ago, I replaced the glass in our house's living-room and dining-room windows (which a painter had damaged through careless sanding) with reproduction cylinder glass made by a New Jersey company called S. A. Bendheim. Bendheim sells two kinds of restoration glass: one with pretty many bubbles, waves, and imperfections in it, and one with very many. Because I esteem characteristics that old craftsmen disliked or were ashamed of, I chose the kind with very many. Those windows are wonderful to look through on sunny late-October afternoons, when the glass smears the autumn foliage into a bright blur—although I hardly ever remember to notice.

In the late sixteen hundreds, various Frenchmen began casting high-quality glass plates by pouring molten glass onto iron tables, then rolling, grinding, and polishing the surfaces until they were smooth. (Plate glass was actually invented by the Romans, but their crude, unpolished version was barely translucent.) Around 1800, English glassmakers thought of using steam engines instead of muscle power or water power to accomplish the grinding and polishing—a major improvement, which brought down prices and made possible an epochal breakthrough in the history of retail marketing: the invention of the storefront window. Beginning around 1900, plate glass was made by drawing it in a continuous ribbon from a vat of viscous glass and pressing the ribbon between rollers as it emerged from the vat. Today, most window stock and other flat glass is manufactured by floating molten glass on a bath of molten tin, a method that produces perfectly smooth sheets of uniform thickness (and creates the hottest factories in the world). The float process was invented in 1952 by Alastair Pilkington, a British engineer, who is said to have thought of it while washing dishes. Making his idea commercially viable took most of a decade. Pilkington—later Sir Alastair—was employed by Pilkington Brothers, an industrial glassmaker; surprisingly, he was not related to the company's early-nineteenth-century founders. He died in 1995. Today, Pilkington Brothers is called Pilkington PLC. Its products include Pilkington Activ, a self-cleaning window glass, which has a microscopically thin, permanently bonded titanium-oxide coating that causes dirt to break down in sunlight and rinse away in rain.

A HYPOTHETICALLY IDEAL piece of glass would be many times stronger than steel, but glass in the real world has even more issues with tension than concrete does. Solid glass is extremely rigid, and tiny flaws in its surfaces can rapidly amplify into cracks when bending forces are applied: early glass broke more readily than the goblets you received as wedding presents. Internal irregularities increase the fragility of glass. When molten glass cools, it usually does so unevenly, with some parts solidifying, and therefore contracting, faster than others. These differences create powerful permanent stresses, which can make glass vulnerable to catastrophic structural failure; in some cases, a gentle tap is enough to make a large piece shatter. Glassmakers eventually discovered that they could reduce the potential for fracturing by keeping newly made glass at a high temperature until the stresses introduced by manufacturing had dissipated—a step known as soaking—then cooling the glass slowly to prevent new stresses. This entire process is known as annealing; the oven in which it is done is called a lehr. Even beads and other very small glass objects usually turn out better if they are annealed.

There's a double-hung window at floor level on the landing near the foot of the staircase in the cabin; per the local building code, it is glazed with tempered glass, which is significantly stronger than ordinary annealed glass and is therefore less likely to be broken by someone falling against it after stumbling on a flight of stairs. Tempered glass was invented in 1929. It is made by reheating annealed glass to a temperature just below the point at which it would become plastic again, then cooling its surfaces very rapidly, by blowing pressurized air on them. The air-blown surfaces cool, and therefore solidify and contract, faster than the center; when the center contracts later, it pulls the hardened surfaces and edges inward, creating permanent compression in the surfaces and permanent tension in the center. (Something similar happens in a prestressed concrete slab, in which the tension of the stretched internal tendons strengthens the slab by compressing it from edge to edge. See Chapter 5.) Tempered glass is far stronger than ordinary glass as long as it remains intact, but if a tempered sheet of glass is cut, drilled, cracked, or even chipped, the sheet can disintegrate spectacularly, into hundreds of pellet-like fragments—a failure pattern known as dicing. These fragments, unlike shards of ordinary glass, don't have sharp edges, and for this reason fully tempered glass is also called safety glass. Storm doors, basketball backboards, and the windows in oven doors are made of tempered glass. So are the rear and side windows of most automobiles. If you look at your car's rear window from certain angles, especially while wearing sunglasses, you may notice an iridescent pattern in the glass—an unavoidable consequence of the tempering process.

Automobile windshields, in contrast, are made of laminated glass, which consists of two layers of glass with a layer of strong plastic film bonded between them under pressure (and sometimes, nowadays, with an additional layer of film bonded to the inside surface). The film holds the pieces in place if the glass shatters, and it helps to prevent passengers from being ejected in collisions. It's also the reason that you don't get sunburned through your windshield, since the film blocks almost all ultraviolet radiation. (It also inhibits the transmission of sound.) Laminated glass was invented by accident in 1903, when a French chemist named Edouard Benedictus knocked a flask to the floor of his lab and was amazed to see that the glass held its shape despite being shattered. The reason, he determined later, was that the flask had once been used to hold collodion, a syrupy solution of ether, alcohol, and nitrocellulose, and that remnants of the collodion had dried into a flexible film on the inside surface of the flask.* Benedictus realized almost immediately that his discovery could be used to make safer windshields, and he quickly assembled the first laminated-glass plates. But early automobile manufacturers resisted safety improvements even more assiduously than modern automobile manufacturers do, and Benedictus's idea wasn't used in cars until almost a quarter-century later. The first serious commercial use for Triplex, as his invention

---

* The invention of collodion, in 1846, by a young French chemist named Louis Ménard, was an important early step in the development of modern plastics. Nitrocellulose is the key ingredient not only of it but also of modern gunpowder; in one of its forms it is known as gun cotton. Combining nitrocellulose with camphor produces celluloid, which was first used commercially, beginning in 1869, in billiard balls.

came to be known, was in the eyepieces of World War One gas masks.

Fully tempered glass isn't used in windshields, for several reasons: its great strength makes it more likely to cause head injuries; even small chips or cracks can lead to sudden shattering; and diced tempered glass, if it doesn't fall to the ground in a hail of pellets, is impossible to see through. The glass bits you notice in the street at the scene of a traffic accident are almost always from side and rear windows; shattered windshields are usually held in place by their internal film, with spider-web-like fractures radiating from the places where heads or other solid objects have struck them. People who break into cars for a living do so through side or rear windows, because windshields, although they crack more readily, can be a nuisance to penetrate fully. If you ever have to break into a car yourself, a very sharp object, such as an ice pick, will work better than a broad, heavy object, such as a brick. (With a brick, the force of each blow is spread over a broad area and is therefore easier for the tempered glass to withstand; if you worry about being entombed in your car, you can buy an emergency tool with a spiked tip that is designed to shatter tempered automobile glass.) In recent years, a growing number of (mostly European) cars have been manufactured with side and rear windows made of a form of laminated glass called Enhanced Protective Glass, which isn't as sturdy as windshield glass but is similarly useful at preventing passengers from being ejected in crashes; American carmakers have been slow to follow.

Before laminated glass and tempered glass (and seatbelts) came into widespread use in automobiles, the worst injuries in car accidents were often caused by glass. One such accident was described in 1984 by Roald Dahl, the author of *James and the Giant Peach, Charlie and the Chocolate Factory,* and many other books. The Dahl family bought its first car in 1925, when Dahl was nine. The vehicle was a convertible, and it had two windshields, one in the usual position and the other in front of the backseat. During the car's inaugural outing, Dahl's older sister, who was driving, skidded sideways into a hedge. The car wasn't going very fast, but the impact was sufficient to throw several of the seven occupants out of the passenger compartment altogether and to throw Dahl from the backseat to the front. "But miraculously nobody was hurt very much except me," he wrote in *Boy,* his (excellent) memoir of his early childhood. "My nose had been cut almost clean off my face as I went through the rear windscreen and now it was hanging on only by a single small thread of skin. My mother disentangled herself from the scrimmage and grabbed a handkerchief from her purse. She clapped the dangling nose back into place fast and held it there." A few hours later, the family doctor managed to sew it back on.

THE FIRST GLAZED residential windows in America were casement windows—the kind that are hinged on one side and swing out like a door. Double-hung windows—which have two independent sliding sashes, one above the other, and are sometimes therefore known as sash windows—came later.*

All the windows in our house, and not quite half the windows in the cabin, are double-hung; the rest of the cabin's windows are casements. Reese specified casements for the cabin because they look rustic and have a number of appealing features: they open fully (unlike double-hung windows, which can never be more than half-open), their screens are mounted on the inside (and therefore don't get dirty as quickly), and their swinging sashes can be positioned so that they divert breezes indoors. But they also have a number of big disadvantages, I've discovered. Mounting a window fan or an air conditioner in one is next to impossible, and when a casement sash is swung open its inside surfaces and mechanical parts are fully exposed to the elements. A spider will often weave a web between an open casement window and its screen, and the web then becomes a permanent part of your win-

---

* *Sash,* in its window sense, came to English in the seventeenth century, from the French *chassis,* meaning frame. Renovation snobs often use *sash* as a plural as well as a singular, but I'm not sure why—perhaps because early English users assumed incorrectly that the French word was a plural (because of its final *s*) and so shortened it in addition to borrowing it and mispronouncing it. The Oxford English Dictionary says *sashes,* and so do I.

dow treatment until you remove the screen and whisk away the mess. Casement windows also have to be kept tightly closed in any but the gentlest rain. Shortly after the cabin was complete, I left a few of the upstairs casement windows open during the first few minutes of a big rainstorm and had to run frantically from room to room, using bath towels to mop water from sills, screens, walls, radiators, and rugs. When I look at a casement window, I can't quite figure out why it offers so much less resistance to a downpour than a double-hung window does, but it definitely is more vulnerable—and I have the stains on my walls to prove it. My friend Ken, who used only casement windows in his own house, warned me not to use them in the cabin, saying that I would hate them in the rain. I ignored him, but I now wish that I had followed his advice.

Most of the windows in our house—all but the ones that have been replaced in various recent renovations—are very old and won't stay open by themselves. If you want a breeze or need to fiddle with the screen or storm window, you have to prop up the lower sash with a stick, a book, a wooden clothes hanger, the wand of the vacuum cleaner, the top of your head, or something similar, and if you pull away the prop the sash comes down like a guillotine blade. I once spent a month unable to make a tight fist with my left hand because the bottom sash of the window in my office had fallen across the first and second joints of three of my fingers while I was trying to deal with a hornets' nest up near the top of the storm window.

The double-hung windows in the house I grew up in were kept open by sash weights—torpedo-shaped iron counterweights attached to each side of each sash by a length of clothesline-gauge rope, called a sash cord. The sash weights were hidden inside the window jambs, in covered channels called sash pockets. The weights rose as the sash descended and descended as it rose, and, if properly adjusted, they would keep the window open in any position. Every once in a while, a sash cord would break and my father would have to open a panel in the jamb, retrieve the weight, and attach a new cord. He would then thread the new cord through a pulley at the top of the jamb and attach it to the sash. If I slammed a window in anger, I would hear the sash weights clonking around inside the walls for five or ten seconds afterward—the muffled reverberation of my tantrum.

The windows in Ann's and my house don't have sash weights. Many of the oldest ones have a thumb-operated, spring-loaded latch in one jamb which, if pressed before the sash is opened and released once the sash has been lifted to the desired height, is supposed to grab one of several notches mortised into the side of the sash, holding it in place. This system probably worked great for the first century or so, but the notches in the sides of the sashes eventually wore away, leaving little or nothing for the latches to grab onto. I have removed a number of the latches over the years, during various home-improvement projects. For quite a while, I saved them in a box in the basement, thinking they might be valuable—but then I thought, Who am I kidding? (I don't even know what they're called.) The newer windows in our house stay open without weights or latches, by some friction-related method that I have never bothered to try to understand because it has never not worked.

All the windows in the house and the cabin are of a type known, nowadays, as "divided-light"—a category that wasn't needed in the old days, when there was no other kind. A divided-light window is one that is made of multiple pieces of glass held together in a frame, like a patchwork quilt in which the patches are pieces of glass. (*Light* is the grown-up, window-expert word for *pane;* it's also sometimes used for entire windows.) The first glazed windows had to be made this way because early glassmakers couldn't produce sturdy, affordable glass in sash-size sheets. The stained-glass windows in early churches, in addition to being beautiful, were a technological necessity: small, irregularly shaped fragments of flat glass were about the best that glassmakers could do, in quantity. Panes got bigger as glassmaking advanced, and, in fact, light size is an important clue in the dating of original windows. The windows in the very oldest houses in colonial America usually consisted of very small diamond-shaped panes held together in lead frames. Later windows had larger, rectangular panes, usually mounted in double-hung wooden sashes. A typical house window during most of the eighteenth century had twelve or sixteen small lights in each sash—styles

now known as "twelve over twelve" and "sixteen over sixteen."
(The big windows in several old Congregational churches in my
area are twenty over twenty.) Our house has six-over-six windows,
which began to appear in American houses toward the end of the
seventeen hundreds. By the end of the following century, windows in which each sash held just a single sheet of glass were
common, although many people remain devoted to more primitive styles, for aesthetic reasons. The brand-new double-hung windows in the cabin are six-over-six, and almost all of the casement
windows have twelve divided lights each.

Divided-light windows, no matter how many lights they contain, are sometimes referred to as "mullioned" windows, although in careful usage the term for the wooden dividers
between panes is not mullions but muntins. (A mullion is the vertical piece of trim that divides a pair of doors or a pair of windows, or covers the gap between them when they are closed.)
Manufacturers sometimes fake a divided-light effect on single-
pane windows or doors by adding wooden or plastic grids that
snap into place against the inside surface of the glass. I don't like
that look, because it seems so obviously simulated, but I understand the impulse. In most houses, unblinking expanses of undi-
vided glass seem stark and cold. Dividing a window into smaller
lights, though no longer necessary technologically, does something pleasing to the window's appearance, in the same way that
hanging pictures on a blank wall improves the wall.

Paradoxically, dividing a window into smaller lights can also
improve the view in the other direction. People who install enormous uninterrupted sheets of glass in their houses often squander their views in their very efforts to possess them. One
little-discussed fact about impressive views is that they, like most
nice things, wear out with use. The first time you stand before
your wall-size window and run your eyes over the curvature of the
earth, the scene takes your breath away. The thousandth time you
do it, your lungs scarcely notice. Familiarity inexorably turns the
transcendent into a cliché—like the Mona Lisa. When a view is always on display, it quickly loses its ability to surprise and, therefore, to delight. As a result, a modest window may hold a good
view longer than a two-story wall of glass. The smaller frame re-

tains its power in part because it requires some work from the viewer, the way a book does. An attractive view should flirt with the viewer rather than baldly proposition. It should leave something to the imagination.

THE MAIN QUALITIES of the oldest windows in our house are looseness, draftiness, and rattly-ness. Their upper sashes don't move at all—and it is possible that they never moved—but some of the lower sashes sit so loosely in their jambs that they jiggle when you open or close a door in another room, or even on another floor. Obviously, a window like that, acting on its own, doesn't put up much resistance to icy winter winds, or to anything else. One warm autumn afternoon a few years ago, I walked into the living room and noticed a dark, writhing mass on the ceiling and walls in the room's farthest corner. The mass turned out to be ladybugs—seemingly, bazillions of them. Driven by some instinctual imperative, they had squeezed through the gap between the top of a window's bottom sash and the bottom of its top one, and were now forming a comfortable huddle in which to pass the winter. I quickly closed all the storm windows, then went after the ladybugs with the vacuum cleaner, eventually filling most of a bag. These particular ladybugs were members of an Asian species that emigrated to the United States aboard a cargo ship in the nineteen-eighties and have been spreading across the country ever since. Vacuuming them filled the house, temporarily, with a horrible smell. We've been bothered by ladybugs ever since, but in smaller numbers. During winter warm spells, they emerge from their hiding spots and knock around inside lampshades, where they make as much noise as small birds. One night, while I was working late in my office, I smelled something odd and worried that the house might be on fire. After a few minutes of frantic searching, I discovered the source of the smell: a dozen ladybugs that had clustered in the central cavity of a tubular compact fluorescent light bulb, died, and smoldered until the heat of their incinerating corpses had caused the bulb to burst. (Possible television show: "CSI: Crime Scene Investigation—Funny Smells in My House.")

All the windows in the cabin, both casement and double-hung, are made of wood and have double-glazed lights, each with two panes of glass separated by a hermetically sealed half-inch air space. Inside each muntin, along the edges of that air space, is a perforated aluminum spacer filled with silica gel or some other desiccant. The purpose of the desiccant is to absorb any moisture remaining in the sealed air space after manufacture, and to sponge up any water vapor that sneaks in later on. Early double-glazed windows had a bad habit of permanently fogging from the inside—a hopeless problem that has largely been eliminated by improved design.

Double-glazed windows are warmer and quieter than single-glazed windows, because the air space between each pair of panes acts as an insulating layer, turning a window into its own storm window. This is a swell idea, I think, although its impact on residential energy use is often exaggerated. You can spend almost any amount of money on high-tech windows nowadays, and manufacturers make impressive claims about the energy savings you can expect to enjoy, but what you actually get for your money isn't always clear.

The insulating value of many building materials—as you know if you've ever shopped for insulation—is indicated by a numerical rating known as an R-value, which is an expression of the material's ability to resist the flow of heat. The formula used to calculate R-values contains frightening-looking symbols and operators, and has to do with the time it takes a given amount of heat on the warm side of a material to raise the temperature of the cool side by a given amount; all that you and I need to know, as far as household insulation is concerned, is that higher R-values are better. A thin sheet of metal has an R-value of close to zero, because thin sheets of metal conduct heat very readily. (A house with sheet-metal walls would be very cold in the winter and very hot in the summer.) A three-and-a-half-inch-thick blanket or batt of high-quality fiberglass insulation has a rating somewhere between R-11 and R-13; a five-and-a-half-inch layer of the same insulation is about R-18 or R-19; a foot-thick layer of rock wool insulation is about R-38; a one-inch-thick sheet of expanded polystyrene is about R-4. R-values are additive: If you combine a five-and a-half-inch-thick fiberglass blanket with a two-inch-thick slab of expanded polystyrene, you get an insulation sandwich with a total R-value of about 26. In my part of the country, builders try to achieve an R-value of close to 50 in attics, to slow heat loss through the roof during the heating season and to reduce heat gain through the roof during the summer. They usually do it by combining several insulation systems: loose insulation between the attic's floor joists, plus a layer of fiberglass blankets on top of the joists, plus fiberglass batts between the rafters. (Because warm air rises, the uppermost surface of an enclosed structure is the one most vulnerable to the flow of heat and therefore requires the most insulation.)

All the elements of an enclosed structure—including lumber, wall-hangings, and the film of air adhering to interior and exterior surfaces—resist the flow of heat to some extent and therefore have R-values of their own. You can determine the total thermal resistance of an entire system by adding together the R-values of these elements. A typical modern house wall—with Sheetrock on the inside, wood siding and sheathing on the outside, and five and a half inches of fiberglass insulation in between—has a total R-value of somewhere around R-21. Like most single measures of complex systems, R-values work better in broad comparisons than they do in precise evaluations. The R-rating for a typical house wall really applies only to the parts of the wall between the studs, because the R-value of framing lumber is less than a third that of fiberglass insulation; nor does the wall rating apply to the parts of the wall containing windows, electrical outlets, or other openings, whose R-values are much lower. The true heat retention provided by any wall or other structural element, no matter what its putative R-value, is also affected heavily by how conscientious the builders were about filling gaps and plugging air leaks, and by such external factors as how hard the wind is blowing and whether or not it is raining.

In windows, thermal performance is expressed not in R-values but in U-values, which measure heat conductance rather than heat resistance. (The same measure is also sometimes referred to as a C-value.) A U-value doesn't contain any information that an R-value doesn't, since each number is the reciprocal of the other:

if you know a material's R-value, you can obtain its U-value by dividing its R-value into 1. There may be a compelling scientific reason for classifying windows with U-values rather than R-values, although it's also possible that window manufacturers use U-values because they worry that the R-values of even the most energy-efficient high-tech windows would seem pretty meager to people trying to decide whether such windows are worth the money. An ordinary wood-framed single-glazed window with an aluminum storm window has an R-value of about 2, while a fancy wood-framed triple-glazed window with quarter-inch spaces between the panes (but no storm window) has an R-value only somewhat higher—about 2.5. A triple-glazed window that has a low-emissive coating on the glass and is filled with argon, an inert gas, instead of ordinary air, has an R-value of a little more than 4. That's a large relative improvement over an ordinary window, but it's a small absolute one; you could match the impact of one high-tech window on the overall R-value of your house by adding an extra three-quarters of an inch of fiberglass insulation to one window-size section of one wall. And the saving in fuel consumption from a high-tech window can be negated if you leave it open a crack in cold weather to admit fresh air, or fail to seal all the gaps around its frame during installation. Also, argon has a tendency to gradually leak out of putatively sealed windows (the molecules are very small). Window manufacturers sometimes say that such leakage—which cannot be detected—has little impact on a window's overall thermal performance, an assurance that might make a smart shopper hesitate to pay for the stuff in the first place.

The real-world value of expensive window add-ons can be very hard to judge. Low-emissive glass has a microscopically thin coating that is intended to reflect some infrared and ultraviolet radiation while admitting as much visible light as possible. Theoretically, this should keep a house cooler in the summer (by reflecting solar rays that would otherwise warm the house) and warmer in the winter (by slowing the escape of some interior heat), while also helping to preserve upholstery and wall coverings (which, like paint, wood, and human skin, are damaged by exposure to ultraviolet light). But a coating that reduces solar heat gain during the summer, and therefore decreases the load on your air conditioner, also reduces solar heat gain during the winter, and therefore increases the load on your furnace. And if you're planning to fit your windows with curtains or shades—which are far more effective at blocking solar radiation than low-e coatings are—you may receive less actual benefit from the coatings than the manufacturer claims you will, because the curtains will make the coatings at least partly redundant. And the same can be true for other costly features.

The difference in price between an old-fashioned but tightly fitting single-glazed window, used in combination with a good-quality storm window, and a top-of-line multiple-glazed window with low-e coatings, suspended inner films, and an inert gas between the panes can be many hundreds of dollars per window. Does investing in such features pay for itself? In many cases, it doesn't. For most homeowners, a far more cost-effective (and environmentally friendly) long-term strategy would be to specify fewer and smaller windows, and to make better use of curtains and other window coverings. The fanciest high-tech residential windows available today have R-values of 7 or so. That's amazing for a window, but it doesn't approach the thermal performance of a plain-old windowless Sheetrock wall filled with a few inches of fiberglass insulation. For almost any house, spending an additional twenty thousand dollars on energy-related window features would have much less impact on actual energy use than spending two thousand dollars on more insulation for the attic.

GAINS IN BUILDING technology, including window technology, have made our homes immeasurably more comfortable and energy-efficient, but they have also reduced our ingenuity at directly managing our interior environments. My grandparents lived in a hot part of the country without air-conditioning, triple-glazing, or low-e coatings, but they still managed to survive virtually a century apiece—and even in August my grandfather never took off his tie. They controlled summer temperatures the old-fashioned way, with awnings over their windows and venetian blinds behind their curtains, and with a big whole-house fan, in the basement, which looked like a propeller salvaged from the *Titanic*. When I spent the night at their house during the summer, I would sleep on top of my covers with my head by the open window at the foot of my bed, and the basement zephyr would carry me off to sleep. I liked lying with my head by the window, because that way I could directly observe the many personal problems of my grandparents' neighbors, a large dysfunctional family.

In Ann's and my house, we have neither central air-conditioning nor a basement fan, but we still manage to stay comfortable most of the summer. We have borrowed a trick from Ann's parents, who cool their own un-air-conditioned house by opening most of their windows at night, then closing all the windows and most of the curtains during the day. In my part of the country, even a poorly insulated old house, like mine, will stay fairly cool well into the afternoon if it's buttoned up in this way before the temperature starts to climb. Ann and I have a portable fan that fits snugly inside the opening of our bedroom window. We turn it on low when we go to bed, and it cools the room so thoroughly that by early morning I usually find myself groping for a blanket. The only rooms with air-conditioning are Ann's and my offices, which are directly under the roof and become unpleasantly oven-like in very hot weather. We both keep our air-conditioner use to a minimum, though, by closing the shades in our offices when the sun is shining directly on our windows, by keeping our office doors closed when our air conditioners are running, and by shutting down our computers when we knock off for the day.

People whose houses have robust central air-conditioning systems seldom think about employing these and other strategies, but they would reduce their energy use and live in greater comfort if they did, just as they would reduce their energy use during the winter if they accustomed themselves to putting on a sweater rather than adjusting the thermostat when they felt cool. In coming years, as the cost of heating and cooling our homes rises dramatically, all of us are going to have to rediscover creative ways of managing our comfort zones. During the winters, we will need to re-learn our grandparents' strategies for shepherding heat inside their homes. And during the summers, perhaps, we will rediscover the screened porch.

THE FIRST HOUSE my parents owned was a one-and-a-half-story, three-bedroom Dutch colonial on a suburban street lined with other small houses. Poking through our roof were three little dormers: the one on the right as you looked up from Huntington Road belonged to my room, and the one in the middle belonged to my closet. I remember that room fairly well, despite never having seen a photograph of it—photographs being the main source of memories of early childhood. Part of the ceiling sloped. My bed was in the back corner, on the left as you went in. Near the bed was a radiator under which the Christmas Mouse, an invention of my mother's, left me a gumdrop on a Candy Land game card on Christmas Eve. There was a white bookcase against the front wall, and I kept my toys and books in that. When I was two or three, I had a nightmare in which I had to squeeze into the inch-wide space between the back of the bookcase and the wall, to get away from a pirate.

Other rooms in that house seem less vivid to me, although I remember details: the wallpaper in my sister's room, Wedgwood blue with small white figures, maybe fleurs-de-lis; my mother's little built-in dressing table and its chintz-covered stool, under the third dormer window, which I used as a cowboy hideout; the hand-cranked ice crusher screwed to the jamb of the door between the kitchen and the little breakfast room, used mainly when my sister or I had a sore throat; the detached one-car garage, on the roof of which my father once caught two local juvenile delinquents using a Coke bottle filled with gasoline to burn our hula hoops.

Some of my clearest memories are of our screened porch. We ate dinner out there almost any evening when the weather was room temperature or higher. In the era before central air-conditioning, your porch was where you made your final stand against the thermometer. It was not quite inside, not quite outside—a transitional zone between the furnace of your bedroom and the convection oven of outdoors. Occasional breezes and the sounds of the neighborhood came through the screens, but you nevertheless felt enclosed, and after dark the light from the old wrought-iron floor lamp somehow didn't leak away into the blackness. I remember playing on our porch at night before going to bed, in the almost liquid heat of a Kansas City summer, while cicadas made a sound that still seems to me like the aural dimension of being hot. The turning ceiling fan cooled nothing; it was a visual placebo. Moths the size of humming-birds thudded against the screens.

Both my parents had grown up in houses with screened porches—and I knew both those porches, since I inhabited them when I visited my grandmothers, both of whom had the same zip code we did. My mother's mother's porch was dark and cool, as she was; the woodwork was painted brown, and the view through the screens was filtered through dense shrubbery. She had a big wicker chair and a card table on which she kept her reading glasses and whatever she was reading, along with a few pencils of a type I never saw anywhere else and associated only with her: ones with erasers that were rectangular and narrow rather than cylindrical. My father's mother's porch was light and open and welcoming, as she was, and you could step down from its back door into her little rose garden. Canvas awnings blocked the worst of the sun. There was a woven rug on the concrete floor, and I remember how it embossed my knees as I knelt over various games. At some point, my sister and I discovered that if you pressed your cheek against the screen for a minute or so, the screen would make a grid pattern in your skin which was more regular, though less durable, than the pattern made by the rug.

Wire screening of the type used in screened porches and window screens is one of the great technological triumphs of the past century and a third, although hardly anybody thinks of it that way now. Before the first window screens appeared, in the late eighteen hundreds, opening a window to cool a stifling house turned the house into a seething insectarium. Horse-manure-covered streets, open sewers, and uncovered garbage dumps were breeder reactors for flies, and in high summer a kitchen ceiling could become so thickly covered as to appear almost black. Mosquitoes whined in everyone's ears, always. Dried plants called "strewing herbs"—rosemary, lemon balm, lemon verbena—were sometimes spread on wood floors in the hope that the fragrance they released when trodden upon would be obnoxious to insects. The most important kitchen appliance, after the stove, was the pie safe, a cabinet with door- and side-panels made of pierced tin, which admitted air but not flies. (The holes were punched from the inside out, creating sharp edges that further frustrated infiltration.)

The insect problem stimulated human ingenuity. A major innovation, around 1880, was fly paper: sheets coated with a sticky, oleaginous substance that lured flies, then permanently trapped them. Because the ingredients were finicky and perishable, fly paper was handmade to order, a few sheets at a time, usually by pharmacists. In 1887, four brothers named Thum, in Grand Rapids, Michigan, patented a durable version that could be manufactured in bulk and shipped to other places. They called their product Tanglefoot, after its intended effect on its victims. An early advertisement depicts a smiling patriarch sitting at a formally laid dining table, with a fly-encrusted sheet of Tanglefoot lying on the tablecloth, next to his plate. The popularity of this product made *Tanglefoot,* for a time, as widely recognized a trademark as *Kleenex* and *Xerox* would later become.

The Tanglefoot Company still exists and is still engaged in what it refers to today as "adhesive pest management." (Among the company's current products: sticky insect traps, tree banding strips, and bird repellent.) Classic fly paper is mostly a thing of the past, however. It, along with the Tanglefoot name, was made largely obsolete by the rise of the automobile, which removed horses and therefore horse manure from American streets; by the widespread use of chemical pesticides, especially DDT, which was introduced in the nineteen-forties; and by window screens.

Wire screening, which is a loose-weave fabric in which the threads are metal wire, was probably invented in the mid-seventeen hundreds, for use in papermaking. (So-called laid papers are made by pressing a broth of pulverized plant fibers against a sieve-like mesh screen, to drive out excess water.) In 1818, Benjamin Gilbert, a Connecticut tanner, began making sieves out of woven horsehair. He and a partner, Sturges Bennett, later acquired a mill on the Norwalk River and eventually wove wire cloth in the same manner. By the late 1800s they were using their wire cloth in a variety of products, including window screens.* The Roebling family, builders of the Brooklyn Bridge, began manufacturing wire fabric around 1870. In 1873, Chester Wickwire, who owned a grocery-and-hardware store in Cortland, New York, received two dozen dog muzzles, three dozen egg beaters, two rat traps, and a carpet loom from a customer who owed him money. He added the muzzles, egg beaters, and rat traps to his inventory, and installed the loom on the second floor of the store, where he used it to weave wire fabric. He sold it by the yard, in various gauges, and also turned it into meal sieves, coal sieves, popcorn poppers, and window screens.

The woven wire fabric used in window screens was once known generically as insect wire cloth. The standard mesh today is eighteen wires to the inch in one direction by fourteen in the other; the mesh of Wickwire's first screens was twelve by twelve. All his first window screens were painted either green or black, to inhibit rust; later, he figured out how to weave screens from bronze wire. He also manufactured landscape wire cloth, which had scenes painted on it. This material, according to a local history written by a Cortland resident, "was generally used in store fronts a few feet back from the glass to keep the public from looking in." Woven-wire products made Wickwire rich. In 1890, he built a thirty-room limestone mansion in Cortland and hired Tiffany & Company to decorate it. The house was a close replica of (and was designed by the same architect as) a mansion that Wickwire had seen and admired in New York City: the Harlem residence of James Anthony Bailey, who was the cofounder, with P. T. Barnum, of the Barnum & Bailey Circus. Both houses still exist: Wickwire's, which retains many original furnishings and decorative features, was occupied by descendants of his until 1973 and is now a museum, called the 1890 House; Bailey's is a funeral home.

---

* Gilbert & Bennett Manufacturing Company, makers of fencing and other woven wire products, went bankrupt in 1998. Two years later, the U.S. Environmental Protection Association undertook a two-million-dollar cleanup of the factory site, where until 1987 the company had dumped "waste acids, alkalis, solvents, oils, lead and zinc galvanizing waste and metal hydroxide sludge," according to the E.P.A. The cleaned-up factory site is being converted into an attractive mixed-use development.

The contribution to residential comfort made by window screens is second only to that made by central heating, and the impact of window screens on human health is comparable to that of quinine and penicillin, since screens created a comfortable hot-weather barrier between people and disease-bearing bugs. Today, we take screens for granted, as we do most of the astonishing blessings of modern life, but we would be uncomfortable, unwell, and unhappy without them.

WHEN I WAS in second grade, my family moved to a bigger house. One of the first major improvements my parents made—long before they got rid of the off-white nylon wall-to-wall carpeting in the living room, dining room, and den—was to add a screened porch. This was a major construction project, and my father superintended it. The new porch had a poured-concrete foundation, and it was several times the size of the porch at our old house. It was too sprawling to be cozy, but it was a good place to have parties and poker games and family dinners with both the grandmothers, and it was a good place to read on summer nights, especially if it was raining. My girlfriend and I used to sit on the couch in the dark and smoke cigarettes, watching the smoke disappear through the screen. The porch opened onto an elevated brick patio with heavy iron furniture on it. The patio was also a good place to sit and smoke, until the mosquitoes drove you back behind the screens.

My parents sold that house after my sister and brother and I had grown up and moved away. Almost immediately, the people who had bought it did something that unthinking people often do: they ruined the screened porch by enclosing it in glass. There are people who view the changing of the seasons as a kind of poverty, and when such people see a screened porch their first thought is often to make it work for them year-round. They add glass and heat and air-conditioning, and soon the porch is no longer a transitional zone between the kitchen and the yard, but is just another room with furniture that can't be rained on and a big-screen TV. A porch enclosed in glass isn't a porch anymore; it's a solarium, or worse.

Despite what people seem to think, a room that can be used only half the year isn't a waste; it's a sanctuary that you get to re-discover every spring. When Ann and I bought our house, I was pleased to report to my father that it had a screened porch—though a very small one, with torn screens and a sagging floor. The first meal we served on it was Easter dinner, six months after we moved in, with some friends from New York who were visiting for the weekend. That porch was so narrow that you almost had to lean against the screens to get up from the table. A little over a year later, Ann and I hired a contractor to replace our leaky roof, and almost as an afterthought I asked him to enlarge our screened porch, too, as long as he was ripping things apart.

The porch project, like most old-house construction projects, turned out to be more complicated than it had seemed initially. The old porch couldn't simply be extended—my naïve assumption at the outset—but had to be demolished entirely so that a sound new porch could be built from scratch, and the demolition exposed several unexpected problems, which then had to be dealt with, too. The existing floor boards were rotten, and the feeble joists that held them up were resting on stones. Most of the roof framing was in bad shape, too. When the carpenters pulled it down, they found mouse nests and acorn shells and galleries of carpenter ants. I saved an old chestnut timber that was twelve feet long, fourteen inches wide, and more than two inches thick, and I later gave it to a woodworker friend, who turned it into a coffee table. Everything else went into the Dumpster.

The new porch measures about fifteen feet by eighteen feet, and is screened on two and a third sides. The principal furnishings are a heavy old dining-room table that belonged to one of my grandmothers; a large cedar-lined trunk that belonged to the house's previous owner; a half-dozen canvas director's chairs, purchased on sale at the hardware store; an old rocking chair with a cane seat; a small, portable pulpit that was used for dock-side church services by a nineteenth-century itinerant minister in Maine and that Ann found in the backyard of an antiques shop; a wooden bookcase that was the second piece of office furniture I ever bought, back in New York; an old table lamp with a white glass shade and an old floor lamp with a burlap-covered shade; a white enamel-top table that belonged to my other grandmother; a very unglamorous but serviceable couch, which we purchased fifteen years ago from a company called This End Up; and our very first coffee table, which we bought from the Bombay Company in 1979 and which is now held together by angle brackets, glue, and drywall screws. Ann uses the enamel table as an annex to the refrigerator and freezer when she's preparing big meals during cold weather; occasionally, we forget that we've left a six-pack of beer out there, too, and the bottles freeze and explode. I used to bring the couch cushions indoors for the winter, but for the past ten years or so I haven't bothered and they seem to be all right, although the sun has faded their nubby red fabric. During the summer, we place a dog bed in the sunniest corner, and our two dachshunds spend hours out there, watching the cats on the other side of the screens and developing their own ideas about solar heat gain. Sometimes, they are so contented they don't bother to get up to bark at the UPS man.

At our house, you enter the porch through a door at the far end of the kitchen, in the part that used to be the playroom. A bank of three double-hung windows looks into the porch from the kitchen; the windows are just a little bit too high and out of the way to be useful as pass-throughs, but they facilitate inter-room hollering. The porch's ceiling is made of one-by-six tongue-and-groove pine boards and is painted white, like the rest of the house. The floor is made of one-by-four tongue-and-groove fir flooring and is finished with an untinted exterior wood preservative, which I ought to renew every two or three years but don't. A screen door connects the porch with a stone patio and the yard beyond it.

The screens on the porch are made of aluminum and have a flat black coating. The black coating makes them virtually invisible in almost any light—an important quality, since the first role of a screen is to disappear. When the porch was under construction, a friend strongly recommended that we use bronze screens. Bronze is the most durable screening material, but its bright, reflective surface makes it too conspicuous for my taste. (It's also very expensive.) I could have chosen plastic or vinyl-coated-fiberglass screens, but I don't like the way they feel when you brush against them, and I don't like the way they stretch when you accidentally hit them with a golf ball or the back of your chair.

The screened porch at the cabin has roughly the same floor area as the screened porch at our house but is longer and narrower—about eleven feet by twenty-four. It connects to the kitchen through a single double-hung window, which we use as a pass-through, and it serves as the cabin's fair-weather dining room. Like the porch at the house, it has a wooden ceiling and a fir floor, although its ceiling is finished with an exterior wood preservative rather than painted. In both porches, the bottom rail of each screen panel is raised about three-quarters of an inch above the surface of the floor—an innovation of mine. This gap, which is not screened, allows air to circulate under the bottom rail and around the posts, and it prevents water and dirt from creating a rot-prone seam along the outer edge of the floor. Rudy was skeptical when I told him I wanted him to leave a gap, feeling that it would defeat the purpose of the screens, but I assured him that the same feature had always worked well at our house and that few insects ever seemed to find it. I also told him that the gap would be especially useful after heavy rains, since it would provide an escape path for any rainwater that had been blown in through the screens. Reese designed the floor of the cabin's porch so that it slopes away from the building in two directions— another useful feature. At our house, I use a squeegee on a broomstick to push puddles out onto the patio.

There are three doors in the porch at the cabin: one opens into the living room, one opens onto a set of steps leading down to the ground, and one opens onto another porch. This second porch is really more of a balcony. It's about seven feet deep and twenty feet wide, and it runs along the front of the living room, on the side facing the big hill across the river. It isn't screened, and its floor is made not of tongue-and-groove fir flooring but of five-quarter-by-six cedar boards, which are spaced about an eighth of an inch apart so that rain will drain through them. (The ground beneath them is covered with pea gravel.) It also has a ceiling—the underside of the bedroom above. This porch's only semipermanent furnishing is a hammock chair, called an Air

Chair, which hangs from a hook in the ceiling. The Air Chair is extraordinarily comfortable. It has a sling-like extension for your feet and another for your beer. On several happy occasions, I have fallen asleep in it—once, during a summer thunderstorm when I was staying at the cabin by myself.

The drop to the ground from the front of the open porch is about ten feet, so the porch has a railing. Reese drew a very simple one in the plans, as a sort of placeholder, but I wanted something more distinctive, if I could find it. Rudy had a few ideas, and we discussed them occasionally. The simplest option would have been to knock together a standard railing from ready-made parts, which are available from any decent lumberyard. Such railings are easy to build, but they all look the same. While I cogitated, Rudy put up a temporary railing made of two-by-fours—a handy surface on which to rest a hand or a cup of coffee while urinating over the edge on days when the wind was favorable.

I finally found what I was looking for in a book called *Cabin Fever,* by Rachel Carley. (I learned from the dust jacket that Carley lives in my little town, although we've managed never to meet.) *Cabin Fever* is full of color photographs of the exteriors, interiors, and decorating details of log cabins, hunting lodges, Adirondack great camps, and other rustic getaways, of all vintages and from many parts of the country. Dreamily turning its pages in my office when I should have been working gave me many ideas for the cabin, including a few that, thank goodness, were not too expensive to be carried out. I was struck in particular by some photographs, in the back of the book, of rustic furniture and outdoor structures. Especially appealing was a fence that had been made from unpeeled cedar branches instead of orderly ranks of stiles, rails, and pickets. Many of the branches seemed to have been arranged almost at random—like strands in the web of a drunken spider, or cracks in a shattered glass plate.

The fence I admired was the work of a company called Romancing the Woods, whose headquarters, I noticed, were in Woodstock, New York, not all that far from where I live. I didn't need an entire fence, but I did need a twenty-foot-long railing, and it occurred to me that something like the fence in the book might be perfect—a style in harmony with the design of the cabin, and a simple but eye-catching structure in a spot to which the eye of anyone sitting in the living room would naturally be drawn. I made contact by e-mail, then sent measurements and photographs. The construction crew—two carpenters and two helpers—arrived on one of the coldest days of the year, with the temperature near zero and the wind chill at least twenty degrees below. "We cut the pieces in the woods yesterday," one of the men told me. The wood was eastern red cedar, and there was snow clinging to some of it.

The railing that those men built that day is divided into three sections, each a bit less than seven feet long. There are four posts: one attached to the side of the cabin, one attached to the side of the porch, and two that descend through the floor and are bolted to the two-by-twelve pressure-treated joists below. The top, bottom, and diagonal rails are made of straight cedar branches about four inches in diameter; the interior pieces, which are arranged in the same chaotic manner I had admired in *Cabin Fever*, are an inch or two in diameter. (In compliance with the building code, none of the gaps between branches exceeds four inches in width.) The finished railing looks both striking and just right, and it may be the feature of the cabin that pleases me the most.

ROMANCING THE WOODS, the outfit that built my railing, was founded in the early nineties by a retired New York City advertising executive named Marvin Davis. In 1989, Davis and his wife built a weekend house in Woodstock, on a mountainside near the eastern edge of Catskill State Park. "The house has a hundred-mile view," Davis told me recently. "And just below the house there's a kind of a rocky ledge, with a twenty- or thirty-foot drop. It's a wonderful place to sit, but it's exposed, and any chairs that I put on it would blow off. After a while I decided that the answer would be to build some kind of a small structure on the outcropping—a gazebo."

Davis knew what he wanted. He had seen numerous examples at Mohonk Mountain House, a quirky 135-year-old resort

Cabin, rear porch, rustic cedar railing.

not far from where he lived. Mohonk is hard to describe to someone who's never seen it. (Ann and I have stayed there twice: once
with friends shortly after we were married, and again to celebrate
our twentieth anniversary.) The hotel is a "sprawling Victorian
castle," in the words of its owners, and it stands at the edge of a
crater-like mile-long lake near the top of a mountain. (*Mohonk* is
an Indian word meaning "lake in the sky.") The whole formation
looks as though it almost has to be volcanic in origin, but it isn't.
The hotel has a rocking-chair-filled porch that overhangs the
water, and inside there are half a dozen parlors, with high ceilings, dark nineteenth-century woodwork, and the kind of furniture in which you half-expect to find William Howard Taft taking
a nap. Many of the guest rooms have a working fireplace; none
has a TV.

Mohonk sits near the center of a thirty-thousand-acre natural
area. There are eighty-five miles of hiking trails, and some of
those trails run along the edge of the lake, with cliffs falling away
below. Precarious points near the trail are protected by rustic railings made of unpeeled cedar, and there are numerous benches,
lookouts, and shelters made of the same rough materials. It was
this style of construction that Davis had in mind for the gazebo at
his house in Woodstock.

"I talked to a carpenter who had done some interior work for
my wife and me," he told me. "He said he had never built anything like what I described, but he said he would jump at the
chance. So I took him over to Mohonk, and we walked around,
and I said, This is what I want. I made a drawing, and we worked
out a price, and he promised not to tell my wife what it was, because she would have had a fit. My wife's father lives in this area,
and there is a grove of cedar trees on his property, and I had access to those trees and we were able to take what we needed."
The carpenter built the gazebo with help from an associate. It's
five-sided, and it has built-in benches on four of the sides and a
small built-in table in the center. The roof, which looks a little
like a pentagonal straw hat, is made of split cedar logs in varying
sizes. (You can see a picture of this first gazebo, which is called
the Overlook, at Davis's Web site, romancingthewoods.com.)

The rustic style that Davis copied for his gazebo is a nineteenth-century American invention. The builders of the Adirondack great camps of the eighteen hundreds would occupy themselves during the long winters by embellishing the simple buildings with imaginative porches, railings, and other features made of unfinished tree branches from the surrounding woods. "There are hundreds of people today who still make furniture in this style," Davis told me, "but I didn't know of anyone who was building exterior structures. Well, one thing led to another. In 1991, I suggested to the carpenter that we form a small business. I said, If we get any customers, you'll do the building and I'll put up the money, and we'll see if we can't turn this craft into something of value."

A lunchtime conversation with a New York *Times* editor in 1991 led to a brief mention in the newspaper, and many commissions followed. "The technique—the thing that sets us apart— also keeps us unprofitable," Davis told me. "We have to go into the woods at least twice a week, and we have to pay for every tree we cut, and then we have to bring them back to the shop and clean them up and prepare them and cut them in the shapes that are required for the particular job." Davis has a varied clientele. At the time I spoke with him, his crew was building a hundred and fifty feet of fencing, two gates, and five arches for an architect in Lawrence, Kansas, and after completing that, they were going to begin six benches and a twelve-foot shelter for Animal Kingdom, at Disney World. And the year before, they had done a major project at Frank Lloyd Wright's Fallingwater, in Pennsylvania.

A couple of years after my Romancing the Woods porch railing was installed, I noticed a few small piles of sawdust-like powder on the porch floorboards directly beneath the bottom rail. I recognized this powder as the frass, or excrement, of a wood-destroying insect of some kind. The most widely known such insects are powder-post beetles, a category that includes a large number of species. Adult beetles of this type lay their eggs on trees, chairs, floorboards, logs, rafters, or other wooden items. When the eggs hatch, the larvae eat their way into the wood, creating meandering tunnels that increase in diameter as the larvae grow. When the larvae reach adulthood, they eat their way back

to the surface, creating a tiny round exit hole and ejecting a
shower of frass. Then they begin the cycle again by laying eggs of
their own.

If wood-boring beetles are left undisturbed, they can eventually do great damage. A friend showed me a photograph he had
taken in Costa Rica of a restaurant building that the owner had
attempted to protect from termites by tightly wrapping its beams
in Saran Wrap. Rather than trying that (or anything else), I ignored my problem for a full year, hoping that if I did nothing it
would go away all by itself, the way a cold does. But it didn't go
away, and every time I swept away the little piles of frass more little piles of frass appeared. On a couple of occasions, I even found
dead beetles, which looked like caraway seeds. Finally, I e-mailed
Marvin Davis and asked him what I should do. He recommended
treating the railing with Bora-Care.

Borate-based wood treatments, of which Bora-Care is a widely
used one, sound much too good to be true. They are easy to
apply, and can usually just be swabbed on with a brush. They fully
penetrate bare wood. They kill existing infestations of termites,
carpenter ants, powder-post beetles, cockroaches, and wood-
destroying fungi, and they prevent new infestations for decades,
without retreatment. They leave no toxic residue on the surface
and don't cause permanent discoloration. They make wood
somewhat fire resistant. (Borate solutions are used to fight forest
fires.) They don't damage or weaken phenolic resins and can
therefore be used on plywood and other engineered-wood products. They don't smell bad, and they don't give off toxic fumes.
They are not known to cause cancer or contaminate ground
water. They are approved by the Environmental Protection
Agency for sale to ordinary people, and they can be used indoors
and around pets and children. They kill fleas.

I ordered a gallon of Bora-Care online, and it was delivered a
few days later by UPS. As sold, Bora-Care is a clear liquid that is
similar in appearance to, but somewhat more viscous than, corn
syrup. Before using it, you dilute it with water, in proportions
specified in the accompanying instructions. I mixed my batch in
a bucket in the kitchen sink—after first putting on rubber
gloves—and spread newspapers on the porch floor under the

railing, to catch drips. Then I worked my way from one end of the railing to the other, coating each piece of cedar as thoroughly and carefully as if I were basting it with melted butter. Occasionally, I would put down my brush and, using a medical syringe, directly inject Bora-Care into some of the larger exit holes—an entirely unnecessary step and (as far as I know) not recommended by anyone, but the most appealing part of the entire operation, to me. As soon as I had finished, I basted the entire railing again—another unnecessary step, I'm pretty certain.

The active ingredient in Bora-Care is an inorganic borate salt called disodium octaborate tetrahydrate—also known as DOT— which is synthesized from borax and boric acid. When applied in solution, it penetrates bare wood to a depth of several inches, killing bad stuff that it encounters along the way and then remaining in the wood to discourage (and, if necessary, annihilate) any successors. DOT eradicates wood-destroying insects by killing the cellulose-digesting protozoa and bacteria that live in their guts and by disrupting various enzymatic processes, and it has a similarly devastating effect on fungi. Repeated studies by the U.S. Forest Service and others over the past decade (and in Australia and New Zealand for decades before that) have shown it to be extraordinarily effective: termites won't even cross the surface of borate-treated wood to attack untreated wood beyond it, and you can kill the termites in an infested piece of wood simply by placing a treated piece close to it.

The only significant weakness of borate wood treatments is their solubility in water. This means that they are ineffective in marine applications and in wood structures that remain in prolonged contact with water or wet soil, and that they are most effective in wood that isn't regularly exposed to the elements. In most exterior uses, though, this weakness can be overcome by sealing treated wood with a preservative shortly after treatment. That's what I did to my porch railing—after first making certain that the beetle problem truly was gone, and after basting the whole railing one more time, just to be sure.

7

WALLS, CEILINGS, AND FLOORS

DURING THE WEEKS when Rudy, Joe, and Mark were closing in the cabin, the weather was unusually cold, with many days when the temperature scarcely rose above zero. The men came to work in heavy coveralls and did what they could to stay out of the wind. They felt relieved when they had installed the last of the windows and could turn their main attention to the interior.

The plumber and the electrician roughed in all the pipes and vents and cables, and then Rudy subcontracted the job of insulating the cabin to a local specialist. Windy sub-zero weather is actually the perfect time to install insulation, because you can easily detect air leaks both before and after the batts go in, by running a hand along interior seams and edges, checking for drafts. I didn't think of doing this until long afterward, when it was too late for me to try it, but I wish I had, because even small breaches can make a significant difference in the heating efficiency of an enclosed structure. Gaps in the framed envelope, if you find them, can be eliminated by caulking them from the inside, and air leaks along the edges of installed insulation can be plugged with insulation scraps—although you have to be careful. During an early remodeling project at our house, I used a putty knife to work fiberglass insulation into the narrow gaps between some new windows and the rough openings inside which they had been installed. Insulating such spaces is a good idea—I was mentally congratulating myself as I worked—but I crammed in so much fiberglass that the window frames bowed inward, impeding the free movement of the sashes. Fortunately, a contractor showed me the problem, and I was able to remove the excess before the window casings were installed.

At the cabin, the walls and ceilings in the bedrooms, kitchen, bathrooms, and basement were all going to be covered with gypsum wallboard. The walls and ceilings in the main room, dining alcove, mudroom, stairwell, and upstairs hall were going to be finished with pine planks, but before the wood could go up those walls and ceilings had to be covered with wallboard, too. This doubling up was done to satisfy the building code (wallboard is far more fire-resistant than wood is) and to reduce the transmission of sound between rooms.

Gypsum wallboard—which is often referred to generically by its best-known trade name, Sheetrock—is the most visible indoor building material in the United States. It consists of a plaster-like gypsum core sandwiched between layers of heavy paper. The most commonly used wallboard panels are a half-inch thick, four feet wide, and either eight or twelve feet long, although other sizes and thicknesses are available. For rooms with nine-foot ceilings, you can order panels that are fifty-four inches wide and nine feet long, enabling you to fill the entire space between floor and ceiling with either a single panel installed vertically or two panels installed horizontally, one over the other. Using the larger panels on taller walls reduces the number of seams—a good thing.

Wallboard panels are attached directly to wall studs and ceiling joists, ideally using screws that were manufactured for that purpose. The joints between the panels are then covered with paper tape embedded in multiple coats of a spackle-like gypsum-based material called joint compound—"mud," to the trade—which is also used to conceal the heads of the screws. If your house is like everyone else's house, it contains a lot of gypsum wallboard. You can probably reach out and touch some from where you are sitting right now.

People often make fun of gypsum wallboard because it seems so crummy and cheap in comparison with old-fashioned plaster surfaces, such as the ceiling of the Sistine Chapel, but without wallboard modern domestic life would be even more expensive and inconvenient than it is already. Wallboard can be, and often is, installed poorly—you can probably reach out and touch a wallboard defect from where you are sitting right now, too—but its value and versatility as a building material greatly exceed its minimal cost, and the most common problems associated with it can be prevented if the people who install and finish it are careful. And for those who are willing to pay, highly satisfactory upgrades are available.

Hanging and finishing gypsum wallboard are jobs that patient, ambitious do-it-yourselfers can usually handle. I've done a fair amount of Sheetrock work in our house over the years and, through trial and error, I have achieved what I consider an acceptable level of handyman-caliber competence. Professionals almost always do better work, however, and even if they don't they are so much faster that it usually makes sense to use them for all but the smallest jobs. It also makes sense to use wallboard specialists rather than general contractors, I think, for the same reason that it makes sense to use an experienced cardiac surgeon rather than your regular internist for operations on your heart. Guys who hang Sheetrock for a living can knock off an entire room almost before you or I could finish lining up our tools, and skilled professional tapers don't step into open buckets of joint compound, as I once did while patching some big cracks in my daughter's bedroom. Even the pros need guidance and supervision, however. Here are the main things to look out for:

Fastener problems: In the old days, gypsum wallboard was always installed with nails, and there are stubborn old-timers who insist on using them still. But nails are immensely inferior to screws. The main failing of nails is that they lose their grip as the wood they're attached to shrinks. Eventually, this can cause their heads to protrude above the surface of the wall, creating highly conspicuous defects known as nail pops. I once saw a room in which virtually every nail had popped. The pattern looked almost like an intentional decorative effect, except that it wasn't decorative at all. Nail pops can show through wallpaper, and they can even penetrate the human subconscious: I once had a dream in which pressing my thumb against a popped nail caused a fist-size section of a wall to crumble.

Wallboard nails are still manufactured, for use by the few stubborn holdouts, and the modern versions are superior to the types widely used in the past. (The best wallboard nails are relatively short and have annular rings on their shafts, two features that help them stay put.) But even the best nails work less well than wallboard screws, which hold panels tight against the framing as it shrinks and, if used properly, are far less likely to wander into view.

Wallboard screws are installed with a specialized tool, called a wallboard screw gun, which is a variable-speed electric drill equipped with a magnetic screw bit, an adjustable depth guide, and a clutch that engages the bit when the tip of the screw is pressed against the panel and releases it once the screw has been driven to the proper depth. A skilled professional can "screw off" an entire panel in a minute or two. (Sheetrock installers work fast because they are paid by the panel.) A properly installed wallboard screw is driven about a sixteenth of an inch below the surface of the panel, causing the face paper to twist tightly beneath the screw's bugle-shaped head. This creates a depression that is known in the trade as a dimple, which is later filled with joint compound. Screw dimples are much smaller and therefore easier to conceal than nail dimples, which are made by giving the nail an extra hammer whack. Amateurs tend to drive wallboard screws too deep, tearing the paper and thereby eliminating virtually all of the screw's holding power. (The tensile strength of a wallboard panel is in the paper; score the paper with a utility knife and you can easily break a panel with your hands.)

Some professionals who swear by screws also use a few nails on virtually every panel anyway, to hold it in place as they are getting started. This is a very bad idea, since most of these nails will eventually pop. Rudy subcontracted the cabin's Sheetrock work to a very good local crew, and before they began I asked them not to use even one nail. They laughed as dismissively as they would have if I had insisted that they wear safety goggles and earplugs; then, under continued harassment from me, they promised to use only screws. They used some nails anyway, though, as soon as I had left. I know they did because I later found nail pops on several walls. The number is fairly small—but it could have been zero if those cocky workmen had complied with my request. Come to think of it, it's possible that they used nails only because I had challenged their authority by asking them not to. Whatever the reason, the cabin has a few popped nails.

It is possible to get rid of existing nail pops, if you are one of the millions of homeowners afflicted by them. (If you didn't realize until now that you were afflicted, I apologize for bringing this up.) The best treatment is to press the wallboard panel firmly against the framing with your shoulder, drive a wallboard screw to the proper depth within an inch or so of the popped nail, hammer the nail back below the surface of the panel, fill the resulting dimples with joint compound, and repaint the room. A far simpler alternative is to hide the worst nail pops behind pictures or furniture, move the light fixtures that make them visible, or decide they don't bother you. I have decided to believe that the small number of nail pops in the cabin—they are in the bedrooms and the basement—don't bother me.

Cracked joints: The joints between wallboard panels are covered with joint compound and two-inch-wide paper tape, and the process of applying this treatment is known as taping. A wallboard taper, using a tool that looks like an extra-wide putty knife, spreads a thin, uniform layer of compound over the joint, then uses the same tool to embed the paper tape within it. Once this has dried thoroughly, the taper uses wider knives to apply two or more additional thin layers of compound, eventually creating a smooth surface beneath which the tape is concealed entirely. People often assume that the strength in a finished wallboard joint comes from the compound, which seems sort of like cement, but it actually comes from the paper tape, which acts like a bridge between panels and is much stronger than compound alone; if you left out the tape, seasonal wood movement and ordinary household stresses would cause most wallboard joints to crack fairly quickly. Amateurs (and a few misguided professionals) sometimes use plastic-mesh tape, rather than paper tape, with ordinary joint compound, but they shouldn't. Mesh tape looks high-tech and therefore appeals powerfully to the inborn male fascination with reinforcement (see Chapter 5), but it adds virtually no strength to ordinary joint compound and is meant to be used only with plaster and with so-called setting joint compounds, which—like concrete but unlike spackle or ordinary joint compound—harden by undergoing a chemical transformation rather than by merely drying.*

Wallboard joints can also fail for reasons that have little or nothing to do with taping. Wall areas near the corners of doors and windows are especially vulnerable, because any large penetration in a wall is a source of weakness, and doors and windows exert powerful stresses on surrounding surfaces as they are repeatedly opened and closed. There is a door in our house above which thin vertical cracks have formed between the top corners of the door casing and the ceiling. Those cracks exist because the person who hung the wallboard on that wall (not me!) cut a small piece of wallboard to fit the rectangular space directly above the door opening and, by doing so, created a crack-prone joint on each side of the opening, exactly where the stresses are the greatest. The installer could have prevented this problem by spanning the entire top half of the door opening with a single sheet of wallboard—after making a cutout for the opening, of course. Experienced wallboard installers don't put joints where stresses are great.

Visible seams: The long sides of wallboard panels have gently tapered edges, which form a shallow trough when two panels are placed together. Concealing paper tape and joint compound inside such a trough is relatively easy. The butt ends of wall-

---

* USG Corporation, the world's leading manufacturer of wallboard systems, recommends paper tape for most applications. The most recent edition of USG's very informative *Gypsum Construction Handbook* says, "Repeated joint strength tests conducted at the USG Research Center have shown that joints taped and finished with conventional fiberglass leno-weave mesh tape and conventional joint compounds are more prone to cracking than joints finished with paper tape and conventional joint compounds. This is because fiberglass mesh tapes tend to stretch under load, even after being covered with joint compounds. Permanent repair of these cracks is difficult." There's no reason not to believe USG on this subject, since the company manufactures both kinds of tape, and fiberglass tape is more expensive—and therefore more profitable.

board panels, however, are not tapered, and, as a result, they are nearly impossible to hide completely, even if the person doing the taping is extremely skillful. (The eye can detect a ridge or bulge just a fraction of a millimeter high, especially if light is raking across it or striking it at an angle.) The best way to avoid visible butt joints is to keep butt joints to an absolute minimum, by using long panels and taking advantage of architectural features, such as moldings and trim pieces, that make it possible to break up long runs of empty wall. Lumber yards often don't stock twelve-foot panels, which weigh more than eighty pounds each and are tricky to maneuver, and they are even less likely to stock fourteen-foot panels. But using long panels on long expanses is worth the trouble, if you can find them, and sweating a little during installation is easier than living with wall defects for years afterward.

All joints can suffer an unsightly problem known as joint ridging. This occurs when humidity-related expansion or contraction of the framing lumber creates stresses that cause wallboard panels to deform along their seams, creating a small but bothersome ridge. Ridging can often be prevented with careful installation; once it has occurred, it can sometimes be concealed with light sanding followed by an additional application of joint compound. As with mild nail-pop problems (and most of life's other minor disappointments), the simplest and, in the long run, the most satisfying remedy is not to care very much.

Visible joint compound: The final step in wallboard installation is sanding, which eliminates trowel marks in the dried joint compound and makes the finished wall surface smooth. Even after careful sanding, though, taped joints and filled dimples don't always disappear completely. Joint compound and wallboard facing paper have very different textures, especially if the sanding has roughened parts of the paper, as often happens. These texture differences may not be noticeable until after painting, and even then they are usually obvious only in certain kinds of light, but once you've spotted them they can drive you crazy—assuming that you're susceptible to that sort of thing. I've seen walls (in other people's houses) on which I could easily pick out every

joint and dimple. These blemishes showed through the paint as
clearly as if they had been painted a different shade.

A good way to eliminate texture differences is to apply a very
thin coat of joint compound to the entire wallboard surface, filling in all the empty spaces between taped joints and filled dimples. This technique is called skim-coating, and it's not as hard or
as time-consuming as it probably sounds. You can ask the taper or
your painter to do it, or you can try it yourself. Skim-coating is a
good way to deal with certain other cosmetic problems, too.
Many of the ceilings in our house had ugly sand finishes when we
moved in—the result of the previous owner's misguided desire to
make them look extra old. Over a period of five or six years, I
eliminated all the sand-finished ceilings, one by one, by skim-
ming joint compound over them. Sanding all that joint compound was a nightmare—gypsum dust is one of the most
exasperating materials in the world to clean up, because it gets
into everything and turns to paste if you attack it with water—but
the ceilings are greatly improved.

Getting rid of ugly "popcorn"-textured ceiling finishes requires more ingenuity. Popcorn finishes were introduced in the
fifties as a low-cost alternative to careful taping and painting,
and they are still practically universal in new construction in
some parts of the country. The best removal technique is probably to wet the material, then scrape it with a taping knife. After
the popcorn is gone, you have to deal with all the issues that the
contractor was avoiding by using it in the first place: poorly
taped joints, popped fasteners, and bulging seams, along with
the nicks and scrapes that you yourself made with your taping
knife. It's a good job to leave to a professional, who won't like it,
either.

The visibility of superficial wallboard defects can be reduced
by applying paint as generously as its manufacturer wants you to.
Amateur painters tend to push too hard on a paint roller and not
to reload it with paint until after the last drop has been squeezed
out. Painting in this way may save a little money on paint but it creates a "starved" finish, which readily reveals texture differences underneath. Rolling on paint with less wrist pressure creates a more

robust and consistent surface texture, and helps to hide minor flaws. Using expensive, high-quality paint can help, too.

USG, the manufacturer of Sheetrock and the world's largest producer of wallboard and wallboard supplies, recently introduced a product called Tuff-Hide, which is meant to serve as both a skim coat and a primer for wallboard surfaces. Tuff-Hide is essentially a thick, high-solids latex paint. It is applied (after taping and sanding) with an airless sprayer, and it dries to a smooth finish that USG says is equal to that achieved by skim-coating.

Wallboard defects of any kind tend to be especially bothersome on large, uninterrupted surfaces that span more than one story—such as the tall walls in stairwells and entrance halls, and the oversized walls in rooms with very high ceilings. Part of the problem has to do with the way such walls are usually framed, and part has to do with the difficulty of hiding problems on huge, blank expanses. There is a thirty-year-old condominium complex in my town in which most of the units have two-story living rooms. Each of those living rooms has one double-height wall that could serve as an encyclopedia of wallboard problems. There are popped nails, visible butt joints, protruding tape ridges along lateral seams, visible patches of joint compound showing through the paint, and other unsightly defects. All these problems are made more noticeable by light that rakes across the walls from ceiling fixtures placed directly above them, and by sunlight that rakes across them from the extra-large windows in the end walls. Better placement of the ceiling fixtures and the use of design features (built-in-shelves, trim pieces, paneling) to break up all those acres of Sheetrock would have made the problems much less severe. Even better, in my opinion, would have been to skip the miles-high ceiling. Why do people like interior volume they have to heat but can't store stuff in?

A RELIABLE WAY to avoid most common wallboard problems is to upgrade to veneer plaster—which can be thought of either as the modern, high-tech incarnation of old-fashioned plaster or as the fancy, expensive version of ordinary wallboard. A veneer-plaster system consists of one or two thin coats of real plaster applied to gypsum panels that are indistinguishable from ordinary gypsum wallboard except that their face paper is formulated differently. (Veneer-plaster panels are sometimes called blue board, after the bluish tint of the paper.) When veneer plaster is installed by skilled professionals, it yields a hard, smooth, durable finish that is free of common wallboard blemishes.

In the old days, plaster (often mixed with horsehair) was spread on narrow wood strips, called lath, which were nailed horizontally across the studs, with small gaps in between.* As the wet plaster was smoothed on, it would ooze through the gaps, droop over the back of the lath strips, and harden, keeping everything in place. Ann's and my house still contains a couple of original, late-eighteenth-century plaster walls, in which the lath strips were split by hand, and a number of mid-nineteenth-century replacement plaster walls, in which the lath strips were sawn. During the mid-twentieth century, plasterers switched from wood lath to metal lath, which is made by cutting small, evenly spaced slits in sheet metal and then pulling the sheet metal apart to form a sturdy mesh. The holes in such mesh perform the same function that the gaps between wooden lath strips do. Today, most conventional-plaster systems use gypsum lath—paper-faced panels that are similar in appearance to Sheetrock but are only a third as wide—although expanded metal lath is sometimes still used in industrial applications and on walls with complex decorative details or curves.

Veneer plaster falls somewhere between gypsum-lath plaster and ordinary Sheetrock in complexity of installation. It was invented in the nineteen-seventies and has been refined and improved since then. I first saw it a dozen years ago in the house of a friend, who had just completed a major kitchen renovation. During cocktails, I carefully studied the friend's new walls from

---

* In the even older days, plaster was sometimes applied directly to the interior side of the exterior sheathing boards, which the plasterer would first score with an ax, to give the plaster something to grip—an exceedingly primitive technique that I once saw in a very old house on Martha's Vineyard.

every possible angle, and even surreptitiously ran my hands over them, but could detect no seams or fastener bumps or other imperfections. The walls had been left unpainted—a possibility with veneer plaster, for people who like the look—and they felt smooth and cool to the touch. (Veneer plaster can also be painted in the ordinary manner, or tinted before it is applied.)

There are two drawbacks associated with veneer plaster: it is anywhere from 20 percent to 100 percent more expensive than ordinary Sheetrock, and experienced plasterers are often difficult to find, especially in areas where plasterwork is uncommon. Proponents usually say that installing veneer plaster is less messy than installing regular wallboard, because there's no sanding and therefore no choking blizzard of joint-compound dust, but a veneer-plaster installation is usually far from mess-free. Plaster hardens quickly and therefore has to be mixed in relatively small batches, and the mixing involves hoses and buckets and dust and sloppy stirring (usually with a high-torque electric drill that has a paddle attachment). And because the volume of plaster required for a veneer-plaster job greatly exceeds the volume of joint compound required for a wallboard job of the same size, there tend to be many more drips and splatters. Proponents also often say that veneer plaster is faster than regular wallboard, because it can be painted the next day, or even the same day, but this is misleading, too. Plastering a wall takes far longer than taping it, so a large job can stretch out for days even though the plaster itself hardens very quickly. The real advantage of veneer plaster is that it yields a finished wall surface that is superior in every way to that produced by an ordinary wallboard job.

Ann and I chose veneer plaster for our big kitchen-and-bathroom renovation in our house, and ordinary Sheetrock for the cabin—and in both cases I think we made the right decision. The new veneer-plaster walls and ceilings in our house are beautifully smooth, without a nail pop or a bulging butt joint or a visible ridge anywhere; in my opinion, they are well worth the extra cost. Nevertheless, we chose Sheetrock for the cabin, and, given how we use the cabin, I'm glad we saved the money. For people torn between the two systems, a good compromise might be to use veneer plaster in public rooms with tall, uninterrupted walls and huge ceilings—the kinds of spaces where wallboard defects usually cause the most trouble—and to use ordinary wallboard and joint compound everywhere else.

The man who did the plasterwork in our house was a hyper-kinetic ex-hippie named Max, and he was fun to watch. Once he had started on a wall or ceiling, he was a flurry of nonstop motion until he had reached the other side, because plaster works best when it's applied continuously, without allowing the leading edge to harden before the next batch is applied. For the ceilings, he stood on short stilts, which he strapped to his calves. To stay out of his way, I would usually crouch in an adjacent doorway and do my best to dodge the splatters once he had worked his way down to my end of the room. Watching him was exhausting—and so was cleaning up the mess he left behind. After he had knocked off each evening, I made a careful inspection of my floor defenses in the areas where he had been working, mopping up spilled water and replacing rosin paper that had been soaked or covered with spatters.

———————

FIFTEEN YEARS AGO, I swore to myself that if I ever built a house from scratch I would be sure to ask the framers to add wood blocking between the studs in strategic locations in the bathrooms so that I would later be able to attach towel bars, toilet paper holders, and the basins of pedestal sinks to solid wood instead of to Sheetrock or plaster. Well, I completely forgot to do that when we redid the bathrooms in the house, and I almost forgot to do it when we built the cabin. And at the cabin I remembered only at the very last minute, so that Rudy was able to add blocking only for the toilet paper holders. But it's still a good idea, and if I ever build another house I'm really going to do it.

You can securely hang a framed picture anywhere on an ordinary Sheetrock or plaster wall by using an ordinary picture hook, but if you need to attach something really heavy (like the stuffed head of a wild boar) or something that people are likely to pull or push or jostle (like a towel bar), you need to anchor it more firmly. The best way to do that is to screw it to the underlying studs. But screwing things to studs can be hard to do because the wall itself prevents you from seeing where the studs are situated. Even if you had X-ray vision, you would probably still have a problem, because standard studs are just an inch and a half wide and are spaced sixteen inches apart, meaning that the chance of a stud's being exactly where you need it to be is small. And if you need two studs—well, forget it. The most recent Restoration Hardware catalog (for example) offers towel bars that are eighteen, twenty and a half, twenty-four, twenty-six, twenty-six and a half, and thirty inches long—none a multiple of sixteen.

To screw something into studs, you have to know where the studs are. If you are the kind of person who can cheerfully spend a weekend shopping for a stepladder, you probably already own or covet an electronic stud sensor. These devices locate studs through wallboard by measuring the ability of wall materials to store an electric charge—a quality known as capacitance. The capacitance of Sheetrock backed by a stud is higher than the capacitance of Sheetrock backed by nothing, and the sensor detects that difference. Some electronic sensors are quite sophisticated, and can also be used to find electric cables, rebar, vent ducts, and other invisible items of possible interest. For most homeowners, though, these devices, which can cost anywhere from twenty dollars to seventy dollars, are unnecessary extravagances. A better choice in almost all applications is the Stanley 47-400 Magnetic Stud Finder, which is the size of a Ping-Pong ball and costs less than three dollars—or about what you'd pay for the batteries for an electronic model. The 47-400 consists of a bar magnet mounted on a pivot inside a little plastic dome. You slide the dome over the wall, and the pivoting magnet jumps and sticks straight out when it passes over a Sheetrock screw or nail (or anything else magnetic). I bought an electronic stud sensor years ago and quickly decided it was more trouble than it was worth, but I use my Stanley thing all the time.

Even without a stud finder, you can usually find studs if you know what to look for. Shining a bright light across a Sheetrock wall will almost always reveal the location of at least a few fasteners; they'll be either slightly protruding or slightly sunken, or you'll see evidence of the joint compound covering them. The vertical seam between two butted Sheetrock panels is also usually conspicuous, especially under raking light, and it will almost always be directly above a stud. Baseboards are almost always nailed only into studs, and nail holes are easy to find even if they've been filled. And finding any one stud will narrow your search for the others, because you can measure sixteen-inch intervals away from it in both directions.

When you absolutely have to mount something heavy on Sheetrock alone, you need to use more than just a screw. The most common items used for this purpose are slender plastic anchors, which you insert into a hole in the wall and then drive a screw into. The screw pushes the plastic against the Sheetrock, supposedly holding it firmly in place, but these fasteners are worthless for anything much heavier than a smoke alarm. Far more effective are self-tapping plastic wall drillers, which screw into the wall and work better because their larger circumference spreads stresses over a broader area. For loads that are heavier still, you need molly bolts or toggle bolts designed for use with Sheetrock.

But the best thing—did I mention this already?—is to have the carpenter place solid-wood blocking in the places where you know you're going to need it.

―――――――

FOR THE WALLS and ceilings in the main public rooms of the cabin, I didn't want either Sheetrock or veneer plaster; I wanted wood—the same rustic look that I had shown Reese in that magazine photograph of the dude ranch in Colorado. (See Chapter 4.) I also had two other models in mind. The first was the main upstairs bedroom in Ann's great-aunt's house, which was built by an eighteenth-century New England sea captain. The captain had wanted to re-create the feel of his berth at sea, so he covered the walls and the (low) ceiling of his bedroom with wide pine boards, each of which had a simple round bead cut into each of its long sides. This room played a semi-mythical role in Ann's childhood imagination, and it made a big impression on both of us when we stayed in it one night shortly after we were married. About ten years later, when we remodeled our own bedroom, we copied the captain's room as closely as we could. I gutted and insulated the room myself, then hired two local carpenters and showed them a few seriously underexposed photographs of the sea captain's room which I had taken during a recent visit to the great-aunt. The carpenters found a supply of appropriately wide pine boards at a local mill—the finished boards range in width between ten and fifteen inches—and used an industrial-strength woodworking tool called a shaper to create the beads. They nailed these boards to the walls and ceiling using some huge, ancient-looking nails that I had ordered from Tremont Nail Company, a Massachusetts manufacturer of cut nails and other reproduction hardware. Tremont has been making nails on the same site for almost two hundred years. (The building that serves as its main nail mill was partially burned by the British during the War of 1812.) The Tremont nails I bought have big, lumpy, irregular heads, which look like the heads of the hand-forged nails in the sea captain's old room and like the heads of the hand-forged nails in a couple of very old floors in our house.

For the cabin, I wanted a more rustic look, with no beading on the edges of the boards, and I wanted the boards on the walls to be installed horizontally, rather than vertically as they are in the sea captain's room and in Ann's and my room. Rudy and I independently investigated a couple of local lumberyards, and it was Rudy who found the wood we used: some nice knotty pine boards about eleven inches wide, the kind you might use to panel the tack room of a horse barn. The boards had been dressed smooth on one side and left rough on the other, and they were shiplapped; that is, each one had a half-inch-deep, step-shaped recess, called a rabbet, running along the top of one long edge and the bottom of the other. These recesses would overlap each other when the boards were placed together.

Shiplapping is one of several methods of creating continuous joints between pieces of wood. Floorboards usually have tongue-and-groove joints, in which a protruding flange—the tongue—is cut into one edge of a board, and a corresponding groove is cut into the other, so that when two boards are nailed in place, side by side, the tongue on one board fits snugly into the groove on the other. The pine paneling in Ann's and my bedroom in our house was put together using a similar method, called groove-

and-spline, in which grooves are cut into both edges of every board, and the boards are locked together with wood strips, called splines, which are inserted into the grooves. Both methods help to join individual boards into a continuous surface; they also enable the boards to expand and contract in response to changes in humidity without creating open gaps between them.

When the lumberyard delivered the pine for the cabin, Rudy, Joe, and Mark stacked the boards on the plywood subfloor of the main room. "We'll let them dry out for a week or two before we nail them up," Rudy said. "That will make them fit together better, because the boards will have done their shrinking already."

Actually, *drying* isn't always the best term to describe what lumber does when you let it sit around. What actually happens is that its moisture content moves toward equilibrium with the relative humidity of the air around it, and if the air is wetter than the wood, the wood will actually take on moisture rather than giving it off. Because the air in the cabin was very dry—this was winter, and the furnace was running—these particular boards, which had been stored in an open shed at the lumber yard, were definitely becoming drier. But if I had moved them into an enclosed space in which the air was very humid, they would have absorbed moisture instead.

Contrary to what many people believe, cut wood doesn't permanently "dry out," no matter how long ago it was cut. All the wood in a house—from the framing in the basement to the furniture in the living room to the firewood in the yard—has a moisture content that fluctuates with local conditions (assuming that local conditions fluctuate, as they do in most places). A living tree, by weight, is about two-thirds water. Once the tree is cut down and sawn into boards—or cut and split into firewood—that water content drops until the moisture level of the wood has reached equilibrium with its environment. From that point on, the water content of the wood changes in response to changes in relative humidity. The water content of a piece of seasoned lumber might be 5 percent during a dry season and 25 percent during a wet one, moving between those two extremes as the seasons change. If you took a log from your wood pile and baked it in your oven at 250 degrees for a few hours, you could get its moisture content down pretty close to zero, but when you returned that desiccated log to the woodpile it wouldn't stay dry. It would absorb water from its surroundings, and its moisture content would gradually rise until, once again, it was about the same as that of the other logs in the pile.

This affection for moisture is a consequence of wood's cellular structure. The parts of a living tree that aren't water serve mainly to move water around. Water in the ground (along with nutrients dissolved in it) enters the tree through its roots, travels up through the trunk to the farthest limbs, and exits the tree, in the form of water vapor, through tiny openings in the leaves. The process actually begins at the tiny openings: as water in leaves evaporates into the atmosphere through them, water from below is drawn upward to take its place. This natural pumping process is remarkably powerful. A large tree can move a hundred gallons a day—as people sometimes discover when they cut down the big old maple out back and end up with a wet spot in the yard or even a wet basement. Trees don't just stand there all day long; they're doing something.

As wood becomes drier, it shrinks, the way a kitchen sponge does; as it becomes wetter, it expands—and this phenomenon continues indefinitely. There are some 150-year-old doors in our house that are easy to open in the winter, when the low relative humidity has caused them to dry out somewhat and therefore shrink, and hard to close in the summer, when the high level of moisture in the air has made them and the jambs surrounding them swell. Those doors, despite their great age, expand and contract throughout the year. In fact, the entire house moves from season to season, growing larger in the damp months and smaller in the dry ones. I see signs of this movement everywhere: in doors and windows that operate differently, in gaps that open and close between baseboards and floors, in cracks that appear and disappear along grout lines at the edges of tiled bathroom floors. Waiting for wood to "dry out" is futile; it will keep shrinking and expanding as long as the relative humidity of the air surrounding it continues to change—and it will do so even if it has been painted. What Rudy was doing by stacking those pine boards indoors was allowing their moisture content to approximate that of all the other wood in the cabin, so that everything would move in sync, more or less, from then on.

In all species, moisture-related movement takes place mainly across the grain, so that a board will shrink and expand far more in width and in thickness than it will in length. This is because the cellular pathways that carry water in a living tree are aligned in the same direction, and when they absorb moisture they get thicker but they don't get longer. Because of this, I knew, the boards that would cover the walls and ceilings in the cabin would always be essentially the same length but would repeatedly become wider or narrower in response to seasonal changes in relative humidity. Rudy had to plan for this cyclical movement when he nailed the boards in place. Because this was the driest season of the year and because the boards had been allowed to acclimate themselves to the cabin's interior, Rudy knew that the boards were now almost as narrow as they would ever be, and that during humid summers they would become measurably wider. He had to make room for that expansion, by leaving adequate gaps between the boards when he nailed them up. The half-inch shiplap on the edge of each board gave him plenty of margin; he overlapped the boards by a little more than half of that distance, leaving a gap on either side to accommodate summertime swelling. If he had been installing the boards during a humid season instead, he would have nailed them up with smaller gaps, knowing that those openings would grow during dry months.

During the time when the pine boards were stacked inside the cabin, I used a small paint brush to stain the half-inch-wide recesses on their edges. I stained them the same color that I would later stain the finished walls and ceilings—a tedious but necessary project. By staining the rabbets in advance, I relieved myself of having to try to work stain into the narrow spaces between the boards after they had been nailed up, and I made sure that bare wood would never become visible in the gaps between boards if the boards shrank further.

———————

BEFORE RUDY BEGAN work on the cabin's interior, I told him that I didn't want him to use any caulk on any of the woodwork. He chuckled at this, but agreed to do as I requested. I made myself swear, too.

Caulk is a wonderful invention, but it's often abused—not so much by guys like Rudy, but definitely by guys like me. The individual components of my early carpentry projects tended to fit together somewhat approximately, with joints that you could have fit whole packs of razor blades into. I hid my errors with caulk, and I felt extraordinarily clever as I gunned the stuff on. The caulk made all the joints appear tight and professional, especially after I'd wiped away the excess with a wet rag and buried everything under a couple of coats of paint. In the nude, my project had looked pretty dodgy, even to me; now, with the accidental spaces all filled and hidden, it impressed strangers.

The problem didn't become apparent until later, when seasonal changes in humidity caused the wood to move. When the wood expanded, during the humid months, the gaps between pieces of wood became smaller, compressing my caulk into wrinkly protrusions. When the wood later contracted, during heating season, the joints opened up again, and my wrinkly caulk looked even worse: some was stuck to this side, some was stuck to that side, some was stuck to nothing at all. I tried to solve this new problem by recaulking and repainting, but doing so only made things worse in the long run. As more seasons came and went, the wood continued to swell and shrink, and the wrinkly protrusions became even more noticeable.

I made the same mistake the first time I installed crown molding. The ceiling of the room in which I was working wasn't perfectly flat, so I couldn't always fit the top of the molding flush against the ceiling. The gaps seemed like a reproach, so I filled them with caulk—and while I was at it I touched up the coped joints at the inside corners, and the far less noticeable seam between the bottom of the molding and the walls. Then I painted the room, and, once again, marveled at how good everything looked—until a few months later, when all the gaps I had stuffed with caulk opened up again, and looked much worse than they would have if I had left them alone. I would have been much,

much better off if I had used no caulk at all. Painting the molding with primer and two finish coats would have narrowed the bothersome gaps, and any space that remained after the paint had dried would have been far less annoying than the ragged mess that I'd created. If some caulking is unavoidable, it should be saved for the painter, who will use less and apply it later in the process.

Caulk also causes trouble when well-meaning imbeciles—I include myself in the category—attempt to repair old furniture. Ann and I own an old school desk with a hinged top that's made of two wide pine boards mounted in a frame. There's a gap between the pine boards, right in the middle of the desktop, and the gap is partly filled with fragments of cracked, jagged, rock-hard material. Here's a likely explanation: The boards in the desktop, like all boards, have always shrunk and expanded in response to changes in humidity, and at some time in the past a previous owner of the desk became annoyed that the boards didn't fit together tightly throughout the entire year. (Maybe the tip of his pencil kept breaking off in the crevice.) One winter, when the boards had shrunk (and therefore pulled apart), as usual, he filled the yawning gap with wood filler, which he had selected carefully to match the color of the wood. The result looked great at first: no more broken pencils. A few months later, though, the local humidity rose again, with the change of season, and the pine boards swelled, as they always did at that time of year. The expansion of the boards now exerted a powerful compressive force on the hardened strip of wood filler that separated them. This caused the filler, which was less resilient than the pine, to act like a wedge. As the swelling boards pushed harder and harder against that wedge, the wood fibers at the edges of the boards on both sides became crushed, so that when the boards shrank again, a few months later, a new, wider gap appeared. As the shrinking boards pulled apart, furthermore, the filler cracked and came away from the wood in several places, since it was now being pulled, rather than pushed, by the movement of the wood, and some of it fell away altogether. The owner, perplexed, decided that the problem must be insufficient determination on his part, and that the best approach would be to add more filler. This he did, cramming the gap as completely as possible. Once again, the repaired crack looked good initially. But as soon as the wood swelled again, the problem reappeared—only more so this time, since the wedge between the boards was now bigger and denser than before. This is the classic home-handyman repair cycle: dealing with small problems by conscientiously turning them into big ones.

Some well-meaning people, including some professionals, try to deal with this kind of wood movement by attacking it from the other direction. Instead of filling the seasonal gap between moving boards, they join the two boards together as tightly as possible at some moment when they have swollen to their maximum extent. If the previous owner of our old pine desk had settled on this course of action, he would have waited until the gap between the boards had disappeared (when the August humidity was at its most unbearable) and then placed a couple of wood or metal braces across the gap, like Band-Aids, on the underside of the desktop, and screwed them firmly to the boards. Once again, a job well done—until the boards shrank again, in dry weather. Now the boards would be held together too tightly to pull apart as before, so the forces that previously had caused the gap to appear would have to find relief somewhere else: the boards themselves would have to crack, or they would have to pull away from the frame that was holding them fast on the other side.

The same effect can be seen in some nineteenth-century panel doors in our house. Each of the doors has four panels, two above and two below, and those panels are set into a grid of vertical members, called stiles, and horizontal members, called rails. This method of construction is very attractive, in my opinion, but it was invented mainly for practical reasons rather than aesthetic ones: frame-and-panel construction is intended specifically to accommodate the movement of wood. The panels fit loosely into channels in the edges of the stiles and rails, allowing them to freely expand and contract as the local humidity rises and falls.

That, at any rate, is how those old panel doors worked when they were built. Over the decades, though, repeated applications of paint worked their way into the channels and effectively glued the panels to the stiles and rails. Eventually, the wood, when it ex-

panded and contracted, could no longer slide freely in the channels, and something had to give. Sometimes, the thing that gave
was the paint along the seams—which would form moraine-like
ridges near the edges of the stiles or would flake away entirely.
Occasionally, the thing that gave was the wood. Some of the panels, held fast by accumulations of hardened paint, have simply
cracked longitudinally, in the direction of the grain. The cracks
widen during the winter, when humidity in the house is low, and
they close during the summer, when humidity is high. Filling the
open cracks with caulk or wood filler would only make them
worse, eventually. Slapping on more paint doesn't help, either,
since it just adds to the existing accumulations of adhesive gunk.

People will sometimes tell you that painting wood—or priming it with a sealer—will prevent moisture-related wood movement, but it won't. Paint may slow the movement of water vapor
somewhat, but it can't prevent it, and painted windows eventually
stick as much as unpainted ones do. The only way to prevent
wood movement altogether—other than living in a place where
the humidity doesn't fluctuate—is to use engineered wood products, such as plywood or medium-density fiberboard, rather than
solid wood. During our big kitchen renovation, Ann and I hired
a local carpenter to install raised-panel wainscoting in our central
hall, one wall of which had had to be torn up during construction. He made the panels from medium-density fiberboard,
which is a more sophisticated cousin of particleboard, and is essentially made from sawdust and glue. Those panels—unlike the
two-hundred-year-old ones in our living room—will never shrink,
expand, or crack.

———

AS SOON AS the pine boards had all been nailed up on the
cabin's walls and ceilings—using the same Tremont nails I had
used in Ann's and my bedroom—I began staining and finishing.
Sometimes, I worked when Rudy, Joe, and Mark were around and
doing other things, and sometimes I worked at night and on
weekends, when I had the place to myself. The stain I used was a
combination of two standard Minwax shades: two parts Colonial
Maple and one part Early American. I had tried this combina-

tion, along with several others, on some wood scraps in the basement, and I had decided that it came pretty close to the deep, warm tone I had been imagining: the color of some exceedingly lovely old pine floor boards on the second floor of our house. Colonial Maple alone was too orange; Early American alone was too brown; the two together were just right. Applying the mixture to an actual wall for the first time took some courage, though; once you commit, there's no easy way to undo what you have done. I chose a single board on a small, relatively inconspicuous section of one wall in the mudroom, and after I had stained it I nervously asked Rudy for his opinion. Then I finished the entire section and studied it for a long time before proceeding.

Mixing stains is tricky because the color comes from solid pigments in suspension, and the pigments settle to the bottom of the can. If you're combining partial cans you have to be sure to mix each one thoroughly before pouring them together, and you also have to stir your finished mixture constantly while you work, to keep everything in proportion. In the cabin, I tried to mix relatively small batches and to use only whole cans—say, by combining two quart cans of Colonial Maple with one quart can of Early American in a single gallon bucket, and carefully scraping the bottom of each can to make sure I'd gotten all the solids—but I sometimes had to improvise. A couple of times, I forgot to stir my mixture as I worked. Late one night, I resumed work in the main room after eating dinner back at our house, and decided, with a stab of horror, that the mixture with which I had just stained three long boards was noticeably darker than the mixture I had been using earlier that day. My fear that I had made an uncorrectable mistake kept me awake through much of that night. A week or two later, though, I realized that I couldn't really see much of a difference. And today I can't see any difference, because those boards are completely hidden by a couch and a couple of lamps. (Mistakes that are heartbreakingly obvious in an empty room often become undetectable once the room has been inhabited.)

Sometimes I applied the stain with a brush, and sometimes I applied it with a folded cloth diaper, embracing or re-embracing each technique after becoming exasperated with the other. The stain ran down my arm as I worked, and it got all over my shirt, my pants, and my glasses. It also ruined a pair of sneakers, which I sometimes still wear, even though Ann wants me to throw them away. The most tedious part was the ceilings. I made a movable scaffold by resting two ten-foot-long two-by-twelves on the cross braces of a pair of sawhorses, and I scooted this contraption along the floor as I worked my way across the room, two or three ceiling boards at a time. To reach the ceiling above the stairs, I had to lean a short extension ladder against the high wall at the bottom of the stairwell and run a two-by-twelve between one of its uppermost rungs and the top step. Doing this created a precarious platform that bounced menacingly as I inched across it. I was virtually positive that at some point I would fall, although I never did.

Before the cabin project began, I asked Rudy if he didn't want me to rent a portable toilet for him and his crew. "Nah," he said. "We'll use the woods." Then he looked thoughtful. "The painters will want one, though," he said. "They always do. All day long, they have nothing to do but think." By the time I had finished my staining, I knew what he meant. As I worked my way from one side of the main room to the other, the same closed thought loops cycled through my brain. One morning, as I was working on the muntins of what seemed like the ten-thousandth window, a phrase I had read in the newspaper the day before crept into my consciousness and stayed there, muttering to me between strokes. I couldn't get it out of my head until I knocked off that evening, when I promptly forgot all about it. But it was right back in my skull the following morning, waiting for me to pick up my brush again. (Now I don't remember what it was.)

For those who are able to maneuver themselves into the proper frame of mind, the wavelike rhythms of painting can promote a meditative sense of inner peace. That must be what pro painters learn to do, and I myself have experienced it on several occasions. But even the pros have to be careful. No painter should ever go to work without having resolved all outstanding domestic disputes. If you had a screaming fight with your loved ones at the breakfast table, the last thing you should do is spend eight hours alone with your thoughts and a China bristle brush.

With every stroke, your irritation winds itself a little tighter. By the time you return to the scene of the crisis, you are unfit to find a solution.

The radio can help, by drowning out some of the more disquieting inner voices. But radio only goes so far. As one of the painters who worked on both our house and the cabin told me, "You can listen to the same station for two or three days in a row, but after that the playlist starts to drive you crazy." He was right. One morning, I found an oldies station that I liked a lot, and I spent the rest of that day enjoying the nostalgic time travel that old songs inspire. By the third day, though, I was beginning to fantasize about strangling individual Beach Boys, so I switched to an AM sports talk station. Radio sports talk is the most depressing form of human communication, but listening to that station for a day was a relief just the same.*

NOWADAYS, THE USUAL way to finish stained wood is with a varnish made from a synthetic resin (such as polyurethane, phenol, or alkyd), or with a natural drying oil (such as tung oil), which hardens when it's exposed to oxygen. I decided to use something different: shellac. I had learned about shellac a dozen years before, from James Boorstein, a restoration and preservation specialist in New York City. At the time I met Boorstein, he and his crew—which had sometimes included as many as thirty craftspeople—had been working for three and a half years on a single apartment in the Dakota, the legendary building in which John Lennon lived and outside of which he was murdered. The first room Boorstein showed me was typical of the project. Its deteriorated floor (made of oak and cherry) had been taken up, reinforced, and relaid, with some new boards, which were cut to the exact dimensions of the old ones. The door and its jamb and

---

* A friend of mine told me: "My brother and I listened to a classic-rock station while we were painting. We each made a list of 'essential' classic-rock songs, and whoever got the most in an hour won. Hint: always pick 'Smoke on the Water' and something by Lynyrd Skynyrd."

casing had been stripped of innumerable layers of paint, then repaired with dozens of inlaid patches, called dutchmen. The plaster walls had been repaired and then embellished with an ash
baseboard and picture rail. A plaster cornice had been run by
hand above the picture rail, with knives made by Boorstein's
crew. The walls and ceiling had been prepared as if for a meticu-
lous paint job, painted, and then covered with five different wall-
papers, selected from nineteenth-century pattern books. A
period chandelier had been hung from the eleven-foot ceiling.
The only atypical thing about this room was its size: eighteen
inches by forty inches. It was a closet. Boorstein explained, "The
clients told us, 'Don't cut corners just because the door is going
to be closed.'" As a result, even the cramped hallway near the service elevator had been treated like a primary space. "I like to
think that there are levels of restoration," Boorstein told me.
"There is high-quality restoration work, which is expensive, and
which you don't see very often. A step above that is museum-
quality restoration work. And then there's this, which is really
something else again."

Boorstein was born in Manhattan and raised on Long Island.
In college, at Colgate, he majored in art and archaeology, and
learned welding on the side. After graduation, he moved to New
York and worked as an ice-cream store manager, a furniture re-
finisher, a plumber, and, intermittently, a sculptor. Sculpture was
his first love, and he sold a number of pieces, but he felt increasingly uneasy in the art world, in part because he didn't like to
hustle his work. "I don't feel very comfortable saying to someone,
'I'm a good artist,' whatever that means," he told me. "But I don't
mind saying, 'I can take this nineteenth-century brass doorknob
and make a copy of it that is literally perfect.'" In 1980, he was
hired by the Metropolitan Museum of Art to create an old-
looking finish for the new frame of a Tiffany window that would
eventually be displayed in the courtyard of the American Wing,
which had just been completed. Later, he was asked to help install some of the wing's period rooms, one of which was a reproduction of a parlor in a Greek Revival house, built in 1837, on
West Eleventh Street. Partly as a result of his work on that re-cre-
ation, he was hired to take part in the restoration of the house—

in effect, to bring the original up to the level of the copy. His restoration business, which is called Traditional Line, Ltd., grew out of that project.

In the Dakota apartment, most of the wood surfaces that weren't painted, excluding the floor, were finished with shellac, which Boorstein had formulated to his own specifications. He told me that he liked shellac because it was versatile and easy to handle, and because it produced strikingly rich, durable, and historically accurate finishes that would have been impossible to duplicate with synthetic varnishes. I spoke to him again recently. He told me that he was still using shellac, and that during the early nineties he had taken a trip to India during which he had watched it being made. He also said that he had considered writing a book about shellac, but that he had decided ultimately that the market would be too small. He's probably right, but if he changes his mind I'll want a copy.

Shellac is made from a natural resin, called lac, which is the only commercially valuable resin that is produced by an animal. (All other natural resins—rosin, amber, mastic, and dammar among them—are produced by plants; most synthetic resins, including the ones in most plastics, are derived from petroleum.) Lac is secreted by a tiny red scale insect that abounds in parts of southern Asia and feeds on the sap of certain trees. The word *lac* is probably derived from a Hindi word meaning "one hundred thousand" and "extremely many"—a possible reference to the teeming profusion in which the insects cover their hosts. As lac larvae extract sap, they secrete a protective resinous shell over themselves, and the shells merge into a continuous coating. Lac insects live for about six months. They molt twice as they mature, shedding their legs, antennae, wings, and eyes as they do. Newly hatched larvae dig out through the coating and move on to uninhabited branches.

Lac can be found on trees growing in the wild, but most of the world's supply is cultivated, mainly in India and Thailand but also in Myanmar, China, Bangladesh, and elsewhere. Shortly before the larvae emerge from the lac shell, growers remove some of the encrusted twigs and tie them to uninfested trees, to establish the next crop; the lac on such twigs is called brood lac. The workers scrape or knock the resin from remaining branches. The harvested material contains many impurities—living larvae, dead adults, dirt, twigs, bits of bark—and is known as stick lac. It is crushed, rinsed, winnowed, and dried, yielding a semi-refined substance, known as seed lac, which is then processed further, either by hand or in factories. In the hand method, workers fill a long cloth sleeve with seed lac and suspend the sleeve over a fire. As the lac softens, the workers twist the sleeve tightly, as though wringing a wash cloth, and a liquefied, amber-colored resin oozes through the weave, leaving most of the remaining impurities behind. In the factory method, the seed lac is melted in large vats or dissolved in alcohol, then filtered. The purified lac is either drawn and stretched into thin sheets, then broken into flakes, or formed into disks, which are called button lac. Shellac varnish is made by dissolving purified lac in alcohol.

The first lac-related human product was probably a bright red dye, later known as lac dye; it was first made more than three thousand years ago. Until the rise of synthetic dyes, in the second half of the nineteenth century, lac dye was used all over the world, in textiles, cosmetics, paints, the uniforms of Indian soldiers, and innumerable other items. The dye comes not from lac resin but from chemicals in the bodies of the dead insects; it is precipitated from the water in which stick lac has been washed. A small quantity is still produced today. It's used mainly to dye rugs in regions where lac is cultivated.

The most significant uses for lac have involved the resin. Ancient peoples shaped it, carved it, used it as an adhesive, and made jewelry, abrasive tools, medical instruments, and other items from it. Sealing wax (used in the olden days to seal letters and official documents) was made mainly of shellac. The Old Masters protected their paintings by coating them with shellac varnish. Daguerreotypes were often kept under glass in hard, ebony-colored "Union cases"—intricately decorated flat boxes that were molded from a mixture of shellac, sawdust, and dark pigments. On my desk I have a small daguerreotype of an unsmiling and now long-dead female relative; its Union case, which has a patented "embracing riveted hinge," was manufactured in the late 1850s or early 1860s by Littlefield, Parsons & Company, whose founder, Alfred P. Critchlow, invented the material. (He called it Florence Compound, and it was also used to make buttons, hairbrushes, and revolver cases.) Hats were once stiffened with shellac, and shoe polish and floor polish often contained it. The scientists who invented the first synthetic polymers, early in the twentieth century, were trying, in part, to replicate the natural properties of shellac. An early form of electrical insulation consisted of paper coated with shellac. Hairspray used to contain it, and some other cosmetics still do, including some kinds of lipstick and mascara. The first 78-rpm phonograph records were made of shellac that had been mixed with various fillers and dyes. If you shatter an early 78 and soak the pieces in alcohol, you may be able to create a useable imitation of black shellac, a dark wood finish that was popular in the nineteenth century but is very hard to find today. (You can also make your own by adding ten fluid ounces of black universal tint to a gallon of ordinary shellac.)

Shellac is non-toxic. It is an FDA-approved ingredient in many foods and medications, a fact that complicates the lives of vegans, the strict vegetarians who attempt to live without consuming or using animal products. Grocery-store apples, tomatoes, oranges, and other fruits and vegetables are often given a shiny protective coating that contains shellac. Part of the reason that certain chocolate candies don't melt in your hand is that their shells contain shellac. Some nuts are coated with it, too. It is added to medications to make them easier to form into pills, and it is an ingredient in the coatings of some coated tablets and time-release drugs.

The main use for shellac is as a transparent finish for wood. In the United States, it was introduced for that purpose around 1850 by William Zinsser, who had worked in a shellac factory in Germany before emigrating to New York. The business he founded is known today as Zinsser Company. It is a subsidiary of a conglomerate called RPM International, Inc.—whose many other products include Day-Glo fluorescent paints and Rust-Oleum—and is the world's largest manufacturer of shellac-based coatings. (Somewhat eerily, James Boorstein dated one of Zinsser's direct descendants when he was in high school.) William Zinsser's first product was bleached shellac, a clear varnish that is made by chemically removing shellac's natural color.

In the cabin, I used Zinsser Bulls Eye shellac. It comes in two varieties: clear, which has been bleached, and amber, which has not. (Until fairly recently, Zinsser called these shades white and orange; I assume that the name change was a marketing decision—and a good one.) I used the amber version, which had been manufactured in what is called a "three-pound cut," meaning that each gallon contained three pounds of shellac resin. Zinsser also sells one-pound aerosol shellac, two-pound "sanding sealer," and—although these can be hard to find—four-pound clear shellac and four-pound and five-pound amber shellac. Zinsser's popular B-I-N primer-sealer, which I have used to prevent Magic Marker from bleeding through new paint on a playroom wall, among other things, is shellac varnish to which titanium dioxide and other white pigments have been added. (When B-I-N was introduced, in 1946, it was called Bulls-I-Namel.)

Shellac's main appeal as a wood finish is aesthetic. It enhances the natural color and grain of many varieties of wood, and it doesn't dry to the dead, filmy sheen of polyurethane. It's also extraordinarily easy to use. It adheres to almost anything (except wax), dries to the touch in minutes, can be recoated in less than an hour, cures to an extremely hard finish, and can be removed from a brush with alcohol or ammonia. A shellac coating is easy to repair, touch up, and renew because shellac bonds permanently to itself: a second coat melts into the first, creating a single, homogeneous layer. (The same is not true of polyurethane, which sticks well to almost anything except itself; to recoat polyurethane you have to either sand the first coat, to roughen it, or apply the second coat before the first coat has hardened completely.) A very light wash coat of thinned shellac makes many types of wood receive stain more uniformly, and it also makes the wood easier to sand smooth. Shellac is not damaged or discolored by sunlight. It is virtually impermeable to water vapor, and it is the only sealer that will permanently prevent resinous wood knots from bleeding through paint. (If you need to paint wood with knots in it, spot-apply multiple coats of three-pound or heavier shellac directly on the knotty areas, then prime and paint.)

People who restore burned buildings often use shellac or shellac-based coatings to seal in soot, smoke odors, and water stains. De-waxed shellac—a premium product that consists of ordinary shellac from which all natural wax has been removed—can be used as a sealer under other transparent finishes, including polyurethane; it can also be applied over other finishes. It can even be applied over old finishes that have been harmed by silicone oil, a common ingredient in popular furniture polishes.

In the cabin, I applied two coats of full-strength shellac to the walls, and one or two coats of thinned shellac to the ceilings. On the doors, door trim, and some of the walls, I sanded lightly between coats, then wiped away the dust with a rag that I had dampened with alcohol. I also lightly rubbed down the final finish with super-fine steel wool, to control the shine. Today, the walls look as though they'd always been there. The natural amber color of the shellac becomes extraordinarily warm and deep when sunlight hits it, and the pine doesn't appear to have been dipped in plastic, the way it would if I had used polyurethane instead. Because shellac is a natural product, its color can vary somewhat from can to can; if I had been insanely fussy, I could have made sure that all the shellac I bought was from the same production batch, or mixed all the cans together before I began.

Boorstein and other serious craftspeople don't use shellac out of the can, the way I did. They make their own, by dissolving shellac flakes or button lac in alcohol. Premixed shellac has a finite shelf life, especially if it has been bleached, and if it's too old it will dry more slowly than it should or, if it's very old, may never harden completely. Old shellac also loses some of its ability to resist water. If you have a can of shellac that's been sitting in your basement for a long time, you should check the date on the bottom and test the shellac on a piece of wood before using it on anything important. Homemade shellac can be made in a broad spectrum of natural shades—raw lac ranges from nearly clear to deep brown—and it can be mixed with pure alcohol, which produces a more durable finish. (Most of the alcohol for sale in a hardware store or drugstore will contain a fair bit of water, among other fillers.) The best alcohol for making or thinning shellac is probably two-hundred-proof ethyl alcohol, also known as grain alcohol, although it can be hard to find. Denatured alcohol, which your hardware store probably sells, is ethyl alcohol to which a small amount of something nasty has been added to make it undrinkable; often, the nasty additive is gasoline, which isn't an ideal ingredient for a wood finish. For the vast majority of users, however, the difference is close to meaningless.

Shellac's one significant weakness as a finish is that it can be damaged by alcohol, water, and alkaline liquids like ammonia—good reasons not to use it near the kitchen sink. You've probably seen a shellac-finished table on which a wet glass has left a white ring; the ring is caused by the water's penetration into (but not all the way through) the finish. A reasonably good shellac finish will resist water for a very long time, though, and white marks can almost always be removed by padding the area gently with a cloth that has been dampened with alcohol or with fresh shellac. A shellac finish, unlike a polyurethane finish, is also relatively easy to repair, using alcohol, fine steel wool, more shellac, and patience.

———————————

THE FLOORS IN the bedrooms in the cabin are carpeted (and the carpeting is installed directly on top of the plywood sub-floor). The floors in the mudroom, the kitchen, and the bathrooms are covered with slate tiles—big ones downstairs, small ones upstairs. The floors in the main room, the dining alcove, and the upstairs hall are made of eight-inch tongue-and-groove white oak boards, which Rudy ordered from a local hardwood supplier that I had recommended. Most of the boards have small, tight knots, and a number of them have other minor imperfections, including holes made by the (no longer operative) larvae of boring beetles. Boards of this type are more interesting to look at than ones that are entirely free of defects—which are also more expensive—and are sometimes referred to as "character grade." Less expensive still is "rustic grade," in which the defects are more than visual.

Rudy left the new oak floorboards stacked in the main room, as he had with the pine boards, to allow their moisture content to reach equilibrium with the relative humidity inside the cabin.

This didn't take very long, because the oak had been thoroughly kiln-dried by the hardwood supplier and the finished boards had been stored indoors before being delivered to us. Rudy was impressed, because hardwood flooring (like all the other wood used in construction) often has a high moisture content when it's delivered. He told me that I wouldn't have a shrinkage problem— and he was right. The worry, if anything, has been expansion. Rudy installed the flooring very tight, and during the summer, when the relative humidity is high, the boards expand and press against each other, producing small ridges along the seams between them which are visible if you look closely. (He left a gap around the edges of the rooms to allow for expansion, but not all the forces in an expanding floor can be relieved at the edges.)

Because wood never stops moving in response to changes in humidity, the effects upon it of either expansion or contraction are almost always detectable to some extent. The house of a friend of mine contains adjacent rooms with floors made of two-and-a-half-inch-wide maple. The floor in one of the rooms was laid during the summer and has very visible gaps during heating season; the floor in the other room was laid during the winter and shows a little bit of ridging during the summer—same wood, same house. The best way to keep wood-movement issues to a minimum in floors is to closely monitor the moisture content of the wood and the relative humidity of the house during installation, and adjust the spacing of the boards so that neither extreme will be too conspicuous—but that's hard to do, even for a professional.

One cabin job that I had no interest in attempting myself was sanding, staining, and finishing those new oak floors. It's very easy to rent a floor sander, but it's almost impossible for a first-timer to do a decent job with one. The machine is enormous and hard to control, and it's always trying to take off on its own. A couple of years ago, a friend of mine told me that he had decided to refinish the wood floor in his kitchen by himself, to save money. I told him that I was sure he could save a lot more money by hiring someone else to do it. He ignored me, but I was right. My friend had trouble maneuvering the sander, and he couldn't figure out how to sand the parts of the floor next to the walls or under the front part of the range. He ended up having to call a professional floor finisher after all—who re-sanded the entire floor (to get rid of waves and burn marks that my inexperienced friend had made by mishandling his rented machine) and took care of all the hard-to-reach spots (by using a floor-edge sander, a piece of equipment designed for that purpose). Simply hiring the pro in the first place would have been less costly and would have spared my friend a great deal of irritation.

The man who sanded and finished the oak floors in the cabin had been in the business for decades. When he arrived to start the job, he looked at the walls in the main room and said, "If I didn't know better, I'd swear that was shellac." We had a nice little chat about the good old days, and then he went to work. He spent about a week sanding, staining, and applying three coats of satin polyurethane. If I'd thoroughly thought things through beforehand, I might have decided to try using high-quality, hand-mixed shellac on the floors instead—something that was done very often in the past, and is still done occasionally today. On the whole, though, it's probably a good thing that I decided not to bother. A month or two after the final coat of polyurethane had dried—and after I had spent some time admiring them and sliding around on them in my socks—I did what most people do to their beautiful new hardwood floors: I covered them with rugs.

8

THE WET PARTS

IN MY PART OF Connecticut, which is largely rural, few towns have municipal water systems. My own town has two private water companies, both of which are more than a century old and neither of which serves even a hundred customers. A few years ago, one of the companies suffered a major line break in the middle of our village center. A golf buddy of mine, who was the company's (pro bono) attorney, noticed a commotion from his office window and walked across the street to see what was going on. He ended up helping to restore service by running a garden hose across the driveway of the gas station to a spigot at the grocery store. A few years before, at a rate-increase hearing, a state commissioner had asked him to describe the company's emergency systems, and he said, "When Mrs. Eames can't get water in her upstairs bathroom, we know the reservoir is low." (Only the court reporter laughed, my friend told me.) And the "reservoir," in those days, was actually more of a spring-fed puddle, with a rotting wooden roof over it. The company's water-treatment protocol consisted of hiring a local man to remove drowned mice from the reservoir with a net. He was paid by the carcass.

Because public water is essentially nonexistent in my area, most homeowners have wells. A few wells date back to the nineteenth century and are just hand-dug holes in the ground. Usually, the holes are lined with stones, bricks, or sections of concrete pipe, to keep dirt from slumping into the water. My friends Rex and Polly have a well like that; it's twenty-two feet

deep and three feet in diameter, and it is covered by a heavy concrete lid. During a very dry summer several years ago, the water
in their well dropped below the outlet pipe, and they took advantage of the drought by hiring a man to clean out the bottom of
the well. The man lowered himself into the hole, removed many
buckets of muck, and charged them twenty-five dollars.

Nowadays, new wells are drilled rather than dug. There are
three principal methods: rotary, cable percussion, and rotary percussion. Rotary drilling is what you probably picture when you
think of well-drilling: a turning steel shaft with a cutting tool on
the end, like a super-size version of your cordless electric drill.
Cable percussion drilling—which is also known as churn drilling,
cable-tool drilling, and pounding—employs a chisel-like bit that
is slowly beaten into the ground. Rotary percussion drilling,
which is also known as compressed-air percussion drilling, is a
high-tech hybrid of the other two methods, and uses tremendous
pressure to rapidly hammer a spinning drill bit. (A cable percussion drill bit rotates, too, but very slowly.) Each method has advantages and disadvantages. Much of the bedrock in my area is
granite, a dense metamorphic rock, through which groundwater
travels mainly in cracks and fractures. Rotary drilling, though fast
and cheap, is ineffective in granite unless it directly penetrates a
water-bearing crack. Pounding, in contrast, creates its own cracks
and fractures, and therefore sometimes produces good wells in
unpromising strata—but it's very, very slow. Rotary percussion
drilling is many times faster than pounding and is more effective
than ordinary rotary drilling, but the equipment is complicated
and expensive. The rapidly turning bit also grinds rock chips into
a fine, pasty powder, which can seal up small fractures as quickly
as they are created.

The summer before the cabin got under way, my little nine-
hole golf club drilled a well near the irrigation pond, as an emergency backup source of water for the course. The well was drilled
by a local pounder, a grizzled guy in overalls whose family has
been in the well-pounding business for many, many years. Before
he began to drill, he spent several hours leveling his rig, a large
truck with a collapsible derrick on the back. Leveling is a crucial
step in any drilling operation, because even a small deviation

from verticality can cause the bit to wander disastrously, ruining both the equipment and the well.

At last, when he was happy with the position of his truck, he fired up the motor, and the pounding began. A winch on the derrick raised a cable, then let it drop, causing the bit to gnaw into the rock. *Kachung.* Then it did it again. *Kachung.* And again and again. *Kachung. Kachung.* The rhythm was unvarying, and it went on for days, for weeks, for centuries. When three friends and I passed the pond during a round of golf on the day he began, he was there, standing beside the machine, his right hand holding the cable, his arm rising and falling with it. *Kachung. Kachung. Kachung.* When we passed the pond again two hours later, on our second nine, he was still there. When we returned a few days later, for more golf, he was still there, still pounding. He looked to be in his early fifties, and had therefore presumably spent at least the past thirty years in the company of this awful metronome, with maybe another twenty or thirty years to go. You could hear the sound all over the golf course, and midway through my round I noticed that I had begun to swing at its tempo. *Kachung.* (Backswing.) *Kachung.* (Follow-through.) If the sound had that effect on me during a single round of golf, what had it done to him over decades? Had he internalized it, so that it was now the rhythm at which he breathed, chewed, walked, talked, and made love to his wife? *Kachung. Kachung. Kachung.* Nor could he escape it by wandering into the woods with a good book (my first thought when I saw him working), because (it turns out) a well pounder has to listen constantly to the sound of his rig, and stand for long stretches with a hand on the cable, the better to detect any change in pitch or vibration that might indicate trouble in the hole. I felt depressed on his behalf every time I saw him, or thought of him, or heard that *kachung.*

Nevertheless, when the time came to put in a well at the cabin, I myself hired a pounder, one recommended by Rudy. His name was Ralph. After he had gotten his rig into position—with three of the four wheels lifted off the ground by hydraulic jacks and blocks of wood—he began pounding. He pounded through ten or twenty feet of soil and sand and gravel, and then through forty feet of sandstone. By the time the well was sixty feet deep—

several days after Ralph began—it was producing a gallon and a half per minute. Ideally, Ralph told, me, you'd like to have five or six gallons a minute, so he kept going. He pounded through forty feet of shale and black granite. Still a gallon and a half. Then a hundred more feet of black granite. Still a gallon and a half. We consulted, briefly. Well drillers charge by the foot. I told him to keep going.

Before Ralph began, a friend had told me that I ought to hire a dowser to show him where to drill. A dowser, or diviner, is someone who uses a forked stick, a pair of metal rods, a pendulum, a coat hanger, or some similar pointing device to search for water, oil, gold, gems, or other subterranean treasure. In the classic technique, the dowser walks around a site while holding his pointer in front of him, and when he feels its tip being tugged by an invisible force he stops and says, "Dig here." There's a highly regarded retired well driller and dowser in my area with the unimprovable name of Oden Foss. When Foss dowsed a well for my friend Bob, a few years ago, he cut his divining rod from a tree on the property, and, after using it to identify what he said was the ideal drilling spot, he let Bob and his daughter use it, too. They both felt the pull of the water, Bob told me. Some dowsers don't even need to be on site. They work from maps, and are known as map dowsers. Another friend of mine sent a topographical map of a building lot he had just bought to a celebrated map dowser in Maine and, he told me, was very satisfied with the results.

The only problem with dowsing, of course, is that it's a fantasy. There is no force in nature that could cause an aquifer, oil dome, gold coin, or dead body (the quarry of a forensic dowser) to pull a forked stick toward it, whether in situ or through a map. All the so-called evidence that people cite in its support is either spurious or flimsily anecdotal; scientifically controlled studies have invariably shown dowsing to be bogus. The James Randi Educational Foundation, a nonprofit organization whose purpose is "to promote critical thinking by reaching out to the public and media with reliable information about paranormal and supernatural ideas," has long offered a large cash prize, now a million dollars, to anyone who can conclusively demonstrate the existence of "any paranormal, supernatural, or occult power or event," including dowsing. Randi—who received a MacArthur Foundation "genius grant" in 1986 and established his own foundation ten years later—hasn't come close to having to pay up.

At a gallon and a half a minute, though, I was tempted to hire a magician. Actually, I had no objective basis for feeling deprived, since I didn't know how much water my family needed, or even how much water the well at our house produces (and I still don't). But I felt stricken with well envy nevertheless. The well at the golf course produces thirty gallons a minute, enough to keep the pond full even in a drought. (Naturally, in the six years since that well was dug, the club has never had to use it.) My friend Ken has a well that produces so much water—sixty gallons a minute—that he had to register it with the state as a potential public water source for emergencies. The well that Oden Foss located for my friend Bob ended up producing "such an abundance of water that we could bail at only 26 gallons per minute and could not keep up," Bob told me later.

So I instructed Ralph to keep going. Even if he found no more water, I rationalized, I would at least have a capacious reservoir, since a well shaft six inches in diameter holds almost a gallon and a half of water for every foot of depth. Ralph ended up going to 362 feet, by which point the yield had risen to two gallons a minute. I was disappointed, of course—but I now had a five-hundred-gallon storage tank.

There was a problem, however. Drilling the well had taken longer than expected, and neither Ralph nor Rudy nor I had anticipated how cold the weather would be. December's temperatures had hit record lows and stayed there, and by the time we were ready to run a water supply line from the well to the house, a distance of seventy feet, the ground had frozen solid to a depth of more than a foot. My friend Ray—whose excavating company had also dug the hole for the foundation—had agreed to dig the trench for the water line, but he found that he couldn't penetrate the frozen ground with the bucket of his backhoe. Everything would have been fine, he said, if we had thought to cover a strip of ground between the well to the house with a thick layer of hay before the weather turned cold, to keep the dirt from freezing, but we hadn't thought of that. Ray had to hire two guys from a local blasting company to use jackhammers to break up the earth, which was now almost as hard as concrete, so that he could chip out pieces with his backhoe. Digging the trench was almost as slow as digging the well had been. It took all day in temperatures near zero, and it left Ray and the two guys with the jackhammers looking like cadavers.

They finished just before dark. The next day, the plumber ran a plastic supply line through the trench and through the small round hole in the foundation which the concrete guys had left for the water line. The plumber attached the end of the line to the inlet valve of a blue-painted metal tank that looks a little like a hot-water heater but isn't. The tank is a pressurized storage tank; an air-filled rubber bladder inside it compresses as water from the well is pumped in, creating the pressure that moves water through the cabin.

A couple of days later, the cabin had one working toilet, which Rudy, Joe, and Mark had installed in an unfinished bathroom. For the first time since construction began, they could stop going to the bathroom in the woods.

THE MODERN TOILET, as every schoolchild knows, was invented by Thomas Crapper, a British sanitary engineer. Crapper devised a silent flush valve, which enabled Queen Victoria's son Prince Edward to go to the bathroom in Sandringham Castle without waking the other residents, and he was rewarded with a knighthood. Sir Thomas's story—including an account of his death, which occurred shortly after he had risen from his sickbed to repair a client's malfunctioning commode—is told in his biography, *Flushed With Pride*. "There is no question," the book's author wrote, "that Crapper's heart was in the toilet."

Well, not exactly. There really was a nineteenth-century British plumber named Thomas Crapper, and he did receive several toilet-related patents in the late eighteen hundreds, and his name can still be seen on a pair of manhole covers at Westminster Abbey. But he didn't invent the modern toilet, and Queen Victoria didn't knight him, and *Flushed With Pride*, though not completely free of facts, was written mainly as a joke. (The same author also published *Bust-Up: The Uplifting Tale of Otto Titzling and the Development of the Bra.*)

The Crapper legend is fully accurate in one regard, however: many key technological advances in the history of plumbing were made to please monarchs, the only people in the past who were rich enough to enjoy comforts approaching those that you and I take for granted. The first known indoor flush toilet was installed, forty centuries ago, in a royal palace in Crete. (It had a wooden seat and was flushed manually, with a bucket of water.) Various Egyptian tombs contained toilets, for use by departed dignitaries. Leonardo da Vinci, near the end of his life, designed a system of flushable indoor toilets connected to a central sewage system for his patron King Francis I of France, although the plan was never implemented. The first semi-modern flush toilet was built for the first Queen Elizabeth, who had previously relied on a portable potty with carrying handles and red velvet upholstery. Louis XIV couldn't flush but did own more than two hundred and fifty "necessary chairs," and he received visitors (and announced his marriage plans) while sitting on one or another of them.

Among hoi polloi, personal sanitation has a more discouraging history. Until very late in the nineteenth century, almost anyone's serious thinking about waste management ended at his front door, and most European city dwellers dealt with their excrement by throwing it out the window, emptying it in the street, burying it in back, or dumping it into the nearest river or canal. Gwen Raverat, a granddaughter of Charles Darwin, wrote (in her memoir, *Period Piece,* which is probably the book I reread most often) about a visit to Cambridge by Queen Victoria, who noticed many small pieces of paper floating in the Cam River and asked what they were. She was told, "Those, ma'am, are notices that bathing is forbidden."

To a modern time traveler, the most striking characteristic of any European city of the pre-plumbing era would probably be its stench—and much of the mud you'd scrape from your boots before entering a house would be trampled feces, both human and animal. One might think that the unpleasantness of living in

what was essentially an open sewer would have created an overwhelming public interest in finding a solution, but humans can
be shockingly adaptable. Residents of London initially preferred
living in filth to being taxed for a sewage system. The turning
point for them was the summer of 1857, when the Thames
smelled so unbearably bad that Parliament had to recess early.
Modernizing waste management throughout the country took
many more decades.

Civilization's waste problem affected more than convenience.
Several lethal diseases, among them cholera and dysentery, are
spread by contaminated water, and epidemics were (and remain)
common in densely populated areas with poor sanitation. The
rats that carried the fleas that carried the plague flourished wher-
ever sewage did. The scarcity of potable water also aggravated the
great undocumented scourge of civilization, the chronic alco-
holism of people who drank only beverages that had been
brewed, distilled, or fermented. The rise of the modern toilet has
helped to create the only extended period of reasonably
widespread good health in the history of the human race.

Queen Elizabeth's breakthrough toilet was made for her in
1596 by her godson John Harrington, who had built a prototype
in Bath and written a humorous essay about it. Harrington—who
was later knighted, although not because of his invention—also
spent some time in debtors' prison. Elizabeth's toilet was balky,
and it smelled terrible, as most early toilets did, but apparently it
did flush in something like the modern manner—or maybe it
didn't. At any rate, it, like Neanderthal man, was an evolutionary
dead end. Only a queen could afford the accompanying infrastructure, and when Elizabeth died, in 1603, Harrington's flushing mechanism passed out of human memory.

Automatic flushing didn't really begin to be rediscovered
until the late eighteenth century, when several people created
and then steadily improved the true precursors of the devices for
which we routinely fail to be sufficiently grateful. Those devices
eventually had two key elements in common. The first was a
water storage tank, which refilled between flushes. In early toilets, storage tanks were usually mounted on the wall several feet
above the bowl—as they still are, sometimes, in the United King-

dom and elsewhere. The fall from the tank to the bowl, through a connecting pipe, gave the water enough propulsive force to clear the bowl. The second element was a trap, a tightly curving section of pipe between the collection bowl and the waste line. The trap maintained a constant gas-impermeable water barrier in the pipe, even during flushing, and therefore prevented malodorous and potentially combustible sewer gases from escaping into the bathroom and beyond.

Early toilet bowls were made of copper, iron, and other materials. The first one-piece all-ceramic toilet bowl was manufactured in 1885 by Thomas Twyford, whose previous specialty had been teapots. Among Twyford's competitors was another distinguished British pottery maker, Royal Doulton. Twyford's and Doulton's Victorian-era toilets were as elaborately decorated as fine china, and they are prized today by (toilet) collectors. The modern successors of both companies are owned today by Sanitec Corporation, a Finnish plumbing conglomerate—although the non-bathroom part of Royal Doulton remains independent.

Thomas Crapper is treated so much like an urban legend that he may actually receive less credit for toilet-related innovation than he deserves, at least insofar as nomenclature is concerned. Even though Crapper didn't invent the toilet, he probably really is the source of a widely used slang term for it. His name appeared on the iron toilet tanks that his company manufactured, and its prominence probably helped the word drift into generic vulgar use. The word *crap* had been part of English since at least the fifteenth century, and had had several loosely similar meanings, among them "dregs," "residue," and "chaff." All of these meanings are close enough to the word's modern slang sense to have made the transition logical, even inevitable. Use of *crap* and *crapper* in their current meanings dates from the late nineteenth century, the period when Crapper's toilet tanks were becoming common in and around London, and both words may have been popularized in the United States a few decades later by returning American soldiers who had used Crapper-equipped loos in England during the First World War.

Scarcely less important than the invention of the toilet was the invention of its principal accessory. The Romans—who treated defecation as a social activity, and whose public lavatories contained as many as a hundred unenclosed, tightly spaced seats—cleaned up with a sponge attached to the end of a stick. The sponge, which was shared, was lightly rinsed between uses, usually by swishing it in a jar of salt water. Other people, at other times and in other places, employed moss, leaves, grass, sand, clay, snow, smooth stones, straw, corncobs, old rags, wash cloths, fur, mussel shells, coconut shells, newspapers, the pages of mail-order catalogs, and their own left hands. The first people to use paper were paper's inventors, the Chinese, who by the late fourteenth century had devised several versions for the bathroom, including emperor-worthy sheets measuring roughly two feet by three feet. The first modern toilet paper was introduced in New York City in 1857 by Joseph C. Gayetty, whose product was sold in packages of five hundred single sheets, each of which was pre-moistened with aloe. The packages cost fifty cents each—the equivalent of fifteen or twenty dollars today—and were sold by druggists. The first toilet paper on a roll was manufactured in the late eighteen hundreds by the brothers Irvin and Clarence Scott, of Philadelphia. The company they founded, the Scott Paper Company, also introduced paper towels, which were invented in 1907 by Irvin's son Arthur.

THE TOILETS OF my golden youth used as much as seven gallons of water per flush and were capable of disappearing all kinds of unlikely objects, including toy soldiers, golf balls, diamond rings, hearing aids, whole packs of cigarettes, and baggies filled with marijuana. Those toilets, along with their 5-gallon and 3.5-gallon successors, were doomed by the national Energy Policy Act of 1992, provisions of which limited new residential toilets to 1.6 gallons per flush beginning in 1994 and new commercial toilets to the same standards by 1997. (Other provisions of the act dealt with the disposal of nuclear wastes—and not by flushing them.)

The first low-flush toilets didn't work very well, partly because toilet manufacturers initially devoted more energy to griping about the law than to developing good new products. Later models have worked much better, although some users complain that even the newest toilets require so much re-flushing that any reduction in water use must be negligible. Studies of actual water use, however, have shown that low-flush toilets really do reduce water consumption, by a considerable amount. (Users of old-fashioned high-volume toilets were multiple flushers, too.) Government surveys also show that most people are happy with them. Grumpy dissidents sometimes import contraband toilets from countries where high-volume flushing hasn't been outlawed—a toilet I used during a recent trip to Scotland must have used a hundred gallons per use—but cutting back is good for all. Switching from 3.5-gallon to 1.6-gallon models can cut household water bills by a quarter, saving hundreds of dollars over the life of a single toilet. Using low-flush toilets also conserves public water supplies, reduces the energy used by water utilities and waste treatment plants (and well owners), and extends the life of water-related civic infrastructure, among other beneficial environmental effects.

Most residential low-flush toilets operate by gravity, in pretty much the same way those old Crapper models did, although they do so far more efficiently. When you push the flush lever, a chain inside the tank lifts a hinged flapper or ball cock covering an outlet at the bottom of the tank, allowing 1.6 gallons of water, more or less, to run into the bowl. The short drop from the tank to the bowl creates the water pressure needed to scour everything away, at least in theory. As the tank empties, water from the bowl begins to move through the trap, initiating a siphon effect that pulls the contents of the bowl into the waste line and out of local consciousness. At the end of the flush, the flapper falls back over the outlet at the bottom of the tank, which then refills. When the water reaches the prescribed level, the intake valve closes, and the toilet is ready to be flushed again.

The tank of every gravity toilet also contains an overflow tube, which stands vertically on the bottom of the tank and serves as an emergency drain in the event that the water rises higher than it's supposed to. It does this by allowing any excess to flow into the toilet bowl, to which it is connected, rather than onto your bathroom floor. A much smaller plastic tube, called the refill tube, directs a slender stream of water into the top of the overflow tube

as the tank is replenished. Amateur plumbers are often mystified
by this arrangement, because they don't understand how the
water level inside the tank can rise so quickly when so little water
is being added—or how it can rise at all when the new water
seems to be going straight into the emergency drain. The answer
is that the stream from the refill tube doesn't refill the tank; it
tops off the bowl. The water that refills the tank enters it through
several larger, less visible openings, down near the bottom of the
intake valve.

Most gravity-operated low-flush toilets actually hold more
than 1.6 gallons of water in their tank, either because they were
adapted from older designs or because the weight of the extra
water is needed to create sufficient force to clean the bowl. Different models employ different means of preventing the extra
water from leaving the tank. In some, the flapper or ball cock
seals off the outlet before the tank has fully emptied; in others, a
plastic barrier holds back some of the water on every flush. In still
others—including those that plumbers or clever homeowners
have modified to make them less stingy than they are supposed
to be—the water is simply used.

Not all low-flush residential toilets depend on gravity. Some
use compressed air or an electric pump. If you remove the lid on
the tank of one of these toilets—which are usually referred to as
"pressure-assisted" if they employ compressed air and "power-
assisted" if they have a motor—you won't find most of the mechanical viscera you're used to seeing in a toilet, and you
probably won't see any water. Pressure-assisted toilets contain a
sealed tank with an air-filled bladder inside; this bladder becomes
pressurized as water from the household supply line enters the
tank. (These toilets are a poor choice in a house where water
pressure is low or inconsistent.) Upon flushing, the bladder gives
the stored water an extra boost toward the bowl, inaugurating an
event that the toilet manufacturer American Standard calls "a
powerful 'push-through' flush." Power-assisted toilets use an electric pump rather than a pressure tank. Both kinds are usually
more expensive than gravity toilets, and both sometimes startle
first-time users, and even second-time users, because they are
noisier. On the positive side, non-gravity toilets may be less likely

to require multiple flushes, and the exteriors of the tanks of pressure-assisted toilets are less prone to condensation during humid weather because the cool water inside them is isolated from the tank's porcelain shell.

Condensation is a common problem with toilet tanks. Water vapor in the air condenses on the cool outer surface of the tank, then drips to the floor, where it's often mistaken for evidence of a leak. Sometimes the opposite happens, too. Shortly after toilets were installed in the cabin, a puddle formed on the floor behind one of them, and I assumed that the water must be condensation. But then the plumber found a small hole in the porcelain—a leak!—and swapped the toilet for a new one, under warranty. Since condensation and leaks produce identical negative effects—mold growth, rotting woodwork, loosened floor tiles—both need to be addressed. The easiest solution to condensation is to buy toilets with insulated tanks. A somewhat more complicated approach is to add hot water to each toilet's supply line by having the plumber add a device called a mixing valve. Warming the water warms the outer surface of the tank, raising its temperature above the bathroom's dew point. As an interim solution, you can keep a mop and bucket in the bathroom.

When a toilet that has been in place for a while begins to leak, the most likely culprit is the opening around one of the bolts that hold the tank to the bowl. (You would think that the people who design toilets would have eliminated this vulnerability years ago—a water tank with *holes* in it?) Each bolt hole is protected by a rubber gasket, but if the gasket or the bolt deteriorates, the water in the tank escapes onto the floor. This happened in our house not long ago. On my way downstairs one morning, I took a detour into my kids' bathroom to turn off the light and noticed that the joint between two of the vinyl-composition floor tiles looked funny. I knelt on the floor, pressed the tiles with my hands, and watched water ooze up between them. Just a few days before, I had (fatally) said to myself, "Gee, it's been quite a while since we had a two- or three-unit home-repair emergency around here. Maybe this place is finally getting its act together!" Now I noticed that there was also water on the floor near the wall, and that all the tiles within a two- or three-foot radius of the toilet looked peculiar. I picked at the edge of one tile and discovered that I could easily pull it free from the plywood underlayment, revealing a film of water and deteriorated latex mastic underneath. I lifted more tiles, which came free as readily as if they hadn't been stuck down at all, and found water everywhere. (I also discovered some unrelated but far more severe water damage, right next to the tub, where water dripping from freshly showered teens over a period of several years had worked its way past my inadequate caulk job and created a door-mat-size rot zone in the plywood.) Since the toilet was situated at the epicenter of the puddle, I concentrated my investigative efforts there, and soon noticed that water was dripping steadily from the end of one of the bolts holding the tank to the bowl.

I stuck a saucepan under the drip and called the plumber, who had visited us just the day before, for the first time in more than a year, to give our oil burner its annual cleaning. He came over a half-hour later and found that one of the tank's gaskets was shot and that, furthermore, its bolt had partially disintegrated—probably a victim of our well water, whose ultimate source is the acid rain that bathes New England. He disconnected the toilet, bailed the water from its bowl, and moved the whole thing into the bathtub, where it would spend the next month while I waited for the local tile man to find room in his busy schedule. Seeing that toilet sitting forlornly in the tub week after week gave me a little pang of nostalgia, because it reminded me of one of my very first renovation projects, almost twenty years before, during which our downstairs toilet spent a couple of months sitting in our yard, right next to the back door. At around the same time, friends of ours kept a non-functioning toilet in their dining room for a similar reason.

About a month after the kids' toilet self-destructed, I noticed that one of the toilets in the cabin would make an odd whooshing sound every five or ten minutes. After anxiously attempting to ignore the sound for several weeks, I pulled a chair into the bathroom, removed the top of the toilet's tank, emptied my mind of extraneous thoughts, and searched for clues. Eventually, I realized that water was steadily trickling into the bowl—I could see a shimmer on the porcelain and tiny ripples in the water—and I deduced that water from the tank was slowly, steadily leaking into the bowl, probably through the outlet valve. Whenever the water level in the tank had fallen by a half-inch or so, the tank would re-fill itself; that was the whooshing sound I had been hearing and ignoring.

I called a plumber, who, after studying the toilet, told me that the rubber flapper at the bottom of the tank had deteriorated so that it was no longer forming a tight seal against the valve. He also pointed out that the metal arm connected to the flush valve was severely corroded. He replaced the flapper and asked me if I had been using those in-tank chlorine tablets, which are sup-posed to clean your toilet every time you flush. I said that I had placed one such tablet in each of the cabin's toilet tanks a year or two before but had then forgotten to replace them. He said that the concentrated chlorine in even one tablet could do terrible damage to the innards of a toilet, and that I should never use them again. I said that I had thought automatic cleaning would be a good idea for the cabin, where the toilets sometimes went for a week without being used, and he said that infrequent flush-ing made the tablets even more corrosive, because it allowed the chlorine to build up. He replaced the flappers in the other two toilets as well, and I promised him that I would never use toilet-cleaning tablets again.

Dealing with these and other toilet difficulties over the years has often made me think fondly of the toilets in the apartments of several of Ann's and my old friends in New York—toilets that didn't have gravity tanks, pressure tanks, pumps, tank bolts, or rubber gaskets. Those toilets were flush-valve, or "flushometer," toilets—the kind you often see in large buildings and public rest-rooms. They had no tank at all, just a shiny chrome-plated valve with a toggle-like flush lever on the side. Flushometer toilets con-nect directly to a building's water supply pipes, and are therefore appealingly simple and compact. Unfortunately, though, they can seldom be used in ordinary residences, because they require more water pressure than most household systems can produce. Flushometer toilets work best in tall buildings, in which water supply pipes are fed from a storage tank on the roof, the drop from which greatly increases the pressure, although even in such buildings they sometimes work noticeably less well on the top floor than they do closer to the ground.

WHEN THE TIME came for Ann and me to buy toilets for the newly renovated bathrooms in our house and, later, for the brand-new bathrooms in the cabin, we discovered that we had a discouragingly extensive variety to choose from. The idea that a toilet or any other bathroom fixture could pose a shopping conundrum would have surprised people in our grandparents' generation, and ought to disturb people in ours. Thirty or forty years ago, almost everybody's toilet looked pretty much like everybody else's. Even jet-setters who owned such super-modern luxuries as electric carving knives and princess telephones seldom got very ambitious about their potties. The toilets in the house I grew up in were exactly like the toilets in the houses of almost all of my friends, and the four bolts that held each one to the floor were covered by the same semi-mysterious bullet-shaped domes of porcelain. To people in my parents' and grandparents' generations, renovating a bathroom seldom meant anything more ostentatious than buying new curtains and towels.

Nowadays, if you're of a mind to, you can spend almost anything on a toilet. There are ridiculously many shapes and styles and colors and sizes and technologies. You can have a heated seat, a padded seat, a built-in water sprayer, an air drier, an air purifier, a remote control. You can import a Japanese toilet that generates its own white noise, whose purpose is to give you the illusion that no one can hear what you are doing. You can buy a ten-thousand-dollar toilet that looks like a throne and plays a French song called *Le Bon Roi Dagobert* when you lift the lid. You can do what Ben Affleck did for his then girlfriend Jennifer Lopez, in 2003, and spend $105,000 for a toilet seat into which rubies, sapphires, pearls, and a diamond have been embedded (and then covered with plastic, for sitting comfort).

For Ann and me, the one thing that turned out to be tough to do was to find decent modern toilets and other fixtures that didn't seem like major decorating statements or like expressions of social anxieties—fixtures that were functional and reliable yet were sufficiently unadorned to satisfy our nostalgia for the no-nonsense bathroom equipment of the past. For our house we eventually settled on a Kohler model called "Memoirs Toilet With Stately Design." Ordinarily, a name like that would make me want to run in the other direction, but I liked the toilet itself well enough, and I greatly preferred its lines to those of the similar but, to my mind, excessively curvaceous "Memoirs Toilet With Classic Design." The toilets we bought also had what I now consider to be a compulsory feature: a perfectly flat tank cover, from which things like Kleenex boxes and extra rolls of toilet paper won't slide off. In fact, all appliances should be designed so that things can be piled on top of them. My desktop computer printer has a gracefully curved top that makes the printer useless as a storage surface—a serious design flaw, given the way I use my desk.

THE FIRST TIME I used Ann's and my Memoirs Toilet With Stately Design, I realized that I had a problem. Pushing the flush lever on the toilet caused the bowl to begin flushing normally, but after a couple of seconds there was a *thunk* inside the tank— the sound of the flapper falling back onto the outlet valve—and the bowl stopped emptying, or slowed so much that it might as well have stopped emptying. Even worse, flushing the toilet in our bathroom caused some of the water in the toilet in the kids' bathroom, right next door, to be pulled down the drain or to slosh around—on one occasion so violently that it splashed right out of the bowl. Flushing the kids' toilet caused the same pulling and sloshing in our toilet, and the rinse cycle of the washing machine, which was in a little room next to the kids' bathroom, had a similar effect on both toilets. These same activities also produced a gurgling sound in the drains of the bathroom sinks. The plumber and I quickly decided that there must be a problem somewhere in the ventilation of my house's plumbing system.

When you flush a toilet, brush your teeth, or take a shower, waste water moves down a drain, through a trap, and along a waste line until it feeds into a large, vertical pipe, called the soil stack. The soil stack runs straight down into the basement, where it is connected to another large pipe, a nearly horizontal one called the main drain. The main drain runs out of the house and into a public sewer line or (in the case of country bumpkins like me) a septic tank. The soil stack also runs straight up, and through the roof; its upper portion is known as the stack vent. Viewed from the yard a stack vent looks like a little round chimney poking through the roof. Almost every building with plumbing in it has at least one.

A stack vent has two important functions. The first is to provide an escape route for gases produced during the decomposition of excrement—mostly methane, which is also the main constituent of natural gas. Methane is odorless; the smell we associate with sewer gas is the smell of hydrogen sulfide, another byproduct of the decomposition of wastes. (The smell we associate with the natural gas or propane we use in our homes is that of a standard chemical odorant that is added to gas products to make leaks detectable.) Because a stack vent's opening is way up on the roof, the gases that constantly pass through it usually do so without attracting the notice of anyone living below. If the roof is low, however, or if the wind is blowing in the wrong direction, the odor may be conspicuous from time to time—or even most of the time. A friend of mine once caught a whiff of the gases escaping from his stack vent and, in a mild panic, called a plumber. The plumber explained where the odor was coming from, and assured my friend that there was no danger. The plumber said that he might be able to alleviate the problem somewhat by extending the height of the vent. Alternatively, he said, my friend could do what he himself did: learn to like the smell. (Gases from the stack vent at the cabin occasionally waft down over the front step. I am teaching myself to like the smell.)

Some early plumbers, guided by a partial understanding of the need for ventilation, connected plumbing vents to existing fireplace flues, thereby eliminating the necessity of cutting a hole in the roof but creating a fire hazard. In those days, even properly configured ventilation systems were prone to leak. A common way to identify breaches was to pour oil of peppermint into the stack vent, plug up the top, and walk around the house sniffing. A somewhat similar technique is used today to detect breaks in aging municipal sewer lines: non-toxic smoke is blown into the system, and then workers look for telltale plumes rising from yards, sidewalk cracks, manhole covers, and household roof gutters (whose drain pipes are sometimes connected, improperly, to sanitary sewers).

The second important function of a stack vent is to equalize air pressure inside the waste pipes. Water would not flow down household drains, or would do so only sluggishly, if plumbing networks were entirely enclosed, with no openings to the atmosphere. To understand why, consider the difficulty of removing dog food from a can. If you remove one end of the can with a can opener and then turn the can upside down, the dog food will stay where it is, even though gravity is pulling it toward the dog's dish. The reason is that the sealed top of the can prevents the weight of the atmosphere—air pressure—from pushing down on the top of the column of dog food. This allows the force of the atmosphere on the open end of the can to hold the column in place. Another way of describing the same phenomenon is to say that the dog food, as it is pulled down by gravity, creates a partial vacuum between itself and the unopened end of the can, and the vacuum keeps the dog food from falling. To make the dog food slide into the bowl with a satisfying slurp, all you have to do is make a small hole in the closed end of the can. Doing so equalizes the air pressure on both ends of the column of dog food—destroys the vacuum—and allows gravity to pull the dog food free. The same force is evident when you place a soda straw in a glass of water, press a finger over the top of the straw, and lift the straw from the glass, bringing a column of water with it.

To see plumbing's version of the pressure-equalization principle in action, you could climb onto your roof, block the top of your stack vent, then go inside and flush the toilets and turn on the taps. Drains would run slowly or not at all, and the water in all the toilet bowls would slosh around. A number of years ago, my town's elementary school inadvertently conducted exactly this experiment, when a rock, a tennis ball, some old leaves, and a dead bird all somehow became lodged in the building's vent stack, occluding it almost completely and causing the building's bathroom fixtures to go haywire. At last, a custodian correctly diagnosed the problem, then restored the system to good health by removing the foreign objects (with his hand and a metal rod). The top of the school's vent is now protected by a wire cage.

When my brand-new Kohler Memoirs Toilet With Stately Design refused to flush in the normal manner, my plumber and I both thought immediately of ventilation. The plumber was confident that the system had been designed correctly—and the building inspector had signed off on the layout before the walls were closed in—so his first idea was that there must be a blockage somewhere. Shining a flashlight down the vent stack revealed nothing, so he concluded that the blockage, if there was one, must be far down in the stack, or in a branch that he couldn't see. He consulted with another plumber, who suggested running an electric drain-cleaning machine* down the stack vent and then through all branches of the drain system. The consulting plumber guessed that a piece of construction detritus—the plastic lid of a container of caulk, perhaps, or a glob of hardened plaster—had fallen into an open drain before the toilets were installed, and had become lodged somewhere, disastrously reducing the effective diameter of a pipe. The two plumbers removed both upstairs toilets and snaked the drain cleaner's cable through all the lines. Then they put the toilets back and flushed. The problem was still there, exactly the same as it had been before.

My plumber also checked the drain line that runs between my house and the septic tank. He did this by removing the cleanout plug from the main drain, way down in the darkest corner of the basement, and removing the lid of the septic tank to admit light from the other end. "Don't use any water or flush a

---

* The electric drain-cleaning machine was invented in 1933 by Samuel Blanc, an Iowa pump salesman and former telephone lineman. Blanc's first device consisted of a one-sixth-horsepower motor from a Maytag washing machine, a long cable three-eighths of an inch in diameter, and some old roller skate wheels to which he had attached sharp blades. The cable was fed into sewage lines, and the spinning blades chewed through obstructions, including tree roots that had worked their way into the joints between sections of clay drain tile. Blanc's wife, Lettie, thought of a catchy name: Roto-Rooter. The machine was highly effective, and using it was far less expensive and disruptive than the principal alternative, digging up the yard.

toilet until I come back upstairs," he said before going down into the basement. One member of the household somehow failed to receive this message, and a minor crisis ensued. But the plumber recovered quickly, and forgave us. Upon returning, he announced, with sorrow, that the line to the septic tank, though bowed with age, was unobstructed. The problem must lie somewhere else.

From the beginning of our difficulties, I had noticed that both upstairs toilets would flush normally, or nearly normally, if I kept the flush lever depressed during the entire flush. Doing this prevented the hinged flapper from falling back across the outlet at the bottom of the tank as quickly as it was supposed to. That caused the outlet to function throughout the flush as a sort of secondary vent. (Preventing the flapper from closing was like lifting a finger from the top of a water-filled straw.) I also discovered, during a thoroughly absorbing afternoon of hypothesizing and semi-random experimentation, that I could make the toilets flush normally if I removed the threaded cleanout from the trap below the sink in the children's bathroom.*

A sink's trap is the curved section of the waste pipe below the sink's bowl. It looks a little like the letter P lying on its side, and for that reason is known as a P-trap. The function of a sink trap, like the function of the trap built into a toilet, is to retain a plug of water in the waste line at all times, so that sewer gases rising from below can't escape into the house. The sink traps in old houses are often shaped more like a supine S than a supine P and are therefore known as S-traps. S-traps are less reliable than P-traps, because they drain straight down through the floor rather than horizontally into a vertical waste pipe inside the wall—a configuration that makes it easier for the plug of water to

---

* Although a waste-pipe cleanout is obviously meant to be used for cleaning out a drain, it is both too small and too inconveniently situated to be very useful for that purpose. Unscrewing the entire trap (with your hand, while wearing a rubber glove to improve your grip) is usually a more effective approach. After cleaning the removed trap, you can attack both ends of the waste line with your finger, a spoon, a chopstick, a straightened wire hanger, and a small plumbing snake—the five tools I used in succession during a recent attack on a slow-moving drain at the cabin.

be siphoned out of the trap during use, defeating the trap's purpose. Modern building codes forbid the use of S-traps in new
construction.

Removing the cleanout from the trap from the kids' sink
eliminated the water seal in the sink's waste pipe, thereby allowing the waste pipe to act as an additional vent. This wasn't a permanent solution, obviously, but it did prove that the house's
plumbing system needed more venting. What to do? My first
thought was to rip open a wall in some strategic location, remove
a section of the existing waste line, splice an additional vent pipe
into the system somehow, and run the new vent through a hole in
the roof—a hole that I myself would be more than happy to cut,
using a brand-new power tool that I would be more than happy
to buy. The plumber, while acknowledging that doing this might
solve the problem, suggested that we first try something less dramatic and expensive. Somewhat reluctantly—I had already
picked out a wall to demolish, as well as a new reciprocating
saw—I agreed.

The plumber's suggestion was that we add a device called an
air admittance valve, or AAV, to the waste line under one of the
sinks. This valve, which was invented in the early seventies by a
Swedish engineer, is a one-way plumbing vent. When water runs
down a waste line to which an AAV has been attached, negative
pressure in the line causes a valve inside the AAV to open, allowing air to be drawn in. The valve remains open until the pressure
in the pipe has returned to equilibrium with the atmosphere.
Then it snaps shut so that sewer gases can't escape. Because the
valve operates in one direction only, AAVs can be installed indoors—under a sink, say, or in an attic. They are permitted by
most codes, and can be used to create plumbing systems with no
external venting and (therefore) with fewer leak-prone roof pen-
etrations. Mobile homes sometimes have AAVs instead of external vents. The plumbing system at Atlanta's major-league
ballpark, Turner Field, which was built for the 1996 Summer
Olympics, includes more than two thousand AAVs. The devices
can also be used to improve malfunctioning systems, like mine.

The plumber installed my AAV under the sink in the children's bathroom. The device is cylindrical, made of black plastic,

and just two inches in diameter and a few inches tall. It is mounted at the top of a foot-tall section of vertical drain pipe, which is connected to the sink's waste line on the far side of the trap. The whole thing, including connections, takes up about as much room as a four-pack of Charmin. The valve makes a gentle whirring noise whenever a toilet in either bathroom is flushed—a sound that I have taught myself to like.

Installing the AAV stopped the sloshing in my toilets, and it prevented water from being siphoned out of the sink traps. But to get full, effective flushes with the two upstairs toilets, we still needed to hold down the lever for the duration. I asked the plumber why this was so, and he explained that the intake vent on the AAV was smaller in diameter than the sink's cleanout valve, the temporary removal of which, during my "investigative" phase, had caused the problem to go away entirely. We presumably could have put everything entirely to rights by installing a larger AAV in a different location (there wasn't enough room in this particular vanity), or by installing a second AAV on another sink. In the end, though, I decided that the inconvenience was a minor one, and not worth sacrificing under-sink storage space for.

Holding down the flush lever became automatic with me and the other members of my family. (The Kohler Memoirs toilet in the downstairs bathroom—which was the one most likely to be used by guests—had always flushed normally.) Nevertheless, the imposition bothered me, and, to a mildly pathological extent, I became envious of people whose toilets didn't require extra help. I felt especially resentful whenever I stayed in a crummy motel room whose toilet worked better than my toilets at home. Conversely, my heart leaped whenever I discovered a toilet whose handle also had to be held down, as I sometimes did, or when a friend confessed that his house had a problem similar to mine.

Well, I don't feel that way anymore. While I was writing the chapter you are reading, I decided to open the tank on the toilet in Ann's and my bathroom, and take another close look inside. As I was studying the tank's inner workings, I suddenly had an idea. Attached to the chain that connected the flush lever to the flapper was a round plastic-foam float a little smaller than a hockey puck. The float was attached to the chain at a point about three inches above the flapper. Its function was to prevent the flapper from falling back over the outlet valve until 1.6 gallons of water, more or less, had left the tank. I realized that if I could figure out a way to move the float all the way down the chain, so that it rested directly on top of the flapper instead of three inches above it, the flapper would be held open until almost all the water in the tank was gone—the same effect I was producing by holding down the flush lever. The float was held in place by two plastic washers, which snapped onto the chain just above and below the float. Removing those washers required major contributions from my bifocals* and my fingernails, but I managed to get them off without dropping them down the outlet valve. Then I slid the float to the bottom of the chain, replaced the washers, and flushed. For the first time in five years, the toilet worked absolutely perfectly all by itself, just like the toilets in crummy motels! I quickly also changed over the kids' toilet and, for good measure, the one in the downstairs bathroom. Watching those toilets operate normally made me feel so happy and relieved that for several days I flushed them at the slightest provocation. What's this—a leaf on the floor? Into the toilet, and away!

The plumber, from the very beginning, had wondered if the problem might not be the toilets themselves. He had heard of a similar problem with Kohler Memoirs toilets in a new house not far away, and he told me that replacing them with toilets from a different manufacturer had solved the problems there. The new toilets had larger "trapways" than the malfunctioning toilets. A toilet's trapway is the curving channel that leads from the bowl to the waste pipe. In my Memoirs toilets, he told me, the trapway is just two inches in diameter; in the replacement toilets, the trapway was three inches. Small trapways are a necessary feature of most low-flush toilets, because the small opening keeps the water

---

* I hate my bifocals, and I am still learning to live with them. I have discovered a useful trick with them, though. If I'm working on something above my head—trying to unscrew the base of a broken light bulb, say, or changing the battery in a smoke alarm— I turn my bifocals upside down, so that the reading part of the lens is on top.

swirling in the bowl a little longer, and makes it easier to create a forceful siphon effect with less flush volume. (Before 1994, toilets often had four-inch trapways—big enough to accommodate a baseball.)

What's usually true of airplane crashes is also usually true of misbehaving houses: disasters seldom have a single cause. Most big problems arise from a combination of factors, or are the result of a sequence of failures, mistakes, or poor decisions. My flushing problem most likely had a compound explanation: the size of the trapways, plus the amount of ventilation, plus the configuration of the waste pipes, plus maybe even the sag of the waste line.

I'm sure that I, too, contributed—or at least prolonged the tortuous process by which we eventually arrived at a completely satisfactory solution. A little learning truly is a dangerous thing. Like many reasonably ambitious do-it-yourselfers, I have managed to acquire a certain amount of knowledge about home construction, maintenance, and repair. Sometimes that knowledge is useful, as it was the day I correctly deduced that lowering the Styrofoam floats in the tanks of the toilets would make the toilets flush properly. Often, though, I just make things worse, as when I come up with dumb ideas that sound enough like smart ideas to disrupt the orderly ratiocination of an experienced professional.

My most frequent victim in this regard is my regular plumber. The major elements of my house's plumbing and heating systems, which he superintends, are out in the open, where I can see them, and they misbehave frequently enough to have given me many opportunities to study them. By the time the plumber arrives to repair something that has gone wrong, I often have made a preliminary diagnosis, which I am eager to share with him. Sometimes, my diagnosis is correct. More often, though, my ideas merely sound as though they might conceivably be correct—enough so that he can't ignore me entirely and go about his business, as he would if his wife were the one making the suggestions. I am especially dangerous if I have supplemented my half-understanding of the problem with an hour or two spent looking up symptoms on Google.

This happened memorably with a very peculiar, machine-gun-like banging that our heating pipes suddenly developed one winter. I knew enough about heating systems to realize that the sound—which was sufficiently loud to wake up me and my daughter, but not to wake up Ann or my son—wasn't merely the intermittent clicking and clanking caused by the ordinary expansion and contraction of metal pipes as they warm up and cool off. Studying the problem over the course of several afternoons, I noticed that the noise was mainly noticeable in the rooms directly above the furnace; that it was louder on the second and third floors than on the first; that it could scarcely be heard at all in the basement, and not at all right next to the furnace; that it began not when the oil burner kicked on but shortly afterward; that it continued briefly after the oil burner had shut off; and that while it was going on several heating pipes attached to the ceiling near the furnace shook visibly. I decided, with some help from the Internet, that one of the heating system's circulators—the pump-like devices that move hot water through the radiator pipes—was vibrating at a frequency that was causing pipes elsewhere in the house to vibrate sympathetically, and at amplified levels. Resonance of this kind can be an extraordinarily powerful force; it's the reason why marching soldiers break step before crossing a bridge. When I described my hypothesis to the plumber, I used a lot of big words that I didn't understand, including *harmonic, oscillation,* and *amplitude.* As a result, the plumber and his assistant had no choice but to spend a lot of time following my suggestion that they brace and dampen all the vibrating heating pipes in my basement with various straps and hangers. After they left, I added even more straps and hangers, which I had bought at the hardware store the day before and hadn't told them about.

Well, all that strapping and hanging had no effect whatsoever—as I gradually realized after a brief period during which I convinced myself that the banging was now quieter than before. I called the plumber back and told him that the logical next step would probably be to replace the offending circulator, which I had identified beyond a reasonable doubt by gently placing my fingertips on all the circulators in turn while wearing heavy rubber gloves (to keep my fingertips from being burned).

The plumber considered this. Then he said that before spending any more of my money he would like to try an idea of his own, which was to add more air to the heating system's fourteen-gallon expansion tank—a gray metal cylinder connected to one of the main heating pipes, near the boiler. Water expands when it's heated. If it's heated within a closed system, such as a hot-water heating loop, the force of its expansion presses against the pipes and, under certain circumstances, causes them to shake around. To keep this (or worse) from happening, most closed hot water systems are connected to a pressurized, air-filled reservoir that acts as a relief valve when the expanding water has nowhere else to go. The plumber used a tire gauge to check the pressure in my expansion tank, and found it to be close to zero. He then used a bicycle pump to add more air, and the problem went away for good.

———

AFTER THE TOILET, the modern invention for which I am the most grateful is probably the shower. During a ten-day reporting assignment in northern Africa in 2000, I was reminded, not for the first time, that beginning (and sometimes also ending) the day by loitering under a torrent of hot water is a luxury undreamed of in most of the rest of the world. I have often had similar thoughts while traveling in Europe. After playing fifty-four holes of golf one day during a trip to Scotland a decade ago, I discovered that my new hotel room didn't have a shower, just a shallow plastic tub into which a leaky tap dribbled tepid water and dandruff-size flakes of rust. The water in the tub was cold by the time it was deep enough to cover my Advil-depleted legs. The hotel was charming in every other respect—it was a converted country house, with ancient gardens and ivy-covered walls—but at that point I happily would have traded it for a Motel 6.

Good showers rank up there with caffeine, martinis, and Prozac as restorers of human equilibrium, and we are extremely fortunate to have them. One morning a couple of summers ago, I rode my bike past twenty or so members of a girls' high school cross-country team, who were running in the opposite direction. Just after I passed them, I rode through a cloud of shampoo fragrance. This is what I love about America, I thought: our healthy, confident young people and their clean, clean hair.

Three particular showers stand out in my personal experience. The most extravagantly wasteful (and also, therefore, probably the most wonderful) was a shower in the locker room of a private golf club, which I visited as a guest. The showerhead was the size of a manhole cover. It was mounted directly overhead, and its spray was so intense that a plumber had had to enlarge the drain opening in the floor to accommodate the outflow. All the plumbing, in fact, was oversized; the supply pipes, which were exposed, looked less like tubing than like air-conditioning ducts. Each time I turned the thing on, I worried that boats in neighboring counties must be in danger of running aground. The experience was morally inexcusable—less like bathing than like standing in a carwash—but also unforgettable.

Equally memorable, though at the other end of the spectrum of waste, was an outdoor shower at a beach house owned by a friend. The showerhead was held to the side of his house by a rusty iron loop, and it was fed by fifty feet of garden hose, which lay loosely coiled on the ground. If you wanted a warm shower, you had to wait for a sunny day, because there was no water heater at the other end of the hose. The warmth lasted exactly as long as fifty linear feet of hose water took to work its way through the showerhead—not long enough, in other words, to both wash and rinse your hair. But scarcity made that heat seem precious, and while you waited for the inevitable blast of cold you could gaze at the ocean. (Also, there was a regular shower inside the house.)

My favorite shower at the moment happens to be the one I use every morning. It's in Ann's and my bathroom, and it could probably be considered a small room of its own. (We may have modeled it unconsciously on communal gym-class showers in high school.) It's so big that it doesn't require a shower curtain or a door; you just walk in, hang your towel on a hook, and turn on the water. Your knees and elbows don't bang against the sides when you turn around, and you never discover, upon stepping out, that for the past fifteen minutes water has been sluicing down the side of the curtain and onto the bathroom floor. The walls and ceiling of that shower are covered with four-inch white ceramic tiles; the floor is covered with two-and-a-half-inch gray slate tiles. The entire bathroom is heated by a radiant system that runs under the subfloor, so the shower is never icy when you step into it. There's a triangular seat in one corner of the shower which is made from an inch-thick slab of slate set into the wall—a nice place to sit, except that Ann and I use it only for storing our extensive and seemingly self-replicating collection of hair-care products.

Our daughter's collection is far larger, of course. The tub in the bathroom that she shares with her brother when she's in residence has an extra-wide ledge on the long side next to the wall—a useful feature for tub users of any age—but even that isn't capacious enough to contain all her soaps and shampoos and conditioners and rinses and gels. When she went to college, she took her collection with her, and her four roommates took theirs. Each girl had her own hair dryer, too, and all five were plugged into a single power strip, which was connected to an outlet in the hall.

Ann's and my walk-in shower contains many square feet of tile and therefore many linear feet of grout lines. I worried, before the shower was built, that keeping everything clean and mildew-free would be difficult, but it hasn't been a problem. The size of the shower and the absence of a curtain allow air to circulate freely, and I am scrupulous about running the bathroom's two exhaust fans—one in the shower itself and the other just outside it. Most people, if they use their bathroom exhaust fans at all, use them only while a shower is actually running, but to work properly an exhaust fan needs to be kept on until all the excess water vapor in the room has been removed—sometimes a good five or ten minutes after the water has been shut off. Aggressive use of bathroom exhaust fans reduces toilet-tank condensation, helps control mildew, keeps towels fresher, prevents ice from forming on the inside surfaces of storm windows in the winter—and makes paint on the *outside* of the house last longer, since the vents allow water vapor to leave the house without pushing its way through painted siding.

For the cabin, I wanted showers that were even easier to take care of. I chose an unadorned one-piece acrylic shower module for the downstairs bathroom and an unadorned one-piece acrylic shower-and-bathtub module for the upstairs bathroom. Each module is a seamless, leak-proof enclosure with no grout lines and no joints that have to be caulked. They didn't cost very much and they aren't fancy, but they don't make me feel poor when I use them and they clean up with Windex. If people cared only about convenience, they would never use anything else.

THE LAST TEN PERCENT

THE SUMMER AFTER our son was born, Ann and I hired Leah Chapin, the eleven-year-old daughter of friends, to work for us a few hours each week as a sort of junior mother's helper and as a relief playmate for our daughter, who was four years old and was still recovering from the unpleasant shock of no longer being an only child. Leah ended up working for us for twelve summers, with steadily increasing hours and responsibilities. Every hour that Leah was on the premises was an extra hour that Ann or I could spend working, and as long as one of us managed to earn more than we were paying her we came out ahead. During Leah's last summers with us, both of our kids were too old to need a babysitter but were the right age to appreciate having an unofficially adopted older sister with a driver's license who was always happy to take them to the library, the lake, a friend's house, or the mall. When Leah graduated from college, got a real job, and married the guy she had been dating since high school, we were all deeply heartbroken, although we pretended to be thrilled for her, of course. Last year, when she called to say that she was pregnant, my daughter, who was a junior in college, said, "I've been waiting for this phone call since I was six years old!"

After Leah had spent two summers working for us, I suddenly thought: why not a father's helper? Having two young children on the premises had made it difficult for me to keep up with our slowly self-destructing old house, and we now faced several pressing maintenance issues that could no longer be deferred. The paint on the outside of our house had deteriorated until it needed to be stripped down to bare wood, the gutters were a mess, and the yard was overgrown, among a great many other things. Hiring professionals to deal with these problems would have cost a fortune; besides, I knew from talking to friends that all the good local housepainters were booked for months, if not years, into the future. Given enough time, I could have handled everything myself, but I didn't have enough time.

My solution was to hire a home-improvement Leah—a college kid named Will Hardee, also the child of friends, who worked for us eight hours a day, five days a week, for two summers. I paid Will more than he would have earned at a fast-food restaurant, yet the cost of employing him, including Social Security contributions, was a fraction of what I would have had to pay at retail for the many services he ably performed. And we liked having him around. His second day on the job, my daughter, who was then six years old, took him a plate full of crackers and an orange diet soda, as a snack. A few minutes later, her brother, who was three, took him a blueberry Pop-Tart and another orange diet soda. Will cheerfully ate all the crackers and the Pop-Tart and drank both cans of soda, and the children were very, very pleased.

Before Will came to work, I made a long list of tasks that I hoped he would be able to accomplish that summer. On his first day at work, I explained the first chore: disassembling and removing the nonfunctioning stove in the old apartment kitchen on the third floor. I had been meaning to get rid of the stove for a couple of years, but had always been intimidated by the thought of trying to move it down two flights of stairs without scraping the walls or the floors. Taking it apart seemed like a reasonable approach—it was held together with what looked like several hundred screws and bolts—and I knew that if it were in pieces the trash collector would probably be willing to haul it away without complaining or charging me extra. I gave Will my tool box and returned to my office, figuring that he'd be busy at least until lunch.

Half an hour later, he knocked on my door. "What's next?" he asked. I looked out the window, saw a neat pile of stove parts at the end of the driveway, and realized with a shock that my list of chores wasn't going to last the summer. In fact, I worried briefly that it might not last the rest of the day.

Over the following few weeks, Will briskly tackled projects that I'd been putting off since we moved in. He cleaned out the third floor, the basement, and the garage; hauled junk to the dump; meticulously scoured the grubby-looking grout in the downstairs bathroom; cut down all the thorny, rapaciously weed-like locust saplings that were constantly appearing around the edges of the yard; moved a pile of old bricks from one edge of the yard to another; and cleaned the gutters. Will also mowed the lawn each week, weeded the pachysandra, washed and detailed the cars, ran errands, went grocery shopping, kept an eye on the kids for an hour one day when I had an appointment in town, and generally made himself extraordinarily useful.

And he earned his salary many times over. His biggest contributions were two major projects that I had been dreading above all others. The more time-consuming of these two was stripping the house of most of its exterior paint, which was so thoroughly alligatored that the surface resembled the grid-like *craquelure* of a fifteenth-century Flemish panel painting. Yet in most places the fractured paint still adhered so firmly to the underlying clapboards that removing it required concentrated effort. Will's main instrument of attack was an electric paint-stripping tool called a heat plate, which consists of a rectangular radiant heating element attached to a foot-long handle—a depressingly familiar item among the owners of old houses. Will would hold the hot surface an inch or two above a clapboard until the paint had begun to soften, then use a putty knife to scrape away the bubbly goo before it could re-harden. The job was tedious, hot, and very, very slow; hiring professional painters to do it would have cost a multiple of Will's entire salary for both summers. Will made the job tolerable to himself by doing it a little at a time and by ignoring it altogether on the hottest days. When he had finished a section, I would take a few hours off from my own work to sand, prime, and paint the freshly bared surface. In this piecemeal manner, we eventually repainted the entire house.

Piecemeal may actually be the ideal way to paint a house, if you are willing to do the work yourself and don't mind forgoing the exhilaration that comes from seeing a huge, expensive project completed all at once. A common homeowner's rule of thumb is that the outside of a house will need to be repainted every seven to ten years, but those numbers are just averages, if they're even that. (There's no point in repainting the interior of a house until the children have gone to college.) The parts of a house deteriorate at varying speeds, depending on the intensity of their exposure to malevolent forces, mainly sunlight, water, water vapor, dirt, and various life forms. Most houses have at least a few small exterior areas that should be repainted every two or three years, and a few other areas—sometimes large ones—that could be left alone for twenty.

The most efficient approach, if your home-improvement metabolism can tolerate it, is to repaint a little at a time, and only as problems begin to emerge.* Window sills usually peel before siding does, mostly because the sun's rays strike them less obliquely and because water is more likely to stand on them for long periods. The walls outside kitchens and bathrooms—which are the rooms where domestic water use is concentrated—are often quicker than other surfaces to show damage caused by moisture escaping from inside. Siding shaded by vegetation is especially vulnerable to attack by mildew and mold, as is siding that is close to the ground or adjacent to a low-pitch roof. If you repaint your house in its entirety on a regular, unvarying schedule, you will always be too late in attacking the worst parts and too early in attacking the rest.

Many home-improvement challenges become more tractable if you attack them incrementally. When Ann and I moved into our house, we faced so many repair and renovation issues that I sometimes worried we would never ever find our way through them. The solution was to ignore the big picture and simply start somewhere, anywhere. Accomplish something tangible, then

---

* This, incidentally, is the way that the fastidious greenkeepers at Augusta National Golf Club keep their course immaculately green and free of weeds. The club's superintendent, Brad Owen (no relation), told me that his crew inspects the turf continually and deals with trouble only when they see it, rather than trying to anticipate and prevent every conceivable ill. "We don't fix a problem until it appears," he said.

move on to something else—that's the way to handle a job that seems too big to even start. For quite some time, I've understood that if I could force myself to spend five minutes a day straightening up my office I'd soon stop having to wade through piles of old newspapers to get to my computer. I gain nothing from my laziness; the clutter is so thick that I waste more than five minutes a day searching for stamps, scissors, envelopes, a stapler—any of which I would be able to find easily if I could just see the surface of my desk, or the surface of the floor. My office is a mess because I, like most people, ignore chronic problems until they've become acute. Six months or a year from now, the condition of my work environment will finally have deteriorated to the point where it will strike even me as intolerable, and I'll have to spend two or three full days reorganizing my shelves and hauling loads of trash out to the garage. The result will be so refreshing that I will promise myself never to let the mess get out of hand again. But within a day or two I'll be back to my old bad habits.

Early in our marriage, Ann and I decided to implement a daily thirty-minute chore period, during which each of us would clean out a closet, wash the living room windows, rearrange the contents of a kitchen cabinet, un-gunk the trap in the bathroom sink, add four new pages to the scrapbook, or make some other real but painlessly incremental contribution to the orderliness of our lives. (Regular recurring tasks, like paying bills and making dinner, didn't count, because they had to be done anyway.) The arithmetic behind this system was truly compelling: in a week, two people working a half hour a day contribute seven hours of productive labor—the equivalent of employing an extremely conscientious one-day-a-week helper—without feeling unduly put upon. Our efforts were individually insignificant, but they accumulated like compound interest, and after just a few days our apartment magically looked better than it had ever looked before. But then something came up, or we got bored with our youthful idealism, and we went back to being disorganized slobs.*

---

* Recently, while getting the cabin ready for a party, I discovered (and named) a useful form of indoor aerobic exercise: Attention Deficit Housecleaning. The basic idea is to

Occasionally, though, I am able to make myself take the slow, steady approach. Last year, I decided that two windows on the south side of our house (but none of the rest of the exterior) needed attention. The sills were beginning to peel, as were some of the muntins in the sashes. I spent about an hour one Sunday afternoon preparing the surfaces. I scraped away loose paint from both windows with a putty knife and a complicated-looking scraper that I had bought at the hardware store. I wasn't trying to get rid of all the old paint, or to claw deep into the bare wood; I just wanted to remove the bits that were no longer stuck tight. I then lightly sanded the exposed wood and the remaining paint, using a fine-grit sandpaper. Painters will usually tell you that the purpose of sanding is to roughen the surface you're about to paint, to give it more "tooth," but the real purpose of sanding is to remove dirt, sun-damaged wood fibers, and other materials to which paint doesn't adhere very well, and you actually want to leave the surface as smooth as possible. When you apply paint to rough, uneven surface, the finished coating ends up being thick in some places and thin in others, and these differences cause the paint to expand and contract at varying rates, creating stresses that can lead to early failure. On a window, the last paint to peel will almost always be the paint that you accidentally dripped onto the glass, which, of course, has no "tooth" at all. (The phenomenal durability of spilled paint, in comparison with the fleetingness of paint that has been applied conscientiously, is a good example of the perversity of the universe. Another example: I have trouble growing actual grass in my yard, but thick, healthy, weed-free turf sprouts all by itself in my gravel driveway and in the narrow spaces between the stones in my front walk.)

---

clean as inefficiently as possible, at high speed. When you find something under your bed that belongs in the basement (for example), you don't start a pile at the top of the stairs; you take the thing down to the basement immediately, without looking for anything else to take with it. And if you see something in the basement that belongs on the third floor, you grab it and head right back up the stairs. You can work up quite a sweat in this way, and the house shapes up very quickly because you don't waste a lot of time planning your next move. A closely related (and equally healthful) activity: Random Access Vacuuming.

After I had finished my sanding, I put on rubber gloves and washed both windows with heavily diluted bleach, to kill mildew and any other paint-antagonistic life forms that might be lurking there. Attacking mildew with bleach is extremely satisfying, because the dark, splotchy colonies disappear as you watch. I then rinsed both windows thoroughly with a garden hose. Amateur painters will sometimes skip the rinsing, figuring that any remaining bleach will act as an ongoing fungicide, but this is a bad idea. Bleach will damage the paint and the wood if you leave it in place for too long, so you need to get rid of it as soon as it has done its job. (It will also burn right through your skin; that's why you need rubber gloves.)

If I had been painting the entire house, rather than just two windows, I would have hired a local company to clean all the exterior paint at one time, using a piece of equipment called a pressure washer, which sprays water at high velocity. Pressure-washing removes not only dirt but also peeling, deteriorated paint. If you do the pressure washing yourself, with a rented unit, you need to be careful that you don't spray the water up behind your siding, creating reservoirs of moisture that may cause peeling or other problems later. This is a major issue in very old houses, like mine, in which the clapboards are nailed directly to the framing, without an intermediate layer of sheathing. The best way to use a pressure washer is from a ladder, aiming downward, so that the water runs harmlessly to the ground.

After rinsing, I left the windows alone for a few days, to give the wood time to dry completely. I didn't want to leave them alone for too long, though, because prolonged exposure to sunlight would have negated the good I had done with my sanding and cleaning. Ultraviolet light is brutal to bare wood, and the longer the wood remains uncovered the more resistant it becomes to successful painting. Painters will sometimes tell you that new wood on the exterior of a house should be allowed to "weather in" for a few months before painting, but they are incorrect. Paint sticks better to new, clean wood than it does to wood that sunlight has attacked. Before you paint wood that has been exposed for a lengthy period, you should sand any visibly UV-damaged surfaces, which typically appear gray, and wash everything down with a hose. Even if the bare wood appears clean and undamaged, a good washing will improve its ability to hold paint.

When my two windows were dry, I spent about an hour priming them. I used a high-quality exterior primer, which I had bought in the paint department of my hardware store. Primer is paint that contains relatively more of the stuff that makes paint stick and—because formulating paint is a zero-sum game—relatively less of the stuff that resists damage by the elements. Primer's purpose is to adhere powerfully to unpainted (and previously painted) surfaces, forming a stable base to which a finish coat can then be applied. Some painters, when repainting, apply primer only to patches of bare wood where old paint has been removed—a practice called "spot priming"—but the finish coat usually turns out better if you apply the primer to the existing paint as well. In fact, if you are repainting a previously painted exterior surface you should usually use primer for your first coat (assuming that you're planning to apply two or more coats overall), because the primer will create a good bridge between the old paint and the new. You should even prime "pre-primed" building materials—after first washing them to remove surface dirt and other contaminants.

The paints used in and on houses can be broadly divided into water-based paints—which include those containing latex, acrylic, and other synthetic resins—and solvent-based paints—which are usually referred to as oil paints, although all such paints today are made with alkyd resins rather old-fashioned linseed oil. There used to be a lively debate among painters about which was better, latex or oil, but very little solvent-based paint of any kind is still used today. I used to think that only alkyd enamel paints should be used on interior woodwork, but modern high-quality water-based paints create as good a finish and are much easier to use (and, especially, to clean up). The only significant residential applications for which solvent-based paints are still used are priming new wood and recoating deteriorated surfaces on which the existing paint is oil. I used a water-based primer on the windows, but if I had been painting bare wood or repainting old oil paint I probably would have used a solvent-based (alkyd) primer and then a water-based (latex or acrylic) finish coat—as many manufacturers recommend. In fact, following the manufacturer's recommendations is always the best idea. Good paint manufacturers sell paint systems that are designed to work together, and the best way to get good results is to use the combination of products they recommend.

Because most primers have a limited ability to resist damage by sunlight, you should never leave a primed exterior surface unpainted for very long. "I'll prime my house this fall and paint it in the spring" is a formula for trouble, since prolonged exposure causes primers to discolor and deteriorate, often quite rapidly. It's usually safe to leave primed exterior surfaces exposed for a few weeks, but it's best to paint them as soon as possible after the prime coat has dried completely. Water-based paints dry very fast; I was able to apply my finish coat the following day, using a flat acrylic house paint from the same manufacturer.

My entire two-window paint job, from surface preparation through finish coat, took a total of just two and a half hours, or about as much time as I might have wasted by falling asleep on the couch while watching a golf tournament on TV. Yet by dealing with those two windows I brought our house's exterior fully up to date, paint-wise, and could afford to leave the whole thing alone until at least the following year. Each individual task had been so circumscribed that I had actually enjoyed doing it; I certainly hadn't driven myself crazy, as I would have if I had waited to act until all my windows needed complete makeovers and then tried to prepare and paint all of them in a sustained burst. I'm sure that I won't have the stamina to keep up with all of our house's emerging paint problems over the next decade, and will end up, at some point, hiring professionals to repaint the whole thing—as I did half a dozen years ago, when the total paint job that Will and I did finally began to look ragged—but with a minimal investment of time I have postponed that big job by at least a year.

For the cabin, I wanted to spend as little time as possible thinking about peeling paint. I wanted an exterior that, in addition to looking appropriately rustic, would require as little ongoing maintenance as possible. For the siding I chose cedar shingles, which are expensive but long-lasting, and after Rudy,

Joe, and Mark had finished nailing them up I had a painter treat them with TWP, a highly regarded oil-based wood preservative, which I ordered online. Cedar shingles, when used as siding, will usually survive for decades all by themselves; treating them periodically with a good wood preservative can make them last indefinitely. TWP (the initials stand for Total Wood Preservative or Total Wood Protectant) is manufactured by a Missouri company called Amteco, Inc. It is designed to resist mildew, fungus, water, and ultraviolet light, and it is more potent and lasts longer than the water repellants and deck sealers that are advertised on television and sold in most hardware stores. TWP did extremely well in tests conducted at Texas A&M University during the 1980s. It is used and recommended by many manufacturers of log homes, and I myself had used it in the past, with good results. I expect to re-treat the cabin's shingles every eight or ten years, and to re-treat the porch floors—which were also sealed with TWP— every three or four. The only parts of the cabin's exterior that are painted are the windows and their trim. Some of these receive considerably more sun than others and will need to be repainted sooner. I hope to be able to keep up with them myself, by tackling the worst as they begin to peel.

Although I chose cedar shingles for the cabin's siding, I didn't want to use cedar on the roof. The shingles would have looked great (to anyone who bothered to notice them), but they wouldn't have lasted long enough to justify their considerable extra cost in comparison with asphalt shingles. Ann and I had to replace the roof of our house shortly after we moved in, twenty years ago, and we decided then that anything but cedar would have looked wrong on our two-hundred-year-old former dormitory, and never mind the money. We were probably right about the appearance, but when the house needs re-roofing again I won't use cedar. Modern cedar shingles are vastly inferior in quality to the ones that were available even thirty or forty years ago, and they aren't remotely comparable to the ones that eighteenth- and nineteenth-century builders used. Cedar shingles today are almost always cut from young trees that grew rapidly, and, as a result, they are less dense than shingles of old, and their growth rings are much more widely spaced, and they contain less of the natural chemicals that make cedar legendarily resistant to bugs and rot. The carpenter who installed the house's roof (after stripping away three layers of asphalt and one of cedar) guessed that my new shingles would last for forty years, but if they make it to twenty-five I'll be pleased. People tend to replace wood roofs prematurely—because of the way shingles overlap, the total covering is actually about an inch thick, and even a slimy-looking roof with moss growing on it will sometimes last another decade if it's left alone—but, even so, I'm not optimistic.

The cabin's roof is covered with asphalt shingles, the most widely used roofing material in the United States. The shingles are green, and they are nominally guaranteed to last for thirty years, although nobody in the roofing business takes shingle warranties very seriously. Ideally, you should favor premium shingles that meet either of two stringent engineering standards, established by a nonprofit group called the American Society of Testing and Materials: ASTM D-225 (for so-called organic asphalt shingles, which have a core of cellulose) or ASTM D-3462 (for fiberglass asphalt shingles, which have a core of fiberglass). Unfortunately, I can't tell you whether or not I followed this advice at the cabin. The shingles we used were the only green ones that Rudy could find in which the color was fairly uniform from one shingle to the next—a style that doesn't seem sufficiently fancy to most people nowadays, I guess. I chose them because I liked the way they looked.

The main cost advantage of asphalt shingles rather than cedar shingles is that installing them requires a fraction of the labor. Rudy subcontracted the cabin's roof to a local roofing company, and the job was finished in a day; re-roofing our house in cedar, in contrast, required many days' worth of hammering, measuring, and fussy trimming by what sometimes seemed to be an army of carpenters, including the contractor's two teenage sons. And while the cedar shingles were going on, the house was vulnerable to bad weather. When the job was halfway completed, a major rainstorm loosened one corner of the huge blue plastic tarp with which the contractor had covered the exposed deck boards on the part of the roof that hadn't been shingled yet—as I discovered when I heard a strange sound, tracked it to my office, and saw that water was streaming through the ceiling and into my photocopier. I moved the copier and made a frantic telephone call to the contractor, who sent one of his carpenters over immediately to scale the roof and re-secure the tarp. Miraculously, the copier survived for another decade, and the water damage to the interior of our house was cosmetic only and was easy to repair.

The only problem I've had with the cedar shingles at the cabin was caused by a woodpecker, which took a liking to a corner near the kitchen and pecked long gouges in several places, mainly in the gaps between shingles. Woodpeckers peck to create nesting holes, to extract wood-boring insects for food, to announce territorial claims, and to make a drumming sound that woodpeckers of the opposite sex find attractive. When they are just making noise, they will peck on almost any resonant surface—the louder the better. One spring afternoon, I heard an especially determined woodpecker hammering on the cylindrical steel transformer at the top of a utility pole at the edge of our yard. The woodpecker that attacked the cabin was probably trying to sound sexy. I got rid of it by buying four pieces of aluminum step flashing—each of which is roughly the size of a jumbo postcard—and sliding them under the edges of shingles in the problem area so that all the existing gouges are covered. If the woodpecker returns, I will either install more pieces of step flashing or try one of the other deterrents that are usually recommended by woodpecker experts: hardware cloth, tin-can tops, aluminum foil, magnifying shaving mirrors, Mylar sheets, plastic netting, plastic strips, pinwheels, pie pans, and life-size plastic hawks dangling from lengths of fishing line.

THE SECOND MAJOR project undertaken by Will Hardee, during the two summers he worked as my father's helper, was creating an underground drainage system to handle the water collected by our gutters. Making sure that a house has properly functioning gutters and drains is one of the most cost-effective home-improvement projects that a homeowner can undertake. Contractors often skimp on gutters, to reduce costs, and some homeowners, believing that gutters cause more problems than they solve, elect to do without them or even to remove existing ones. People will sometimes tell you, for example, that gutters cause or exacerbate ice dams, but they don't.*

A good gutter system is essential for almost any house (or garage or other building larger than a shed), except in regions that receive minimal rainfall. Correctly designed and well-maintained gutters can prevent basement leaks; extend the life of exterior paint, siding, windows, doors, and roofing material; reduce excessive indoor humidity; discourage infestations by destructive creatures; protect lawns, plantings, and driveways; and reduce or arrest foundation problems.

The roof of a house collects rainwater from a very large area and sends it over the edge in a high-volume sheet. (An inch of rain on a 2,000-square-foot roof—about average—equals 1,250 gallons of water.) If there are no gutters, this water all falls onto a foot-wide strip of earth right next to the house. The concentrated downpour saturates the ground, elevating the hydrostatic pressure of the wet soil surrounding the foundation. The resulting forces can be strong enough to crack concrete, or to push water through existing cracks, and the situation grows more dire over time, since the water falling from the roof gradually erodes the soil near the house, creating a depression that allows surface water to flow toward the foundation rather than away from it. (Ideally, the grade around a house should run away from the

---

* An ice dam forms when heat escaping through a roof melts the underside of a covering blanket of snow, causing melt water to trickle down the shingles until it reaches the roof's cold edge, where it refreezes. As the ice accumulates at the cold edge, more melt water backs up behind it. The dammed water works its way up under the shingles and, often, into the house. Electric heating cables placed along the lower portions of the roof don't help; they just change the shape of the cold edge. Removing snow from the bottom few feet of the roof actually makes the damage worse, by moving the cold edge higher. The only way to prevent ice dams is to reduce the amount of escaping heat, by adding more insulation and ventilation under the roof. Installing a waterproof membrane (such as Grace Ice & Water Shield) on the first few feet of a roof deck, under the shingles, will keep water from leaking through that portion of the deck but won't prevent ice dams from forming. When people see huge icicles hanging from their gutters they often assume that the gutters are to blame, but they're not. In fact, gutters sometimes reduce ice damage, by increasing the effective width of the roof's overhang and preventing ice from building up on top of (or inside) the siding.

foundation at a slope of at least 5 percent, or six inches in ten feet.)

Footing drains (see Chapter 5) don't always work as intended, and older houses often lack them altogether, and even where they exist and function well it's best not to overwhelm them with water from the roof.

In any house with interior moisture problems, the edge of the roof is the first place to look for a solution. People with perennially wet basements sometimes attempt extraordinarily expensive interventions—such as excavating the entire foundation and spraying it with a waterproof coating, or jack-hammering a hole in the basement floor to make a catch basin for a sump pump—when all they needed to do was to install good gutters or clean their existing ones. When I find water on the front left-hand corner of my basement floor, under the oil tank, I know that the downspout in the gutter above it has become clogged.

When rainwater cascades to the ground from the edge of a gutterless roof, some of it splashes back up against the house, bringing dirt and debris with it. This turns the lower portions of the siding into a sort of open-air petri dish, which then becomes colonized by mildew, algae, and other undesirable organisms. A friend of mine, who was determined to live without gutters, noticed and correctly diagnosed this problem along the front of his own house—but then he addressed it by digging a shallow trench around the house's perimeter and filling the trench with gravel. The gravel did reduce the amount of rainwater that rebounded against the siding, but it aggravated a worse problem, since the trench acted as a reservoir, storing roof water next to the house until all of it had been able to seep its way into the soil surrounding the basement.

For gutters to work, the water they collect has to be carried as far away as possible. This can't happen on any house where the gutter system's leaders, or downspouts, simply run straight down the side of the house and empty, at fire-hose volume, on the ground beside the foundation—as they do in many cases. The big gutter project that Will undertook was to dig four gently sloping trenches, each of which began at a corner of the house and ended, thirty or forty feet away, on the side of the hill that the house stands on, at a lower elevation than the house itself. At the bottom of each of these trenches he placed lengths of PVC drainage pipe, which he then connected to the leaders, using elbow-shape PVC connectors. He buried the pipes and replaced the sod he had removed when he began digging, and we both waited with anticipation for a really big rainstorm—which finally did arrive, and which Will's system handled flawlessly.

Diverting roof water underground to daylight in this way is not permitted in all localities, some of which are quite strict about what you can and can't do with water that yearns to escape from your property. Many building lots, furthermore, are too flat to make this sort of drainage possible. In such cases, there are other options. The main ones, in order of increasing effectiveness and desirability:

- *Splash blocks placed on the ground at the point where each leader empties.* Splash blocks are shallow drainage channels made of plastic or precast concrete. They are typically two or three feet long and a foot or so wide, and they slope gently from back to front. If they're installed and maintained properly they're better than nothing, but even then they're not much better than nothing. They don't move water far enough to be truly useful.

- *Horizontal extensions to the leaders.* Gutter installers will often put an elbow joint at the bottom of a leader, then attach a short section of leader to that—enough, say, to carry the water out to the forward edge of the foundation plantings, maybe four or five feet from the house. Leader extensions, like splash blocks, are better than nothing if they're working properly, but they often lie disconnected and forgotten, and they can rapidly become clogged with leaves and pine needles, especially if you crimp them by stepping on them— something that's almost impossible to avoid doing if you spend time prowling around the perimeter of your house. There are several ingenious-seeming variations, including plastic versions that unroll toward the yard as they fill with water, but they have most of the same limitations. And no matter how cleverly designed they are, leader extensions do no good at all unless they are pointed *away* from the structure they are meant to protect. I recently saw a house with very long leader extensions that ran *along* the foundation, rather than away from it—a self-defeating arrangement.

• *Underground connection to a storm sewer or curbside gutter.* This is something found mainly in older neighborhoods. The house I grew up in, which was built in the nineteen-twenties, had gutters that emptied into a system made of clay drain tiles— sections of clay pipe two feet long and four inches in diameter, which were butted together to form a long drainage line that ran under the yard and emptied at the edge of the street. The system probably worked pretty well when it was new, but clay tiles are fragile, and tree roots can easily finger their way into the unsealed joints between them, and I don't think I remember ever seeing water emerging from the far end. Many building codes now forbid systems like this in new construction, because in heavy rains the water they carry can overwhelm storm sewer systems, or even sanitary sewer systems. Some municipalities operate programs to disconnect existing drains and replace them with something else.

• *Collection in cisterns for uses other than human consumption.* Groundwater is increasingly scarce in much of the country, and rainwater from the roof can sometimes be captured and used for things like watering flower gardens. (You wouldn't want to drink water that has rinsed your roof, or even wash your hair in it.) Many attractive, well-designed versions are available. Most are barrel-shaped, are made of heavy plastic, and are intended sit on top of the ground. The best have overflow hoses, to carry excess water away from the house in heavy rains. All need childproof lids.

• *Underground diversion to a drywell.* The simplest drywell is a hole lined with a permeable fabric and filled with rocks and gravel. It acts as an underground holding tank and sieve, allowing runoff water to seep gradually into the ground—ideally, far from the foundation. There are also more complicated versions and variations. Local regulations often govern drywells, so before digging a big hole in your yard you should be sure that what you want to do is allowed.

———————————

NO WATER DIVERSION scheme can work unless the gutters that feed into it are kept clean—a job that no one likes. When I asked a guy who used to mow my lawn—not Will!—if I could pay him to clean my gutters, too, he hesitated and looked around, then said he didn't have a ladder. I said, "I have a ladder." He couldn't think of another excuse quickly enough, so he was stuck. I even helped him carry the ladder from my garage, but he moped the whole time and didn't do a very good job, so I never asked him again. (Eventually, he got tired of mowing the lawn, too.)

When I do clean my gutters, it's almost always in pouring rain, since that's the only time they overflow. I can reach most of the ones at our house without a ladder, by crawling out onto the flat roof above the old addition in back. From there I can reach up to the gutter that runs along the back of the main roof and reach down to the gutter that runs along the edge of the flat roof. Often when I perform this chore I am wearing just my underpants—since the biggest rainstorms always seem to arrive in the middle of the night—and carrying an umbrella. To reach the gutter that runs along the front of the house I need my ladder. That gutter is about forty feet long. From a single ladder position I can reach maybe three feet in either direction without leaning moronically far over the side, and that means that I have to move the ladder five or six times to cover the entire run. Moving the ladder involves picking it up the way lumberjacks carry telephone poles in those competitions you sometimes see on ESPN2, then shuffling sideways for two or three quick, panicky steps. When I was a lad, I loved ladders, but now that I'm middle-aged I hate them. Some friends of Ann's parents once came home to find a ladder, a pool of blood, and some broken false teeth in their driveway—the aftermath of a fall by a housepainter, whose ladder had slipped from under him while he was working. When I use a ladder now, those broken false teeth are never far from my mind.

I'm always careful to raise my ladder at the exact angle recommended in the yellow warning sticker on its side, and I always triple-check the footing and climb as timidly as an old lady. Recently, I invented a tool that enables me to clean the house's front gutter without moving my ladder quite so many times. The tool is an old sponge mop, which I use to push unreachable gutter debris ahead of me.

There are many gutter accessories on the market which are supposed to make gutter-cleaning unnecessary, or at least easier. Most are barriers that are intended to deflect leaves and other potential leader-blockers but to allow water to pass through. Some such accessories seem to do little but make existing problems worse. When our house's gutters were installed they were equipped with downspout basket strainers—bulb-shaped contraptions made of wire which fit into the downspout openings and were supposed to prevent leaves and other debris from forming clogs. In fact, though, the strainers (which looked like kitchen whisks) provided a seine-like framework against which thick masses of leaves and other debris quickly backed up, forming an obstruction that the water couldn't get past. In the middle of a big rainstorm one night, after heaving handful after handful of sodden leaves and pine needles over the side of the house, I decided to remove the baskets, but couldn't yank them out: they were riveted to the leaders. I had to go back inside for wire clippers and then climb onto the roof again. My gutters have been without basket strainers since then, and they are less likely to clog now than they were when they had them.

My experience with the basket strainers made me skeptical of all gutter-improvement schemes—of which there are extraordinarily many. Quite a few of these schemes are variations on the leader-strainer idea, some of them ingenious. Others attempt to deflect debris by displacing a gutter's entire interior volume with porous obstructions. (One such product, called GutterPiller, consists of bristly cylindrical filters that look like giant bottle brushes; these filters "stop everything but the rain," according to the manufacturer.) Still others create a screen-like permeable cap over the entire gutter opening.

With all of these products, my anxiety has concerned leaves

that adhere to the permeable surfaces, either blocking the flow of rainwater or allowing piles of rotting organic matter to remain in contact with wooden parts of my house. I have friends who swear by one system or another, but I've always been unwilling to try them myself, until fairly recently. What happened was that I was stung on the hand by a hornet while I was cleaning the gutters on the garage. (The hornets had built their nest at one end of the gutter, and I mistook it for a pile of leaves.) The sting made my hand swell too much for any more gutter cleaning that day, and it put me out of the mood for gutter cleaning altogether for several months. Then we had a huge snowstorm, and the garage's gutters self-destructed. The weight of the snow and ice sliding off the roof bent down the middle section of each gutter, making it, in effect, self-cleaning, while also making it useless for its intended purpose. The gutters could not be repaired.

Rather than simply replacing those gutters with the same type—they were the standard seamless-aluminum kind that you find on most people's houses*—I decided to try something new and expensive, treating the garage as a field test. After considering many options, I chose a system called LeafGuard, which is manufactured by Englert, Inc., and is sold and installed by franchised dealers around the country. LeafGuard is a "reverse curve" system. It consists of an oversized seamless-aluminum gutter that is covered by a curved aluminum lid, which is attached to the back of the gutter using L-shaped plastic brackets. Water from the roof flows over and around the curve of the lid, and enters the gutter through a narrow opening under the lid's leading edge. LeafGuard depends on the principle of liquid adhesion, which is what causes water to run down the front of a glass when you try to pour it by tipping the glass. Rainwater adheres to the

---

* Seamless gutters are a tremendous invention. They begin as a roll of what is essentially heavy-gauge metal foil, which is fed through a machine that shapes the foil into a gutter—like an industrial-strength Play-Doh Fun Factory. Each section is made to length, on site, so there are no leaky seams, except at the corners. To get seamless gutters, you have to hire a gutter specialist. That's probably a good thing, because gutter specialists almost always do a better job than general contractors do.

curved lid and follows it into the gutter, while leaves and most other debris are ejected.

My LeafGuard gutters are quite a bit more expensive than ordinary seamless gutters would have been, but they and their attached leaders are guaranteed not to clog for as long as I live at my address, and if they ever do clog the installer will clean or replace them at no charge. They have been in place for a year and a half now, and I haven't come close to needing to make a claim. The usual criticisms of reverse-curve systems—aside from their expense—are that they can be overwhelmed by very heavy rainstorms, and that they allow some small debris, such as pine needles, to slip through. LeafGuard gutters are also somewhat larger than most ordinary gutters—an aesthetic problem for some people, although I've never been bothered. In fact, I've never noticed. When the time comes to re-roof our house, I will consider using LeafGuard gutters there, too, although I will continue to explore other possibilities in the meantime.

The cabin's gutters, with one exception, feed into leaders that are connected to underground pipes, which carry the water a good fifty feet away from the foundation, on the downhill side, before dumping it onto the ground. Those underground pipes were put in place by Artie, the excavator, when he dug the hole for the foundation. The one exception is the twenty-foot-long gutter that runs along the forward edge of the little roof above the front step—the roof held up by the two stone columns. Running a leader down either column would have looked terrible, but I couldn't think of a good alternative. Rudy suggested simply skipping the gutter or installing a bracket-like diverter, which would attach to roof shingles above the step, and channel rainwater to either side. (Savetime Corporation makes a self-adhesive diverter called the Rainhandler Doorbrella.) But I didn't want all that water to pour down on the ground near the front step, either.

In the end, we decided to install a regular gutter along the entire front edge of the entry-porch roof. Rather than adding a conventional leader at one end, though, the gutter man extended the right end of the gutter about six inches beyond the end of the roof and left it open, so that all the water it collected would stream down to a single spot on the ground near the right front corner of the entry porch. A mason was building a stone retaining wall on the downhill side of the cabin that day, and I asked him if he could contrive a collection drain of some kind to capture the stream of water from the open gutter. He dug a hole about two and a half feet in diameter and a foot and a half deep, and then used his backhoe to dig a gently sloping trench from the edge of the hole to a point about twenty-five feet down the hill from the cabin. In this trench he laid PVC drain pipe so that the uphill opening of the pipe protruded into the hole. He then lined the perimeter of the hole with stones, making it look like a little well, and covered the pipe trench with dirt. Water from the roof would now stream from the open end of the gutter into the stone-lined hole and, from there, into the buried drain pipe, which would convey it well away from the entry porch, the house, the foundation, and the driveway.

This was the theory, at any rate; in actuality, the system didn't work. During the next big rainstorm, I discovered that most of the water streaming from the gutter was overshooting the stone-lined hole by a couple of inches, and, furthermore, that any water that actually did make its way into the hole was soaking directly into the ground rather than running down the drain pipe. This was because the inlet end of the pipe was six inches above the bottom of the hole, and the water never rose high enough to reach it.

The solution, I decided, was to take things into my own hands. I removed the stone lining and extended the hole so that its perimeter fully encompassed the splash area, then rebuilt the stone lining. That took care of the aiming problem; now I needed to get the water from the hole into the pipe. To do that, I decided, I would use concrete to raise the bottom of the hole and make it watertight. I went to my hardware store and bought two ninety-pound bags of Sakrete Concrete Mix—"a pre-blended, ready to use mixture of concrete sand, pea gravel and portland cement packaged in a convenient bag," according to the manufacturer. Sakrete is like cake mix: all you do is add water. The instructions say that you can mix it either in a wheelbarrow or in one of those portable powered mixers that masons and bricklayers use. I decided to simplify my life considerably (who wants to clean concrete out of a wheelbarrow or a rented machine?) by mixing my Sakrete right in the hole. Why not? I put on rubber gloves to protect my hands, emptied both bags into the hole, and slowly added water while stirring with a trowel. Then I began to play. I used my trowel to smooth the surface of my minislab, and contoured it so that it would direct water into the pipe.

After I had finished playing I searched the woods and the edges of my driveway for smooth stones roughly the size of golf balls, hens' eggs, and new potatoes. By the time I had found about two-thirds of a bushel, the concrete had firmed up so that I could push my hand against it without making an impression. I filled the hole with the stones I had gathered (after leaning a nice flat rock over the open end of the pipe to keep the small stones from clogging it). The stones, I figured, would hide the concrete, break up the stream of water from the gutter, and prevent the hole from filling with leaves.

When you want it to rain, of course, it never does; I had to wait two full weeks for a real storm. As soon as the downpour began, though, I rushed over to the cabin to see how my redesigned drain was doing. The stream of water from the open end of the gutter was firm and steady—yes!—and it was hitting the stones in my rebuilt stone-lined hole and disappearing without big splashes—yes!—and an equally firm and steady stream of water was gushing from the downhill end of the pipe—yes! yes! yes! I felt as proud as if I had just topped off Hoover Dam.

AT ONE POINT when I was brooding about my gutters, I bought a device called Gutter Sense, which its inventor describes as "the revolutionary gutter cleaning tool that makes gutter maintenance a safe, fast and easy task." It looks a little like an extra-large pair of hinged plastic salad tongs, with a rope attached. You screw the device to a mop handle or other pole, position the tongs inside a clogged gutter, and pull on the rope, making the tongs come together like a pair of clapping hands. The hands grab a hunk of debris, which you drop to the ground by releasing the rope. I bought my Gutter Sense, which cost about twenty dollars, plus shipping, because I thought it might enable me to clean the gutters in the front of the cabin by reaching up from the ground, and to clean the gutters in the back of the cabin by reaching down from the bedroom windows. On the day I tested it, my Gutter Sense didn't do a very good job on the first chore, and it couldn't manage the second one at all. I had trouble getting the tongs inside the gutters, which are overhung somewhat by the edge of the roof, and pulling the rope caused the device to gradually unscrew itself from the pole. Also, the pole was hard to hold steady with just one hand, and the tongs worked many times better on dry leaves than they did on wet ones. Eventually, I am sure, I will find a use for my Gutter Sense—perhaps rescuing Frisbees from trees—but I am pretty sure that I will never again try to clean gutters with it.

I ordered my Gutter Sense online, and I did a lot of other shopping for the cabin in the same way. When the time came to buy doorknobs, I searched for "rustic lockset" on Google. A few clicks later, I'd found the perfect choice: a heavy, flat-black wrought-steel knob with a rectangular flat-black wrought-steel rosette, manufactured by a company called Emtek. I typed in my credit-card number. A little over a week later, UPS delivered my order in two big boxes, and a little over a week after that a local locksmith installed them. The doorknobs are an important part of the cabin's décor, although I doubt that many visitors notice them consciously. Door and window hardware make a major contribution to a building's interior, but the contribution is a subtle one. A cheap contractor-type lockset can ruin a wonderful old door, in the same way that a cheap tie can ruin a wonderful suit.

Until just a few years ago, my choice of doorknobs would have been limited by the inventory of my local hardware store, the taste and imagination of my builder, and the catalog collection of my architect. The World Wide Web permitted me to examine the wares of hundreds of manufacturers and suppliers—including many that were too small or too specialized ever to have made themselves known to someone like me through conventional advertising—and then to buy without an intermediary. I took a risk, of course—the same risk I took when I ordered my Gutter Sense—but I would have taken a risk as well if I had relied solely on Reese and Rudy. I knew the sort of door-

knobs I wanted, more or less, and the Internet let me find them
for myself. It let me find a lot of other things, too—including a
Ping-Pong table, which arrived during a snowstorm. I had to help
the deliverer roll it from the road on a dolly because the driveway
hadn't been plowed and he didn't think he could get down it in
his truck, a semitrailer. All the way to the cabin he grumbled
about this imposition, even though delivering things was his job
and I was the one pushing the dolly.

Online shopping isn't a perfect replacement for seeing things
in person. During our big kitchen-and-bath renovation, I ordered
a washer and dryer from the Sears Web site. (Our previous
washer, which was fifteen years old, had stopped working a few
days before the renovation began—like an old man who dies the
day before he's supposed to be moved into a nursing home—and
the dryer, which was the same age, could no longer do much
more than make wet clothes damp.) Ann and I wanted our new
laundry room to have a flat work surface on which we could fold
clean clothes, but the space was so small that the only possible
place to put a counter was on top of the machines. To make that
possible, I ordered a front-loading washer, the controls of which
were on the front panel, above the door. I wanted a dryer with
the controls in the same place but couldn't find one on the Sears
Web site. I ordered a conventional dryer, with the controls on
top, since there didn't seem to be an alternative. Later, when it
was too late, I learned that Sears actually did sell a dryer meant
for installation under a counter, but that, for some reason, it
hadn't been listed on the Web site at the time I went shopping.

We were still able to put a counter in the new laundry room,
but the carpenter who installed it had to make a cutout for the
dryer's control panel. The cutout works fine, although coins, golf
tees, and tubes of ChapStick sometimes disappear into it. The
counter was made of a stock slab of plain white Formica. In order
to cut it to the correct size, the carpenter made a template from
four narrow strips of Masonite. He cut the strips to length and arranged them in a rectangle inside the nook where the washer and
dryer were going to be installed, leaving a small gap between each
piece and the wall beside it. I asked him why he bothered to make
a template, rather than simply measuring the width and depth of

the nook at the height of the finished counter, and he said that wall corners, even in new construction, are seldom perfectly square, and that the counter, although it would look rectangular, would most likely be slightly trapezoidal. Once he had arranged the Masonite strips the way he wanted them, he tacked them together with a hot-glue gun, then placed this template on top of the Formica and traced around it. He later used this same useful technique to make a template for a large wall mirror, which was going to be installed above the sink in Ann's and my bathroom.

When the time came to buy appliances for the cabin, I did my research online, also at the Sears Web site, but I took my shopping list to an actual Sears store so that I could be sure I wasn't missing something—and I'm glad I did. My research consisted basically of writing down the model number of the least expensive refrigerator, range, dishwasher, and combined washer/dryer "laundry center" that Sears offered. When I gave my list to a salesperson in the store, she showed me that I could buy a somewhat better refrigerator for the same price because it was on sale, that if I were willing to pay fifty dollars more I could buy what she said was a significantly better dishwasher, and that the store stocked a similar range that was a bit less expensive than the one on my list. I ended up doing better all around than I would have if I had simply pointed and clicked.

I also ended up doing better than Ann and I did when we ordered far fancier appliances for our remodeled kitchen. The Kenmore stand-alone electric range that we bought for the cabin cost less than the KitchenAid cooktop or either of the two KitchenAid ovens that we chose for our house, yet the range's broiler works better than the broiler in either oven, and the range has simpler controls. If Ann and I suddenly found ourselves involved in another big kitchen renovation, we'd probably still fall for excessively costly appliances, but perhaps readers with more self control will be able to learn from our experience and restrain themselves.

———————

MY FRIEND KEN DANIEL—whose wife, Gina, suggested the stone columns in front of the cabin—makes his living as a lighting designer, mainly. He creates lighting plans for houses and office buildings and student centers, and he once helped to plan the interior and exterior lighting for the homes of two well-known American billionaires. He found his calling accidentally. He went to art school, then worked briefly as an artist in residence at a high school in Maine, then got a job as an art preparator at Bowdoin College. At Bowdoin, among other things, he selected, framed, hung, and lighted works of art for campus exhibitions. That job led to a similar one at a gallery in New York, then to one at the Whitney Museum, then to one at the Union Carbide Corporation, in Connecticut. Increasingly, he became interested in illumination. "Lighting was always kind of trailing me," he told me recently, and he found that when he visited an art exhibit he usually spent more time looking at the lighting than at the paintings. He studied lighting design at the Parsons School of Design, attended lighting trade shows, and went into business on his own. He and Gina built a house in our town, and their children became good friends of Ann's and my children. They moved to the West Coast for a few years in the early nineties so that Ken could take a job as a lighting designer for the Walt Disney Company, where, among other things, he created camp lights for the Indiana Jones attraction and flickering candelabras for Pirates of the Caribbean. Then they moved back.

Over the years, Ken and I have helped each other with various home-improvement projects, an arrangement that has worked out better for me than for him, since he has real professional skills and I don't. He designed the lighting in the new kitchen and new bathrooms in our house, and he made a simple lighting plan for the cabin. Before watching Ken work, I had never thought of lighting as distinct from wiring. I just figured that you picked out fixtures you didn't hate, and then the electrician installed them where the building code said they had to go. But now I understand that lighting is an art, and that it can influence not only how a room looks but also how it functions. Our kitchen works better as a kitchen because it was illuminated by someone who knew what he was doing.

A good, simple example is the ceiling lights above the counters. Standard kitchen counters are twenty-four inches deep, and the wall cabinets above them are twelve inches deep, and most architects and electricians will place ceiling fixtures very close to the cabinets, maybe a couple of inches in front of them, roughly above the centerline of the exposed part of the counter. This seems logical, but it places the fixtures too close to the cabinets, creating parabola-shaped scallops of intense light on the cabinet doors and leaving large parts of the counters in shadows. A better place for kitchen ceiling fixtures, Ken told me, is centered on the forward edge of the counters, twenty-four inches from the wall. From that position, they light the cabinets and work surfaces uniformly and inconspicuously.

Even if you have a good lighting plan, you can't be certain that an electrician will execute it. Ken happened to be at our house on the day the kitchen was being wired, and he noticed that all the ceiling fixtures had been roughed in about six inches too close to the cabinets, even though the drawings showed them in the correct positions. Ken went over the drawings with the electrician, who, after grumbling a little, moved all the fixtures to where they were supposed to be. Ken told me later that this kind of thing happens often, and that contractors tend to do things the way they've always done them rather than paying close attention to written instructions. He also told me that a house's framing often makes it difficult to place light fixtures in the ideal positions. If, for example, there turns out to be a two-by-ten ceiling joist in a place where a light fixture is supposed to go, the electrician will have to either move the fixture or, if the fixture can't be moved, cut out part of the joist (and box off the opening, to transfer the load to the joists on either side). Ken told me that he had once asked a house framer why he didn't adjust his framing layout to accommodate the electricians, plumbers, and other subcontractors who would follow him on the job, and he said, "That's not the way we do it."

A good general lighting guideline, Ken told me, is "Light the task, not the room, because if you light the task you will light the room." (An extreme example is the interior of a typical casino, in which most of the foot candles needed to illuminate the entire space come from the backlit front panels of the slot machines.) Our house's kitchen has correctly positioned ceiling fixtures above the forward edges of the counters, two pendant fixtures with glass shades above the island, and focused halogen ceiling lights aimed at the floor-to-ceiling bookcases that fill one rear wall, along with a number of canister-type ceiling fixtures above the areas where people sit to eat, talk, read, or watch TV. Ken had wanted to put a pendant fixture above the kitchen dining table, but Ann and I weren't certain yet how we were going to place the furniture in that part of the room, so I didn't let him. Each group of similar fixtures is wired on its own circuit, so that each can be controlled individually. (Ken told me, incidentally, that most people can't keep track of more than three light switches grouped in the same panel; with four or more, they forget which switch is which.) When task lights—or lights with specific functions, like the ones that shine on the kitchen's bookcases—are insufficient to light the entire room, Ken said, it's a good idea to preserve the illusion that the task lighting is doing all the work, by positioning the supplemental lighting in places where it's relatively inconspicuous.

Ken has taught me quite a bit about lighting; he's also taught me about darkness. Most summers, our two families spend a couple of weeks together at the same place on Martha's Vineyard. The main structure on the property is an eighteenth-century barn, which serves as (among other things) a living room and a dining room. The barn has huge sliding doors and no electric lights. In the evening, as the sun goes down, you can sit between the big open doorways and look out either at the ocean (in front) or at a meadow and a hillside (behind). Sitting there one evening a few years ago, Ken said to me, "In this barn, you can do something that people almost never do anymore: you can watch it getting dark."

Darkness used to be a powerful force. When it arrived, people stopped doing what they were doing and went to bed; when it departed, they got up and went back to work. Nowadays, we scarcely notice the change. Especially during the cold months of the year, when the days are shorter, we reach for the light switch at the first hint of gathering gloom. Then, as our indoor lamps blaze, the darkness beyond our houses obliterates itself, by turning our windows into mirrors. For most of us, night and day are no longer as different as night and day.

When Ann and I moved to Connecticut, I was astonished how dark the night sky seemed, in comparison with the all-night radiance of Manhattan. To walk up our dirt road without a flashlight on a moonless night I had to move very slowly and try to sense the pitch of the concave roadway by shuffling my feet, following the high ground in the middle. Now that's changed. A few years ago, one of my neighbors installed bright white floodlights on the corners of his house, and decorative lights at the bases of some of the trees in his yard. The floodlights are probably meant for security, although they shine away from the house, rather than toward it; the tree lights are pointed up into the branches, and they cast a cold, greenish glow that is undoubtedly intended to resemble moonlight but looks more like the luminous pall of a gargantuan TV. I doubt that my neighbor can even see his exterior lights from inside his house, which is usually blazing. The outdoor fixtures act as high-powered nightlights on what was once a pleasantly spooky little stretch of country road.

On a moonless, cloudless night a few years ago, the power went out all over my town for several hours. I happened to be outside that night, and I was struck by how full of bright stars the sky seemed to be. My town is very sparsely populated in comparison with most other settled parts of the United States, but we still generate enough nighttime candlepower to obliterate most of the rest of the visible universe. There is no place on earth where the darkness at night is still as complete as it was during the eons before the spread of electric illumination. Galileo was able to make out the moons of Jupiter with a telescope whose lenses were about as powerful as the ones in your reading glasses. Our limitless ability to illuminate our lives has added darkness to the list of our vanishing natural resources.

———————

WHEN KEN WAS living in Maine and trying to earn a living as an artist, he built a small house and studio for himself, using skills he had learned at the Shelter Institute, a hippie-oriented low-cost-construction school near Bath. He sold that house when he moved to New York. A couple of years later, when he went to work at Union Carbide, he bought a piece of land in our town, which is about an hour from the company's headquarters, with a view to building a house on it someday. He often camped on his land in a tent, and commuted from there. (He hung his coat and tie on a tree.) He met Gina in the mid-eighties, and not long afterward they began building a house for themselves on the land. Ken acted as the architect, general contractor, and all-around handyman. "Our original budget was eighty-five thousand dollars," he told me recently, "and as soon as the house was closed in we decided that it was livable. For a long time, before the Sheetrock went up, when you came in the front door you could see all the way across the house to anyone sitting on the toilet."

Ken and Gina's kids grew up with my kids, and, in a way, our houses grew up together, too. I helped Ken with the guest suite under his studio/office, and Ken helped me install some new lights in our old kitchen, and he and Gina added a barn-like garage at about the same time we did, and they redid their kitchen shortly after we redid ours, and we both hired the same stone mason to build our patios. Their house followed the same evolutionary path that ours did, gradually becoming indivisible—in my mind, at least—from its occupants. Their house, like all houses, is partly a physical record of the lives it has contained.

It was a shock, therefore, to learn that Ken and Gina had sold their house and bought a smaller place, one town away. Ken hadn't even gotten around to grouting the new stone tiles in the backsplash above the counter in their swell new kitchen. Recently, I asked him whether selling his house didn't make him feel sad.

"No, no," he said. "If you're an artist, and you paint a picture and hang it in a gallery, you may really like the picture but you still want someone to buy it. So you have to let it go. Set it free. Do something else." I must have looked skeptical, because he added, "Well, I guess there's a certain amount of BS in that—but I do think it's a healthy way of thinking. That house was our baby, but it's time to do something else. We're letting it go."

Actually, I understand this impulse very well, because I have felt it myself. Finally finishing our dining room, and having the pool table successfully installed, gave me an extraordinary sense of accomplishment, and made me feel that our house, though hardly perfect, had finally begun to look quite a bit like the kind of place Ann and I would build if we were handed a piece of land and a blank check. Yet almost before the paint on the dining room walls was dry, Ann and I both suddenly thought that maybe we ought to sell the place and move somewhere else. A big house up the road had suddenly come on the market. It wasn't really our kind of house, and swinging the deal would have made us poor for many years, but we both felt what sometimes seemed to be an almost irresistible temptation. We had several serious discussions, and I did lots of arithmetic. Then the house up the road was taken off the market, and we gradually came to our senses.

Why would we (or anyone else) suddenly be tempted to sell a house into which we had invested years of effort and sacrifice? I think the answer may have more to do with mortality than with fickleness. There's something deeply chilling about thinking that you may have put your life into something like its final order. Finishing the dining room was like turning the last page of a good book: oh, no, what will we do now? As long as there is bare Sheetrock somewhere, you don't have to confront the thought that everything eventually comes to an end. I rebuilt the inside of my closet a dozen years ago, but I still haven't painted it, and very possibly I never will. The closer you get your house to what you think you want it to be, the less power it has to pull you forward through your life. That's why you leave the kitchen tiles ungrouted.* It's also why finally getting the place into decent shape can make you want to sell it—or to build another one six miles away.

Of course, mortality has plans for us whether we give in to our anxieties or not. Even if Ann and I never sell either our house or the cabin, someone else will eventually live in both of

---

* Incidentally, if you are trying to sell your house, a conspicuous but easy-to-fix flaw may be an asset. Ken told me that the people who bought his house loved everything about it except the ungrouted kitchen tiles, and wanted written assurance that he would take care of them before the closing. Complaining about the tiles made the buyers feel like smart shoppers, even though grouting them took Ken less than an hour.

them. Whoever takes our place will have different ideas and different dreams; a moving van is usually closely followed by a
Dumpster. We'll have left our mark on both places, though, and
the future owners, even if they tear down both houses, won't be
able to eradicate every trace of us. Home improvement is an a
ongoing narrative, with many authors; it's not a story with a clear
beginning, middle, and end.

Several springs ago, I played golf during a trip to Kansas City.
Toward the end of the round, a member of my foursome pointed
out a pair of short, shallow depressions in the ground near one of
the fairways. "That was part of the Oregon Trail," he said. In the
mid-eighteen hundreds, it turns out, thousands of hopeful settlers and their oxen trudged over that spot on their way to the
West, and the ruts they made have outlasted more than a century
of suburban development and divot-taking. The trail stretched
for two thousand miles over prairies, rivers, mountains, and
deserts, but somehow its length seems less remarkable than its
depth. Grinding a permanent groove into the landscape requires
a lot of human activity.

The wood threshold of the front door of our house, which
was built a little more than fifty years before the beginning of the
Great Migration, looks like a skinny, tipped-over question mark.
Generations of foot traffic abraded a saddle-shaped depression
on one side, and the hollow is so deep that the bottom of our
new storm door had to be scribed to match its contour. But
there's a puzzle: the human rut is on the hinge side of the doorway, where people seldom tread, and it doesn't extend past the
threshold's center. I was mystified until I saw an old photograph.
Our house, I discovered, used to have a double door, which divided vertically and was hinged on both sides. The right-hand
half was obviously the operative one, since that's the eroded side.
And people in the past clearly used the front door more than my
family and I do now; in twenty years of occupancy, we have
scarcely managed to rub through the paint.

When we redid our kitchen, we eliminated what had previously been that room's main entrance, creating a new kitchen
doorway in a better place, down near the entrance to the old

playroom. No trace of the old doorway remains now—the stainless steel counter is on the kitchen side, and there's a seamless new plaster wall on the other—except on the hallway floor. Very visible in the old pine floorboards between the wall and the edge of the rug is a dark, worn area about the size of a welcome mat. That's where my children's feet used to pound as they ran to grab a snack after school, and where the dogs would slide sideways when they took the turn too fast at dinnertime.

I used to brood about that worn spot, hating to think that someday I might have to refinish the entire floor to get rid of it. Now I like to fold back the hall rug every once in a while and think about how the migratory patterns in my home have changed. The marks on the hallway floor are the only remaining physical evidence of a part of our lives that no longer exists—an abandoned chamber in our still-growing nautilus shell.

THE CABIN WAS completed in 2001. Driving to it from our regular house takes eleven minutes; riding my bike there takes forty. This extreme proximity, contrary to most people's initial reaction, is one of the most appealing features. Getting away from our regular life requires no careful forethought, no last-minute running around, no remembering to stop the newspaper and the mail. Usually when we visit we don't have to pack, and we don't have to guess what the weather will be like once we've arrived. The trip doesn't last long enough for the dogs to get carsick. There's probably milk in the fridge already, because we were over there the day before yesterday. We never get stuck in Friday traffic. If our son decides at the last minute that he'd rather go to a movie with his girlfriend, we don't have a big argument; we just remind him when to be back. Yet when we're there we could be in another country. Also, six miles turns out to be the mathematically ideal separation between a host and his houseguests.

Most of the windows in the cabin face across the river valley to the big hill with the state park on it. I climbed that hill one January day to find out if I could see the cabin from the top of

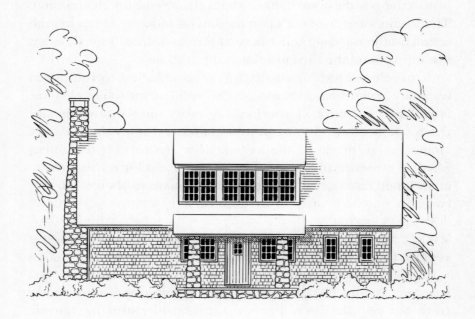

The cabin.

the fire tower; I couldn't. The view from the tower encompasses about three hundred and fifty-five degrees of surrounding countryside, and the cabin is in the missing five degrees, blocked out by a wooded rise. In the cabin, I keep a pair of binoculars on a hook next to the door to the open porch, and on clear winter days I sometimes scan the big hill, looking for deer, foxes, hikers, somnambulating bears, hunters, anything; almost always, I see nothing. Sometimes I spot a hawk circling high above the river and am able to follow him with the binoculars, waiting for him to turn in a particular direction so that the sun will make his tail feathers flash. One cold morning, I looked out the kitchen window and saw two deer lying in frosty fallen leaves, about forty feet away. One of the deer was curled up like a a cat; the other had lifted its head and was staring in my direction, probably awakened by the slamming door of the microwave. I got the binoculars and watched, and during the next ten minutes the alert deer's ears gradually relaxed, and its eyelids slowly drifted closed again. The deer, nodding off, looked like one of our dogs falling asleep in front of the bathroom heater.

During the past couple of summers, an extraordinary fat toad has spent most nights living mainly on the cabin's front step, directly beneath the lamp over the front door. Moths hover near the lamp, become exhausted, and drop to the step, where the toad eats them. The toad doesn't move when we take the dogs out for a walk before going to bed, and the dogs don't notice him, even though they sometimes nearly step on his back. I found the toad's daytime hiding place one day when I was moving a small pile of logs that I had stacked against one of the stone columns. The toad was lying in a bed of dirt and rotten bark between two logs at the bottom of the pile. He was as round and fat as a cow pie, and pretty much the same color. When I reached down to place him on the ground so that I could sweep the step, he held my fingers with his fingers, then slowly stretched a thick rear leg to the grass, like a fat man being lowered into a lifeboat. He sat calmly in the grass until I had finished sweeping. Then I placed him on the step again, and he went back to waiting for night and the return of the moths.

The cabin is an especially welcome retreat for Ann and me

because we both work at home, in the old apartment on the third floor. Commuting for us consists of climbing a flight of steps, a great convenience, but there are times when I feel as though I live under self-imposed house arrest. Like most people with home offices I understand the good and bad sides of having no fixed schedule. When I'm in our house, I seldom fully elude the gravitational pull of my desk, which constantly urges me up the stairs to finish that last paragraph, answer that unanswered letter, reread that discouraging e-mail from my editor, check my most recent book's performance on Amazon. Toward the end of February one year, I realized that Ann and I had spent most of the winter within eight or nine feet of a particular spot on the ceiling of our bedroom, since we had both had pressing writing projects and the wall that separates our desks is almost directly above our bed. Sometimes I turn on CNN or CNBC or the Golf Channel while I'm working, to create the illusion of having colleagues, and Ann and I send each other e-mail during the day and occasionally chat on the phone. Doing such things creates a refreshing illusion of separation between our ordinary lives and our working lives, but we nevertheless often yearn to get away. One winter afternoon a few years ago, as light snow began to fall, we decided to knock off early and take a break by going to the cabin. A few minutes later, we were there. We lit a fire in the fireplace, watched snow collecting on the big hill, read until we felt sleepy, took a nap with the dogs, and woke up in time to be back before the kids got home from school. We felt as refreshed as if we'd spent a weekend in Vermont, yet the knives and forks in the dishwasher at home—which we had loaded and turned on before leaving for the cabin—were still warm to the touch when we returned.

One of the best things about the cabin is that its future is still fully indeterminate. Like Jefferson's Monticello, it remains a work in progress. I have a mental list of possible changes and improvements which I hope will last for many years. I like to turn the rooms over in my mind, wondering where Ann and I would put our offices if we moved there permanently, or how many grandchildren we might be able park on cots near the Ping-Pong table, or what we would do with Ann's bread machine and ice cream maker in a kitchen the size of a closet. The cabin, like the Vagabond's House—and like our regular house fifteen years ago—is still mostly imaginary. It's decades away from its final configuration, its last 10 percent, the part I hope I never get to.

SELECTED RESOURCES, ETC.

1. Rooms and Dreams

My copy of *Vagabond's House* was published by Dodd, Mead & Company in 1930. If, for some reason, you feel like making a Don Blanding pilgrimage, you can visit the Vagabond's House Inn, in Carmel-by-the-Sea, California. The inn was named after Blanding's book. Its Web site is vagabondshouseinn.com. A reprint edition of the book is available at applewoodbooks.com.

Mr. Blandings Builds His Dream House was published by Simon & Schuster in 1946, and an excerpt ran that year in *Fortune*. In 1948, after the movie came out, some engineers at General Electric created real plans based on the fictional house, and a developer built a house based on them, on MacArthur Road in East Natick, Massachusetts. Myrna Loy and 125,000 other fans visited the house in a thirty-day period in 1948. Admission was twenty-five cents.

My book *The Walls Around Us* was published by Villard Books in 1992. My essay about Sheetrock, also called "The Walls Around Us," was published in the May 1987 issue of *The Atlantic Monthly*.

You can read about Thomas Jefferson and his approach to home improvement in *Jefferson and Monticello: The Biography of a Builder*, by Jack McLaughlin. It was published by Henry Holt and Company in 1988.

2. Outside, Inside

If you enjoy thinking about chopping axes and other early American tools, and about early-American life in general, I highly recommend the many books of Eric Sloane, an artist and illustrator who lived in my part of Connecticut and died in 1985. You can find out more about him at ericsloane.com.

Ann's anti-gardening essay, which is called "Give Weeds a Chance," was in the August 2005 issue of *Smithsonian*.

The PaperTiger is made by the Zinsser Company, the main American manufacturer of shellac. (See later.) You can almost certainly find a PaperTiger in the paint department of your hardware store.

Here's what Benjamin Moore has to say about Wall-Grip: "This 100% acrylic product has been designed with the professional in mind using high hiding pigments that deliver an easy to work with foundation for hanging most any wallcoverings including pre-pasted, unpasted or commercial coverings. Moore's Universal Wall-Grip 203 is the ideal primer over unprimed drywall, previously painted surfaces and hard glossy surfaces such as glass and Formica. This universal formula eliminates any confusion when choosing the correct primer to use for your wallcovering project. This primer also protects your Sheetrock from damage when you need to remove the wallcovering. The finish of this primer promotes adhesion of the wallpaper being hung while reducing curling edges and seam splitting." You can find out more at benjaminmoore.com

The shade of dark green that Ann and I used in our library was Saratoga, by Kyanize. I don't think it is still manufactured.

Our decorator friend Polly Roberts, whose design business is called Off-Color Décor, can be contacted by way of her Web site, pollyroberts.com. Unlike virtually all decorators, Polly charges by the hour and doesn't mark up the merchandise she buys for clients.

The vinyl-covered foam-core insert that lets us eat Christmas dinner on our pool table was made by the wife of the guy we bought the pool table from. It weighs just a few pounds, and it folds in quarters, making it easy to store when it's not in use. You can find a very similar insert at seyberts.com.

3. The Big Kitchen Project

The *Reader's Digest* article about Percy Spencer and the microwave oven appeared in the August 1958 issue and was written by Don Murray.

You can learn more about fifteen-thousand-dollar ovens at aga-ranges.com.

Ducci Kitchens, Inc., is at 4 Old Middle Street, Goshen, Connecticut 06756. The company's Web site is duccikitchens.com, and its main e-mail address is info@duccikitchens.com.

You can learn more about ZipWall products at zipwall.com.

Wood-Mode's Web site is wood-mode.com. The cabinets we used are from Wood-Mode's Design Group 84 series, in a style called Embassy Recessed, custom-painted to the Benjamin Moore historical color Bennington Gray.

You can learn more about DuPont Corian at corian.com; the color we used on the kitchen island is called Prairie. The kitchen's Azrock vinyl composite floor tiles are from Tarkett, Inc., in Dusty Green and Bluff; you can see them at tarkett-commercial.com. You can see photographs of the kitchen (and a glimpse of the dining room beyond it) in the March 2000 issue of *Home*. You can study the full range of Emeco aluminum furniture at emeco.net, and you can see selected pieces in the Design Within Reach catalogue, which may be sitting in your mailbox right now. (You can also go to dwr.com.) Our Jeff Covey Model Six bar stools can be found at momastore.org. Ours have metal seats, an option that doesn't seem to exist anymore; the stools that the museum store sells now have wooden ones.

KitchenAid no longer makes the exact ovens that we bought—called Superba, model number KEBS1070667. I would hesitate to buy any oven with complex electronic controls, from any manufacturer.

4. The Cabin

Reese Owen's firm is Halper Owens Architects LLC, 18 Titus Road, Washington Depot, Connecticut 06794, and 225 Mill Street, Greenwich, Connecticut 06830. The Web address is halperowens.com.

5. Backhoes and Concrete Mixers

A good source of information on concrete for all residential applications is the Portland Cement Association, at cement.org.

Rub-R-Wall foundation coatings are manufactured by Rubber Polymer Corporation, 4015 Nine McFarland Drive, Suite 100, Alpharetta, Georgia 30004. The Web address is rpcinfo.com. To find an applicator in your area, you can call 800-860-7721. The Platon Foundation Protector system is manufactured by a division of Armtec Ltd., 33 Centennial Road, Orangeville, Ontario, L9W 1R1 Canada. The Web address is systemplaton.com.

6. Studs, Windows, Screens, and Porches

You can learn more about S. A. Bendheim's restoration glass at bendheimrestorationglass.com.

The 1890 House Museum, Chester Wickwire's old house, is at 37 Tompkins Street, Cortland, New York 13045. The Web address is 1890house.org.

Cabin Fever, by Rachel Carley, was published by Simon & Schuster in 1998.

Romancing the Woods is at 33 Raycliffe Drive, Woodstock, New York 12498. The Web address is romancingthewoods.com. You can e-mail Marvin Davis at davis@rtw-inc.com. For pictures of Mohonk, go to mohonkpreserve.org.

I ordered my Bora-Care from pestproducts.com. The concentrate costs about a hundred dollars a gallon, but it's worth it.

7. Walls, Ceilings, and Floors

An indispensable resource for anyone working with plaster or wallboard is the *Gypsum Construction Handbook,* published by USG Corporation, the manufacturer of Sheetrock. If you register at usg.com, you can order a copy of your own (about thirty dollars) or study an electronic copy online (free).

You can get in touch with James Boorstein, of Traditional Line Ltd., at 212-675-5133.

The Zinsser Company's Web site is zinsser.com. If you feel inspired to make your own shellac, a good place to start is shellac.net.

8. The Wet Parts

Flushed With Pride: The Story of Thomas Crapper, by Wallace Reyburn, was published in England in 1969 and has been reprinted several times since then. The first American edition was published in 1971. You can order a British reprint from Amazon. Be warned, though, that the book is mostly fiction.

The ten-thousand-dollar throne toilet is manufactured by a company called Herbeau Creations. You can order one (with free shipping) at vintagetub.com.

You can browse Kohler's toilet collection at us.kohler.com.

9. The Last Ten Percent

I ordered my TWP from amteco.com.

You can learn more about LeafGuard gutters at leafguard.com, and you can learn more about the Doorbrella at rainhandler.com. I bought my Gutter Sense at guttersense.com.

I ordered my Emtek locksets at thehardwarehut.com. The relevant Emtek Web site is emtekdoorlocks.com.

You can reach Ken Daniel of Ken Daniel Lighting Design LLC at kendld@aol.com.

ABOUT THE AUTHOR

DAVID OWEN is a staff writer for *The New Yorker* and the author of a dozen books, among them *The Walls Around Us, My Usual Game, The Chosen One, The First National Bank of Dad,* and *Copies in Seconds.* He lives in northwest Connecticut with his wife, the writer Ann Hodgman, and their two children.